THE STATUE OF JOHN BUNYAN AT BEDFORD
PRESENTED BY THE DUKE OF BEDFORD TO THE TOWN IN 1874
Sir J. Edgar Boehm, Sculptor

BUNYAN
CHARACTERS

Bunyan Himself as Seen in His *Grace Abounding*

Alexander Whyte

Baker Book House
Grand Rapids, Michigan 49506

Reprinted 1981 by
Baker Book House Company
from the edition published by
Oliphant, Anderson, and Ferrier

ISBN: 0-8010-9647-2

PHOTOLITHOPRINTED BY CUSHING - MALLOY, INC.
ANN ARBOR, MICHIGAN, UNITED STATES OF AMERICA

CONTENTS

CONTENTS

CONTENTS

BUNYAN HIMSELF AS SEEN IN HIS 'GRACE ABOUNDING'

I

'I never went to school to Plato or Aristotle.'

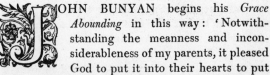

JOHN BUNYAN begins his *Grace Abounding* in this way: 'Notwithstanding the meanness and inconsiderableness of my parents, it pleased God to put it into their hearts to put me to school, to learn both to read and write; the which I also attained according to the rate of other poor men's children; though to my shame, I confess I did soon lose that little I learnt, even almost utterly, and that long before the Lord did work His gracious work of conversion upon my soul.' And in another place: 'I am no poet, nor poet's son, but a mechanic.' And again: 'I never went to school to Plato or Aristotle.' And then when he comes to speak of his married life he says: 'This woman and I, though we came together as poor as poor might be (not having so much household stuff as a dish or spoon betwixt us both), yet this she had for her part, *The Plain Man's Pathway to Heaven* and *The Practice of Piety*, which her father had left her when he died. In these two books I should sometimes read with her, but all this time I met with no conviction.' Now, with such an unlettered and ignorant and unconvicted beginning as that how are we to account for all that John Bunyan afterwards became and accomplished? How did a man with no book-learning at all come to write by far the best-written religious book in the English language?

Well, to begin with, John Bunyan's first step toward the unique place he now holds was taken in his heart-searching and thoroughgoing conversion. No two cases of conversion have ever been altogether alike. Take the greatest of all recorded conversions; take Paul's conversion, and Augustine's, and Luther's, and in our own land take the conversions of Thomas Halyburton, and James Fraser of Brea, and Thomas Boston, and Thomas Chalmers, and it is very remarkable how they all differ in every possible way from one another. And Bunyan's conversion, as he describes it in such pungent detail in his Autobiography, is all his own and is like that of no one else in all the world. There is no subject of study in all the world of study that is so interesting and so important and so urgent to us all as the study of conversion. And when we once address ourselves in right earnest to that supreme study, John Bunyan's *Grace Abounding* will always be found lying on our table beside those masterly writers already named.

The second thing that went to the making and the fitting out of our great author was his absolutely agonising experience of the lifelong pains of sanctification. The life of sanctification follows

on conversion, and both of those experiences have
a kindred character in every man who truly under-
goes them.   An easy conversion is usually followed
by an easy sanctification, and a fierce and a soul-
crushing conversion is usually followed by a fierce
and a soul-crushing sanctification.   In all my reading I have only come upon three cases of sanctification of a fierceness and a crushingness worthy to
be set beside that of John Bunyan.   And they are
all three fellow-countrymen and fellow-churchmen
of our own—Thomas Halyburton, Alexander Brodie
of Brodie, and James Fraser of Brea.   The sword
of truth and love and holiness was driven through
and through the sinful hearts of those four elect
men, and that divine sword turned every way in
their sinful hearts till it laid them down dead men
every day all their days on earth.

In the divine preparation of the author of the
Pilgrim's Progress, both in his great conversion, and
alongside of his great life of sanctification, his
wonderful imagination was always working.   John
Bunyan's imagination was of the very highest order,
and it was all taken up into the hand of the Holy
Ghost and was turned continually in upon the
terrible battle between sin and grace that went on
incessantly in Bunyan's mind and heart and life.
Bunyan's whole soul lay naked and opened to the
eyes of his sanctified imagination till his spiritual
life within him was far more real to him than was
the social and the political and the military life of
Bedford and of England all round about him.   And
till, as Halyburton says about himself, his own sin
and then the grace of God were such real things
to him, that compared with them nothing else in

the world had any reality at all. Dean Church
says somewhere that the original and unique and
characteristic power of Dr. Newman's preaching
lay largely in his extraordinary *realisation* of that
spiritual world of which he spoke. That is to
say, that great preacher's imagination, like the
imagination of Halyburton, and like the imagination of Bunyan, made those things to be absolutely
and supremely real and actual to him which are
only words and names and the fleeting shadows of
things to ordinary men.

And then there was Bunyan's exquisite style.
I have named three men above whose conversion
first, and then their after sanctification, stand out
beside those of Bunyan in their intense interest to
me, and in their deep and continually increasing
power over me. But their books are not known
outside a very small and a fast-decreasing circle of
readers. And that, partly, because of the poor
and stumbling and repelling style in which they
are written. Whereas John Bunyan's *Grace Abounding* will be read as long as the English language
lasts, if only for its incomparably pure, and clear,
and strong, and sweet, and winning English style.

Now, if I mistake not, there are some lessons of
the very first importance and of the very first value
to us all to be taken out of all that. All that was
written by John Bunyan, not for his own sake
alone, but for us also if we will attend and will take
his offered lessons to heart.

1. Dr. Denney has a very remarkable paper in
the *London Quarterly* for April 1904, on 'The
Education of a Minister.' It is a very remarkable
paper in itself, and it is doubly remarkable to be

written by a man who has gone to school to Plato and Aristotle as few men in our day have done. Dr. Denney is all for a learned and a scholarly class among our ministers, but his strong and unanswerable contention is that the door of the evangelical pulpit ought to be set wide open to men who have had no opportunity for laying in themselves the foundations of either classical or philosophical scholarship. And indeed who may have no natural aptitude for such studies, but who may have a great compensation in their conversion, and in their character, and in their experience, and in their practical knowledge of the men and the things among whom they are to live and work, even if they have but little direct knowledge of the men and the things of ancient Greece and Rome. And I am wholly with my able and learned friend in his generous argument. Where it can be got, like him, I would like to see a deep and a broad and a firm foundation of classical and philosophical learning laid in every minister's mind. At the same time, I would like to see our foremost pulpits open and inviting to all men who have had a conversion, and are having a sanctification, and a knowledge of their English Bible, and a passion for fruitful preaching, like all that of John Bunyan.

2. At the same time, like Dr. Denney, I would have every precaution and every guarantee taken that the lack of scholarship in any given student or minister is not due to his own laziness. I would have laziness held to be the one unpardonable sin in all our students and in all our ministers. I would have all lazy students drummed out of the college, and all lazy ministers out of the Assembly.

And all the churches will have to take steps to do
that soon, if they are to live and thrive in this
hard-working world of ours. Genius and grace,
like John Bunyan's genius and grace, are the
sovereign gift of Almighty God; but incessant
industry, and the most conscientious preparation
for the pulpit and the prayer-meeting and the
Bible-class, and daily and hourly pastoral and sick-
bed visitation, are all things of which every minister
will have to give an account, and that by day and
date, to Him who did not redeem us in His sleep.

3. We have a fine lesson as to John Bunyan's
ideal of what a Christian minister ought to be in
his seven ministerial portraits of Evangelist, and
the Interpreter, and Greatheart, and the four
Shepherds on the Delectable Mountains, whose
fine names are Knowledge, and Experience, and
Watchful, and Sincere. They are all portraits so
beautiful and so heart-winning that they must have
been the salvation of a multitude of ministers. Let
all ministers look till they see themselves as in a
glass in Evangelist and in Greatheart. And let
every manse, and every minister's study, and every
pulpit, and every Bible-class be an Interpreter's
House, with its inexhaustibly significant rooms.
And let every minister seek to have the four
portraits of the Delectable Shepherds realised and
fulfilled in himself. All our congregations cannot
have four ministers like the Delectable Mountains.
They cannot all have one minister with the knowledge, and another with the experience, and another
with the watchfulness, and another with the sincerity. But at the same time, happy that delectable
mountain where its very poverty and its other

limitations all compel its one pastor to have all the
knowledge needful, and all the experience, and all
the watchfulness, and all the sincerity in his single
self. As they all so conspicuously met in unlettered
John Bunyan.

4. It may look like it at first sight, but it is not
at all to come down from a high level to a low to
say a word or two at this point about a minister's
written and spoken style. Let all our students be
sure to read and lay to heart all that Dr. Denney
says on that subject also. And if they have not
already learned to distinguish in their own work,
and in other men's work, a good from a bad style,
their divinity professors should take them and
teach them some elementary lessons in that fine
subject. Dear old David White of Airlie was wont
to take me in my teens and teach me just what a
good style is, taking now Hugh Miller's leading
articles in the *Witness* newspaper, and now young
Mr. Spurgeon's early sermons in the Park Street
Pulpit. Till, though I cannot to this day write a
style to my own satisfaction, at the same time a
good style, and especially in sacred composition, is
one of the purest delectations of my daily life.
And it is surely an immense encouragement to us
all to see a man able to write a style which is one
of the high water-marks of the English language,
though he never went to school to Plato, or to
Aristotle, or to Tully, or to Quintilian. 'In the
name of wonder, Macaulay, where did you pick up
that astonishing style of yours?' demanded Lord
Jeffrey of his young contributor. Macaulay we
know had picked up his astonishing style out of all
Greek and Latin and English literature, and out of

many other such sources. But John Bunyan, who
beats Macaulay at English out of all sight, picked
up all his astonishing style out of his English Bible
and out of Foxe's *Book of Martyrs* alone. 'Give
your days and nights to Addison for style,' advised
Dr. Samuel Johnson. But I will rather say to all
our students—Give your days and nights to your
English Bible and to John Bunyan if you would
write and speak a perfect English style for your
purpose.

5. Then, again, let no student nor minister be
downcast about doing good pulpit work and good
class work because he has so few books. Jacob
Behmen, Luther's greatest disciple, and the greatest
mind in all great-minded Germany, had no books;
but then, in his own words, he had himself. And
John Bunyan was quite as badly off as Jacob
Behmen, for he had only his English Bible and
Foxe's *Book of Martyrs*. He had none of our long
shelves of prosy commentaries and Bible dictionaries
and encyclopædias and rows upon rows of ephemeral
sermons gathering dust in his significant rooms.
' Look in thy heart and write,' it was said to
Behmen and Bunyan. And Bunyan looked into
nothing else but into his English Bible and his own
heart till he wrote the *Grace Abounding* and the
Pilgrim's Progress and the *Holy War*, and in all
these set a standard for English composition.

6. Now, with all these lessons out of John Bunyan
for your future ministers, there is still this great
lesson left for yourselves: this great lesson: English
is the key to everything, even to Plato and Aristotle.
For Plato himself is now to be read in the finest
Oxford English, and with all that has been learned

in Christendom since his day added to him. But better far for you than all Plato and all Aristotle taken together, like Mr. Spurgeon, read the *Pilgrim's Progress* a hundred times. And I promise you that you will lay the book down many a sweetened and sanctified midnight saying with Ned Bratts in Robert Browning—

> His language was not ours:
> 'Tis my belief, God spake:
> No tinker has such powers.

II

'I was overrun with the spirit of superstition.'

ECAUSE I knew no better I fell in eagerly with the religion of the times; to wit to go to church twice a day, and that, too, with the foremost. And there should, very devoutly, both say and sing as others did; yet retaining my wicked life. But withal, I was so overrun with the spirit of superstition, that I adored, and that with great devotion, even all things; both the High Place, Priest, Clerk, vestment, service, and what else, belonging to the Church: counting all things holy that were therein contained. And especially, the Priest and the Clerk most happy, and without doubt, greatly blessed, because they were the servants of God, as I then thought, and were Principal in His holy temple to do His work therein. But all this time I was not sensible of the danger and evil of sin. All this time I never thought of Christ nor whether there was one or no.'

Now you must all see from that truly Bunyan-passage just what this thing superstition is and just what it is not. Superstition always sticks fast on the surface of things. Superstition never goes down through the outside skin of things. Superstition never enters into the deep and living heart of things. Superstition always builds both its own house and the house of its god upon the sand. And it fills the house of its god with high places, and with priests, and with clerks, and with vestments, and with services of its own. At any rate it did so in Bunyan's day. But all the time this so scrupulous worshipper still retained all his former wicked life. All the time he remained utterly insensible of the danger and the evil of his sin. All the time, in his own words, he never thought of Christ nor whether there was one or no.

Now you will all expect me to launch out at this point against the superstitions of other Churches than our own, and against the superstitions of other people than ourselves, but I am not going to do that to-night. I am not so much as to name the papists, nor the ritualists, nor any of our own too superstitious fellow-countrymen. A discourse of that kind would do you no good, and it would do me no honour; no honour that I covet after. But to discover to you some of your own overrunning superstitions and to help you to cast them off—what a successful and what an honourable discourse that would be!

And now to take John Bunyan for our forerunner and for our guide into this not very easy subject. Well his chief superstition in those early days of his, and before he had one atom of true religion, was to go to church twice every Sabbath, and that too with the foremost. In those unconvicted and unconverted days of his, Bunyan would not stay away from church in the very worst of wintry weather; no not even when he was threatened with a consumption. No not for a single diet from year's end to year's end. Bunyan was always the first to arrive at the church, and he was always the last to leave it. But all the time—would you believe it?—he led the same wicked life as soon as he went home, and all the week again till the next Sabbath came round. The thought of sin, or of salvation from sin, never once entered his tinker head from Sabbath to Saturday. He left all these things to the priest and to the clerk to manage for him. Now there are multitudes among ourselves who are exactly like poor Bunyan in all that. We, many of ourselves, go to church twice a day. We will not on any account stay away from church, no not for a single diet, if we can crawl on our staff or can get a Sabbath cab. But the cab delivers us at our own door again exactly the same men that we were when it took us up. We still retain our old life, as the people at home know to their cost. We are nothing better after a long lifetime of such church-going but rather worse. Well, *that* is superstition, and rank superstition too. It is the rankest super-stition to think that such going to church as that has anything to do with true religion. Just hear what God Himself has to say about such church-going as that. ' When ye come to appear before Me, who hath required this at your hands to tread My courts? The new moons, and the Sabbaths, and the calling of assemblies, I cannot away with them: it is iniquity, even the solemn meeting. I am weary to bear them. Cease to do evil. Learn to do well. Seek judgment. Relieve the oppressed,' —you know one—' Judge the fatherless,'—you surely know one—' Plead for the widow,'—you must know more widows than one. ' All this while,' says Bunyan, ' I met with no conviction. I did both sing, and say, as others did; yet retaining my wicked life. All this while I was not sensible of the danger and evil of sin. I was kept from considering that my sin would damn me, what religion soever I followed, unless I was found in Christ. Nay, I never thought of Him, nor whether there was one or no.' God does not mean for one moment, neither does Isaiah mean, nor does John Bunyan mean, that we are to stay away from church because of our sinful hearts and lives. Far from that. Come to church, they all three say, twice a day as long as you are able. And twice a day put away some wickedness out of your heart and out of your life before you go home. Twice every Sabbath day become more and more sensible of the danger and the evil of sin. And be you sure, it will take you twice a day all the days that are now left to you on earth to learn the simple a b c of the full danger and the full evil of sin. Yes, come till instead of never thinking whether there is a Christ or no, you come to think and to see that there is nothing and no one else to be much thought about but Christ in all the world.

And then the priest and the clerk and their vestments at that time entirely took the place of God, and of Christ, and of the Holy Ghost, in Bunyan's Sabbath-day devotions. The scales fell off his eyes afterwards till he came to see that there are no such priests and no such vestments in the Church of Christ at all, as he at one time so superstitiously thought there were. By the time he was himself anointed of God to be one of the chief priests of the Church of Christ in England, Bunyan came to see, as clearly as Paul himself saw,

just in what the true spiritual priesthood really
consists, and what a multitude of redeemed men
there are in that holy office on earth, with their
one High Priest in heaven. 'You have no bishops
in Scotland, I understand,' said an English Churchman, with some superiority, on one occasion, to old
Dr. Rainy, Dr. Roxburgh's elder, at Cardwell's table
at Oxford. 'Oh yes, sir,' said the somewhat irate
old doctor, 'I would not like to say on the spot
how many real bishops there are in Scotland;
and, more than that, your humble servant is one
of them himself.' Happily you have not been
suckled into any superstition about bishops and
priests and clerks and vestments, and there is no
fear of your adoring your plain and unpretentious
presbyterian minister with a too superstitious
devotion. You know him too well for that. And
thus it is that your danger lies all the other way.
Indeed, you cannot give your minister a too high
place, or a too frequent place, in your most holy
thoughts. Short of adoring him with Bunyan, all
your way up to church, twice every Sabbath, keep
thinking of your minister, and keep saying things
like this concerning him : ' Cast him not away from
Thy presence this day, and take not Thy Holy
Spirit from him. Restore to him, and to me, and
to mine, the joy of Thy salvation this day, and uphold us all with Thy free Spirit.' And when he
gives out his text in the church, say you all the
time, ' I will hear what God the Lord will speak to
me and mine.' And now and then all through the
week when you are near God mention confiden-
tially to Him the name of your minister. Let
a heavenly spirit like that absolutely overrun your

spirit, and that will extinguish all overrunning superstition out of your spirit. A spirit of love and of prayer like that will fill your mind and your heart and your life, Sabbath day and every day, with a true and a spiritual worship.

Bunyan's superstitions even went the length of regular family worship in those early days of his married life. Partly to please his young wife who had been better brought up than her husband, partly to soothe her conscience for marrying such a man, he held a sort of family worship with her, especially on Sabbath nights. But all the time, his Sabbath night readings in his wife's good books, and his saying a prayer with her, all that was no better than so much hanging up of some of his father's old horseshoes at the door so as to keep away all approaching ghosts during the night. Bunyan would have been uneasy and unhappy and would have been alarmed at the surrounding noises of the night if he had not nailed up that old iron over his threshold. And something like that is the same with ourselves. If our dinner party runs too late into the night, or if some of our guests stay talking too long, or if we know that some of our more honoured guests are not accustomed to it at home, we forego our family worship for that night, out of respect to them and out of regard for their feelings. But we are not quite easy about God all that night till we fall asleep, and then our customary family worship in the morning sets matters all right between us and Him. Not that it makes much real difference in our house any night whether we have family worship or no. The chapter is read, and the psalm is sung, and after we have prayed a word or two on one knee, as that indecent custom is coming in, we rise up light and alert and plunge into the interrupted talk again. The superstition of family worship has enough hold of our habits and of our consciences to make us go through it. But when once it has been gone through, well, Bunyan tells us that for his part he immediately returned to his former evil life.

There is another family superstition that we all go through three times a day and which we call saying grace. This is how they said their graces in William Law's day. 'In one house you may perhaps see the head of the family just pulling off his hat; in another, half getting up from his seat; another shall, it may be, proceed so far as to make as if he said something; we can hardly bear with him that seems to say grace with any degree of seriousness, and we look upon it as a sign of a fanatical temper if a man has not done as soon as he begins.' But worse than even that, I once dined at a nobleman's table where we all fell to like so many famished wolves. Only, I had been so suckled into this superstition of saying grace that I remember to this day how I could scarcely swallow my dinner that evening. I had never eaten a meal all my days till that day, without shutting my eyes and saying something or other to myself before I began to eat. In this connection I remember a young minister once coming to consult with me as to whether he should stay on and finish his intended holiday in the house where he was, because there was neither grace at meals there nor family worship at any time, and he was afraid something evil would happen to him. All the same, it is not so

easy to say grace aright as you would think it is
before you begin to try it.   For one thing, you
might try the freshening-up experience of varying
your grace from meal to meal and from day to day.
You might say a well-selected verse of Scripture at
one time.   And then two or three words straight
out of your own warm feelings at another time.
At one time ask some devout-minded guest, if there
is one at table, to sanctify your meal, and at another
time invite your little boy to say one of his nursery
verses or schoolroom Scriptures.   And when you
say grace yourself, sometimes look up in the twinkling of an eye, beyond all interposing persons and
things, and make your own immediate acknow-
ledgment and say : ' My table Thou hast furnished,
and my cup overflows.'   Say at another time that
you sit down at this full table of yours well remembering Him who had not where to lay His head.

And now to wind up with a word of hope.   We
evangelical Protestants of Scotland look upon the
Church of Rome as being a perfect hotbed of all
manner of superstition in the public worship of
God and in the private Christian life.   And just
because that is our standing protest against her I
was the more arrested by what a dignitary of that
Church said the other day at a Catholic congress in
England.   They had rites and ceremonies in their
Church, he said, not because they thought these
things to be of any real value, but they encouraged
many of these things in order to safeguard their
people against slovenliness and vulgarity and
irreverence and bad taste in the house of God.
Now when a Catholic of position is permitted to
say such things as these there is surely hope for

that Church. At any rate, on the apostolic principle of thinking no evil, but believing all things, and hoping all things, I for one will hail the utterance of such things as these on this so separating subject. At one time that teaching, allowed and practised, would have satisfied John Calvin, and John Knox, and James Melville, and Samuel Rutherford, as to Church ceremonies. As much enriching and good taste and refinement and beauty as is possible and fitting in the house of God, they would have said, so long as it is all sanctified into the beauty of holiness, so long as it is all confessed and taught to be of no superstitious or unspiritual effect. For,—'The hour cometh, and now is, when the true worshippers shall worship the Father in spirit and in truth; for the Father seeketh such to worship Him. God is a Spirit, and they that worship Him must worship Him in spirit and in truth.' Amen.

III

'Before I had well dined, I shook the sermon out of my mind.'

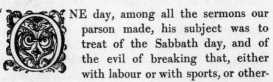NE day, among all the sermons our parson made, his subject was to treat of the Sabbath day, and of the evil of breaking that, either with labour or with sports, or otherwise. Wherefore, I fell in my conscience under his sermon, thinking and believing that he made that sermon on purpose to show me my evil-doings; and so I went home, when the sermon was ended, with a great burden upon my spirit. But, behold, it lasted not. For before I had well dined, the trouble began to go off my mind. Wherefore, when I had satisfied nature with my food, I shook the sermon out of my mind; and to my old custom of sports and gaming I returned with great delight. But all that day I felt what guilt was, though never before, that I can remember.'

The Apostle Paul, next to Jesus Christ, is our greatest possession, and we owe the Apostle to a sermon on the tenth commandment. And we owe St. Augustine, our next possession after St. Paul, to a sermon on the seventh commandment. And we owe John Bunyan—and you all know what a possession he is—to a sermon on the fourth commandment. And Samuel Johnson to a sermon on

that same commandment and to another sermon on
the fifth commandment. Humanly speaking, we
would never have heard the name of John Bunyan
but for that sermon on the sanctification of the
Lord's Day. It is to that sermon that we owe
Grace Abounding and *The Pilgrim's Progress* and
The Holy War. After he had well dined on beef
and greens that afternoon, and after he had revived
his spirits with a large tankard of stout English ale,
the young tinker set off to the village green in
most willing obedience to the Sabbath day commandment of Archbishop Laud. But all the time
Moses had been beforehand with Laud. And
Moses' Sabbath sting was in Bunyan's conscience
all that afternoon in spite of his good dinner and
his game of cat. Dr. Newman in too many things
is a disciple of Laud, but he cannot stomach
the Archbishop's Book of Sports. 'Satan's first
attempt when he would ruin a man's soul,' says
Newman, 'is to prevail on him to desecrate the
Lord's Day.' And let all men listen to Dr.
Samuel Johnson's sermon on this same subject:
' Having lived to my forty-sixth year, not without
an habitual reverence for the Sabbath, yet I resolve
henceforth to attend to it as Christianity requires:
I resolve henceforth—(1) To rise early, and, in
order to that, to go to sleep early on Saturday.
(2) To use some extraordinary devotion in the
morning. (3) To examine the tenor of my life
and particularly the last week, and to mark my
advances in religion or recessions from it. (4) To
read the scriptures methodically, with such helps
as are at hand. (5) To go to church twice. (6)
To read books of divinity, either speculative or

practical.   (7) To instruct my family.   (8) To wear off by meditation any worldly soil contracted in the week.'

Bunyan had heard many sermons from parish ministers and from army chaplains, but the preacher's sermon entered the tinker's conscience that day as no sermon had ever done before.   ' All that day I felt what guilt was, though never before, that I can remember.'   There should be far more preaching to the conscience than there is in our mealy-mouthed and toothless day.   Sometimes the sermon should be on one commandment and sometimes on another.   But there should be no sermon, whatever the text, that does not leave some sting driven deep down into somebody's conscience. There should be much more preaching than there is on the first table of the law, and still more frequent preaching on the second table.   For as Calvin says, ' The second table is better fitted for making a scrutiny into such as we are.'   A bee dies, so I am told, when it leaves its sting behind it, but not so a sermon.   A sermon only begins to live when its hearer goes home ' sermon-sick,' as Bunyan went home that Sabbath forenoon ; only, it is by far the most difficult of duties to preach a sermon right home into the conscience of the hearer.   To make guilty men feel that the sermon was made on purpose to show them their sin and to say to them, Thou art the man, is no easy task. At the same time, ' a sufficiently close word,' says Halyburton, ' will bring even a Judas to ask, Master, is it I ? '   Now, a sermon like that is nothing less than the very sword of the Spirit ; only it is not every hand that can send home that sword

so as to discern the thoughts and the intents of the
heart. As a contemporary of Bunyan has it, ' Here
it may truly be said that of all sermons they are by
far the most difficult that are made concerning the
hearts and the consciences of men. For as no study
is more hard on the student than anatomy, unless
the student has first seen some corpse cut up; so
also is it in an anatomy lecture on the heart and the
conscience. To do this,' he continues, ' will be a
work impossible to those who have never made
acquaintance with themselves : who have never
had their eyes turned inwards upon themselves, and
who, consequently, do not know the first elements
of their own hearts.' At the same time our
preachers must not despair of the success of their
sermons, even though they see them having the
same fate that the preacher's forenoon sermon
seemed to have that Sabbath in Bedford. Even
our Lord Himself had to humble Himself to see His
divine sermons shaken out of His hearer's minds and
hearts Sabbath after Sabbath. Till He determined
to put His experience and His observation and His
indignation into His bitter parable of the sower and
his seed, with the wicked one continually catching
away that which was sown in the hearer's heart.
' But, behold, it lasted not, for when I had satisfied
nature with my food, I shook the sermon out of my
mind.' That was wellnigh a fatal dinner to John
Bunyan ; for, by the meat he ate, and by the ale
he drank, and by the talk he poured out, as far as
in him lay he quenched the awakening work of
God's Holy Spirit that had been begun in his heart
that forenoon. And the last Day alone will declare
how many soul-saving sermons have been shaken

out of men's minds, and how many men have sold
their souls for a good dinner and for a good supper
on the Sabbath day. Though dead, John Bunyan
yet speaks to us in his *Grace Abounding*, and asks
this question at us all: ' Does your minister's very
best sermon long survive your Sabbath day dinner
and Sabbath night supper ? '

I have told you an anecdote before now that I
think is never absent from my conscience a single
Sabbath night after sermon and supper. I was
once spending a Sabbath long ago with dear old
John Mackenzie of Glenisla. The old saint's
memory still sanctifies the glen and draws visitors
of a kindred spirit up to the glen every summer.
Well, that Sabbath night after supper I asked my
friend to read to me out of the manuscript volume
of notes he had taken of John Duncan's sermons
long ago when the future professor was still a pro-
bationer in the neighbourhood, and he was still
reading in his rich manuscript when the bell rang
for family worship. After the worship was offered
I turned to my friend and said to him, ' Let us have
some more of the Rabbi's remarkable sermons.'
' Pardon me,' said the wise old priest, ' but we
always take our candles after family prayers.' He
did not intend that to be a sting in my conscience
I feel sure, all the same it was a real sting all
that night, and after thirty years it still rankles in
my heart and conscience many a Sabbath night and
many a week night after supper and worship. If
we all took our candles immediately after family
worship every week night, and if we could carry to
our own room the full impression of the public worship every Sabbath night, it would be the salva-

tion of countless souls, who as it is simply squander
the whole grace and truth of the public and private
ordinances of God's grace by the frivolous and dis-
sipating talk even of a godly household. I am not
to be taken as preaching salvation by asceticism.
I am not to be understood to be denouncing
Sabbath dinners and Sabbath suppers and the reading of sermon notes of genius after family worship.
Not at all; I am simply stating facts. I am simply
remarking on what I have seen and felt for a long
lifetime. I am simply mourning over what my
Master mourned over as He made, for the instruction of all His ministers, His most painful parable
of the thirteenth of Matthew.

There are many other things besides dinners
and suppers and readings of sermons of genius
that catch away that which has been sown in
our hearts in the house of God on the Sabbath
day. God has appointed the preaching of the
gospel of His Son to be the one and the only
complete cure for all the ills of the human heart,
and for all the ills of the family, and of the city.
But there are mountebanks abroad in our day who
thrust upon us their patent pills for the earthquake.
Are we full of the pains of a bad conscience like
Bunyan? Are we like Bunyan sick to death every
day we live with an evil heart? Then are there not
botanic gardens in which to walk off our sickness?
and picture galleries to amuse us and make us forget our sickness? and bands on the green, and
tipcat, and Sunday clubs, and Sunday newspapers?
Ah, no! Ah, no! Canst thou draw out leviathan
with a hook? or his tongue with a cord which thou
lettest down? Canst thou put a hook into his nose?

or bore his jaw through with a thorn? Wilt thou play with him as with a bird? or wilt thou bind him for thy maidens? Shall the companions make a banquet of him? Shall they part him among the merchants? Ah, no! Ah, no! But we preach Christ crucified.

As my method has been from the beginning of these Bunyan discourses, and as my method will be to their end, I come back to the divinity students before I close. For even one divinity student impressed and directed is worth a thousand of our ordinary hearers. Well then, gentlemen, you have your compensations meantime; you have your compensations for the want of a manse and for the want of family worship. For you have your own rooms standing open and waiting your return to-night, with their tables all covered with the best books in the world, and with your whole time and thought to give to them to-night, and to your own soul, and to your forthcoming work. I often go back to the Sabbath mornings and the Sabbath nights when I was at your present stage. You have no Sabbaths and no sermons such as I had; but such as you have may be used by you and owned by God for your personal salvation and for your pulpit and pastoral equipment. I had the scholarly and saintly Dr. Moody Stuart on the one diet of public worship, and I had the incomparable Dr. Candlish on the other diet, and his sermons still sound in my heart over half a century. But better than that I had such books on my table that I still go back to the same books to draw out of them for my own salvation and yours. I have no books to this day better than those books of my

student Sabbath mornings and Sabbath nights.
And I will plead with you to let no visitor, the best,
and no call of duty even, short of the very best, steal
from you your solitary Sabbath nights with the sermons of the day still holding your heart, and with
the great books of your calling supporting and seal-
ing the sermons of the day. And your present
Sabbath morning and Sabbath night habits, both
intellectual and devotional, will abide with you all
your after days and will help to protect you among
the countless interruptions and distractions and
temptations of your ministerial life. And while
you study to be a pattern of all civility and affability
and hospitality to your people on the Sabbath day,
you will all the time have a holy fear lest you and
they both fall into Bunyan's temptation to shake
the sermon out of your mind. He was a shrewd
king, and he knew the hearts of ministers, who
invited the angry prophet home to dine with him
at his royal table after sermon, for many an otherwise angry prophet has been turned into a dumb
dog by being made trencher-chaplain to a king.
And many an angry conscience has been soothed
to sleep, as the preacher who awakened it has
eaten and drunken and talked and laughed till a
late hour on a Sabbath night.

Among the many conflicts of duties and of
dangers that you will meet with when you are
ministers, this will be one of the most difficult to
deal with aright. You will have to take home
students, and clerks, and tradesmen, and plough-
men, and apprentices with you on Sabbath nights, if
only to make their acquaintance aright, and to make
them to feel at home with you and with the manse.

But with all your wisdom and with all your tact the impression of the day will wholly pass off from both your mind and theirs as you sit and eat and drink and talk late into the night. You will see the impression gradually passing off under your very eyes, till you will be at your wits' end between your clear duty, and the as clear danger that always accompanies that duty. The thing I now speak of will be one of the clearest of your pastoral duties and opportunities; and, in some cases, it will be one of the most fruitful. At the same time, in some other cases, you will have to confess that it has been the death of the Lord's Day, and the burial of all its divine instructions and divine impressions. But all the same do not doubt but that wisdom, and tact, and direction, and discretion, and a rich blessing, will be given you from above as you work your way, Sabbath day and week day, through the manifold duties and the manifold dangers of your ministerial life. God bless you, gentlemen, with His richest and His most effectual blessing! For when you are so blessed multitudes of other men will be blessed in you and with you. Amen.

IV

' Nay, I never thought of Christ, nor whether there was one, or no.'

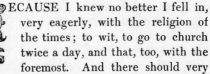 ECAUSE I knew no better I fell in, very eagerly, with the religion of the times; to wit, to go to church twice a day, and that, too, with the foremost. And there should very devoutly, both sing and say as others did; yet all the time retaining my wicked life. Thus I continued about a year; all which time our neighbours did take me to be a very godly man: a new and a religious man. Though, as yet, I knew not Christ, nor grace, nor faith, nor hope. Nay, all this time I never thought of Christ, nor whether there was one, or no.'

Now with Bunyan before us to warn us in this matter it is quite possible that you and I may be coming to this very church twice a day, and may be saying and singing with the foremost, and yet all the time may be, like Bunyan, so insensible to spiritual things as never once all the day really to think that there is a Christ to hear us say and sing and to save us. If that stupidity was so gross with a man of John Bunyan's genius and sensibility it is not at all impossible that it may be the same with some of ourselves. Come away then, and let us all examine ourselves as to this great matter: this by

far the greatest of all matters : our thoughts, yes or
no, about CHRIST. And let us begin like Bunyan
with the Sabbath morning. Bunyan rose off his
bed every Sabbath morning in good time for church,
but he never once said, 'This is the day that
Christ hath made for me, by His arising again
this day for my justification.' The time came when
he said that the very first thing every Sabbath
morning. One Sabbath morning, long afterwards,
he was so in the spirit of Christ's resurrection and
of his own justification, that he says he saw Christ
leaping round His empty grave for very joy that
He had at last finished the work that His Father
had given Him to do. And then before his Sabbath
morning breakfast Bunyan was always scrupulous
to say a special Sabbath morning grace, but that was
all, he never once looked above the bare words of
the superstitious grace. And then he rested, according to the commandment, from his six days' work
with his hammer and his anvil, but his weary soul
had not yet found its Lord's Day rest in the Risen
Christ. And then when the Sabbath morning bells
rang he went up to church and sang the psalms and
sounded out the responses till he honestly thought
that he stood as well with God as any man in all
England.

Now, honestly, what do *you* think about the first
thing on the morning of the Lord's Day ? If it is
indeed His day, should He not have your first
thought in the morning ? That is to say, if He
was indeed delivered for your offences, and was
raised again that morning for your justification.
And to go no farther back did you think of Him,
aye or no, the first thing *this* morning ?   What did

you say to yourself all the time you were washing
your hands and your face this morning? 'This fine
linen,' said one as he put it on, 'is to me a parable
and a sacrament of the righteousness of Christ.'
'I put on His righteousness and it clothed me,'
said another; 'it was to me for a robe and for a
diadem.' Do you ever say anything like that on a
Sabbath morning? And then in after days when
the Gospels were read at family worship and in the
church, 'Methought,' says Bunyan, 'I was as if I
had seen Him born, as if I had seen Him grow up,
as if I had seen Him walk through this world from
His cradle to His cross; to which also, when He
came, I saw how gently He gave Himself to be
hanged and nailed upon it for my sins and wicked
doings. Also, as I was musing upon this His progress, that dropped on my spirit—He was ordained
for the slaughter.' Now has anything like that
dropped on your spirit all this day? It was a large
part of John Bunyan's genius and grace; it was a
large part of his extraordinary success both in literature and in religion, that he always as good as *saw*
everything he read about in his Bible, and everything he sang about, and everything he prayed
about, both at home and in the church. And it
will make you and me to be men of something of
the same genius and the same grace if we also *see*
Christ every time we pronounce His name and hear
it pronounced. But Bunyan, at that early time,
was still a far way from all that. For he quotes, as
describing himself at that time, this text out of the
Preacher: 'Thus man, while blind, doth wander,
and wearieth himself with vanity, for he knoweth
not the way to the city of God.'

But all that was not yet the worst with poor Bunyan. Not only did he never once think of Christ on the Sabbath or all the week; far worse than that, the thought of Christ was 'grievous' to him when at any time a sermon or a book or something else pressed Christ home upon his attention. He could not himself endure the thought of Christ, nor could he endure the company of any man whom he suspected to be much given to that thought. That house, he tells us, was like a prison to him, where he saw lying open on the table a book about Christ. Now the houses of the Baptists in Bedford were full of books about Christ in those Puritan days, as full as our houses are of newspapers and novels, till there was scarcely a house in all the town that Bunyan could enter with comfort and remain in with peace of mind. And there will be some of you exactly like that. The circulating library people never send you a book about Christ. What would you think and what would you say to them if they did? And a text like this and a sermon like this are both grievous to you. There are some kinds of sermons you greatly like and go talking about all the week, but not sermons on the Person of Christ, or on the work of Christ, or on the glory of Christ. You never all your days sat down to read a whole Epistle of Paul about Christ, no not even on a communion week; at any rate, not since you were in your first earnestness as a young communicant. 'As for Paul's Epistles,' says Bunyan, 'I could not away with them. Being as yet but ignorant, either of the corruptions of my own nature, or of the want and worth of Jesus Christ to save me.' But as we read on towards the

middle and the end of *Grace Abounding,* we come
on continual exclamations like this : ' O Blessed
Paul ! O, yes, thou Blessed Paul ! ' And we come
again and again on other exclamations like this :
' O methought CHRIST ! CHRIST ! there was nothing
but CHRIST now before my eyes. To speak as then
I thought, had I had a thousand gallons of blood in
my veins, I could freely have spilt it all before His
feet.' And who knows but that He who made
John Bunyan so to differ from his former self, may
yet in His abounding grace work the same miracle
of grace and truth in you. I hope to live to see
books on Christ lying open on your table and you
will not hide them away as if you were ashamed of
them.

Men and women ! Grown-up men and women !
Take pity on your poor stunted minds and starved
hearts ! For what a mind and heart to be pitied is
that which does not constantly think about CHRIST !
I do not care how great a name any man may bear
among men if he does not constantly think about
CHRIST. Even were his name the name of a Shakespeare, or a Goethe, or a Newton, the humblest
believer may well pity him if he has not yet begun
to think about CHRIST. For, O what splendid, what
soul-saving thinking CHRIST makes to a man !
CHRIST HIMSELF, and then all other things in
heaven and on earth, in God and in man ; what
thinking they all make when they are all seen and
thought of IN CHRIST ! What seraphic minds those
Colossian believers must have had if they indeed
understood and enjoyed the Epistle that bears down
to us their honoured and beloved names. For,
what intellectual and what spiritual heights and

depths are there! What theology! What Christ-
ology! What philosophy, and for once not falsely
so called! And with it all, and as the true riches
of it all, what a Gospel! What pardon! What
peace with God! What present grace, and what
coming glory! Did you ever sit down and read at
a down-sitting the Epistle to the Colossians?
When you do, write me and tell me what you think
and feel as you close the divine book. I will tell
you beforehand one thing you will think and feel
and say. You will say with some in the Church of
Colosse, 'What a man was Paul—if he was a mere
man, and not the very Holy Ghost Himself come
to us in the flesh to talk of the things of Christ,
and to show them to us!'

And now to bring all this to this point. Intending communicants! You of all men are to think of
little else but of Christ all this week. For just
thinking of Christ—that will make you worthy
communicants as nothing else will. The more you
think all this week of His Son the better pleased
the Father will be with you when He comes in to
see the guests. On the other hand, do not come
near His table unless you are prepared to think of
Christ and of little else all your after days. For no
one can possibly sit at His table, and eat and drink
the things of Christ that are there provided, without being so possessed with Christ as to think of
Him above and before all else as long as they live
in this world. If you spend this week wisely, and
then if you communicate worthily next Lord's Day,
you will both understand and will for ever make
your own what Bunyan says about a communion
day of his long afterwards: 'Both again, and again,

and again,' he says, 'I was made to see that day
that God and my soul were made friends by the
Blood of Christ. Yea, I saw that the justice of
God, and my sinful soul, could embrace and kiss
each other through that blood. Now was my heart
full of comfort and hope. Now I could believe that
my sins should be all forgiven. Yea I was now so
taken with the love and the mercy of God to me
that I could not contain it all till I got home. I
thought I could have spoken of His love and of His
mercy to me, even to the very crows that sat upon
the ploughed lands before me.'

And now after the intending communicants, if
the divinity students here present will listen to me
let them do this. Let them borrow from their
library the index volume of Dr. Thomas Goodwin's
immortal works. And next Sabbath morning and
evening let them open that splendid index under
'CHRIST.' Let them ponder those five glorious pages
slowly and thoughtfully and believingly and appro-
priately; and, if they do not leap in their rooms
at the glorious prospect of their soon being
preachers of CHRIST there must be something far
wrong with them. They are surely too far off their
right road in life already. Let them forthwith
choose some other calling. Let them go to the
bar, or to medicine, or to the army, or to the civil
service; but it is only common sense that they
should not go to the Church of CHRIST. They may
make passable advocates, or doctors, or soldiers, but
not preachers of CHRIST to please Him and to edify
His people and to earn His reward. And yet, no!
That is not good advice, and I will take it all back.
Rather than that, let them look well down into

their own sinful hearts; and back, and forward,
into their own sinful lives; and all around at the
world of sinful men round about them. And then
let them read with all their scholarship and with
all their philosophy and with all their personal
experience say, the prologue to John's Gospel and
his seventeenth chapter, and then the Epistle to
the Colossians, and then Goodwin's index again
under 'CHRIST.' And I am as sure as I am standing
in this pulpit that neither the army, nor the bar,
nor anything else in this world will ever get those
men. It is because so few of our able young men
ever think about CHRIST that there is everywhere
such a dearth of first-class divinity students. It is
not the falling Sustentation Fund, nor is it the
Higher Criticism, nor is it the many openings into
wealth and honour at home and abroad that steals
from the Church her choicest sons. No, no. It is
simply this : It is simply because, like John Bunyan
in his blinded youth, they are not yet sensible of
the danger and the disaster of all sin and of their
own sin. And then, as the result of that, it is
because they never think of the Divine Redeemer
from sin, or whether there is one, or no. O come,
all you youths of genius and of learning and of the
beginnings of grace! For here is the proper scope
for you! Your proper field in all this world is the
Evangelical pulpit and pastorate. Here is the one
sphere in this whole world in which to lay out and
to multiply your talents so that both you and they
may be found unto praise and honour and glory at
the appearing of Jesus Christ. 'God,' says Goodwin, 'had only one Son, and He made Him a
minister.'

V

'As for Paul's Epistles, I could not away with them.'

HE time had been when Paul would have hated his own Epistles with a far more deadly hatred than ever John Bunyan hated them. The time had been with the Apostle himself when he was far more ignorant of the corruptions of his heart than ever John Bunyan was, and when he hated the very mention of the name of Jesus Christ far more than ever John Bunyan hated it. But where sin abounded, grace did much more abound. Till, when the scales fell from off Paul's eyes, and when God revealed His Son in Paul, there then began a series of Epistles to the very Churches that Paul had persecuted to prison and to death : a series of Epistles the like of which the world has never seen, nor will ever see, to the end of time. What a man was Paul—'if he was a man!' as was said in the early Church concerning him. And what a work was Paul given of God to do ! Humanly speaking, but for Paul and his Epistles, both the Son of God, and His redeeming work, would have remained to this day an all but hidden mystery to us and to all the world. But as God would have it, when Jesus Christ was elected and predestinated to His redeeming work,

Paul also was elected and predestinated to his apostolic work, after and alongside of Jesus Christ. Jesus Christ was elected and predestinated to do a work that He alone could do; and at the same time Paul was elected and predestinated to preach Jesus Christ and His work of salvation from sin as no other man could have preached it. 'Sun, and moon, and stars, and passages of Shakespeare, and the last greater than the first'—that has been given as a supreme example of the rhetorical figure called hyperbole. But there is no hyperbole in this: Sun, and moon, and stars, and passages of Paul, and the last out of all sight greater than the first. Such passages as this :—'The Church of God, which He hath purchased with His own blood.' And this, 'Being justified freely by His grace.' And this : 'To him that worketh not, but believeth.' And this : 'Who was delivered for our offences.' And this : 'Of Him are ye in Christ Jesus.' And this : 'I am crucified with Christ.' And this : 'In whom we have redemption through His blood.' And this : 'For it pleased the Father that in Him should all fullness dwell.' And this : 'And ye are complete in Him.' And this : 'This is a faithful saying, and worthy of all acceptation, that Christ Jesus came into the world to save sinners, of whom I am chief.' But the truth is, as Hazlitt says of Burke, the only adequate examples of Paul are all that he ever wrote. Read therefore, all that Paul ever wrote ; and like Luther you will read him sixty times, and every time with new wonder and new praise, and you will read less and less every other writer.

The true glory of Paul's Epistles stands in this :

He takes of the deepest things of God and of Christ and reveals them to us as no one else has ever revealed them. 'The Gospels,' says an Egyptian Father, 'supply the wool, but the Epistles weave the dress.' That is to say, it is Paul's Epistles that set forth in all its fullness the complete and the final purpose of God in all that we see taking place in Matthew, and in Mark, and in Luke, and in John. In the four Gospels we see Jesus Christ born, and baptized, and tempted; we hear Him preaching also, so far as His hearers were able to bear it; and then we see Him taken by His enemies, and bound, and tried, and condemned and crucified. But it is Paul alone who comes and takes us down into the divine heart of all that. It is Paul alone who fully preaches out of all that the pardon of all our sin, our peace with God, our holiness of heart and life, and the life everlasting. That was all wrapped up in the four Gospels but was not as yet aright revealed. Yes: the four Evangelists supply him abundantly with the wool, but it is Paul alone who places the warp and the woof in his apostolic loom till both he and all his believing readers can say, 'I put on His righteousness and it clothed me: it was to me for a robe and for a diadem.' Matthew has his Gospel, says Paul, and Mark has his Gospel, and both Luke and John have their Gospels, but better than them all and above them all I have 'my Gospel.' In his holy pride, and rising up to the full height of his holy calling, the Apostle says to us: 'For I certify you, brethren, that the Gospel which I preached to you is not after men. For I neither received it of men, neither was I taught it, but by the revelation of Jesus Christ. For it pleased God, who separated me from my mother's womb, and called me by His grace, to reveal His Son in me, that I might preach Him among the heathen : immediately I conferred not with flesh and blood : neither went I up to Jerusalem to them that were apostles before me.'

Now, with all that, listen to John Bunyan's deliberate and true testimony concerning himself at one time. 'Wherefore, falling into some love and liking for religion, I betook me to my Bible, and began to take great pleasure in reading it ; but especially the historical parts thereof. For, as for Paul's Epistles, and suchlike Scriptures, I could not away with them : being as yet but ignorant, either of the corruptions of my nature, or of the want and worth of Jesus Christ to save me.'

But what exactly is this 'want and worth of Jesus Christ,' of which John Bunyan was still so ignorant ? I do wish that Bunyan had gone to the bottom of all that 'want and worth' himself. For, how impressively and how memorably he could have set forth the want and worth of Jesus Christ, first to God, and then to us. But perhaps Bunyan said to himself, Who can come after the King ? Who can add one word to that which Paul has written so fully in every Epistle of his ? And that is true. For all up and down, in every Epistle of his, Paul exhibits to us what a want Jesus Christ supplied ; first to God, and then to us. First to God, when He came to make a full and an everlasting atonement for sin, and thus to set God's hands free, so to say, to do all that for us which it was in His heart to do. God wanted some one

to come to earth to be a propitiation through our
faith in His blood, so that He might be just, and
at the same time the justifier of him which believeth. I suppose God could have got the worlds
created by some other servant of His than His
Son; but His Son alone could be an all-sufficient
sacrifice for sin. God's want, therefore, was that
His Son should do all that He did, in order that
He, the Father, might be free and safe to justify
the ungodly, which He was determined to do.
'Whom shall I send? And who will go for us?'
'Here am I,' said His Son, 'send Me. Lo, I come,
in the volume of the Book it is written of Me, I
delight to do Thy will; yea, Thy law is within My
heart.' God's great want of Jesus Christ is past
all words of the human mind to contain and to
convey. Words fail the Holy Ghost Himself to
set that want of the Father fully forth.

And, then, there is our want of Jesus Christ to
come to save us. Who shall sufficiently put words
upon our want? Who shall count up the want and
the worth of Jesus Christ to save us who are as full
as we can hold of all corruption and abomination?
The Son of God puts that to us in His own incomparable way when He demands of us in one place:
'What shall a man give in exchange for his soul?'
And we reply to that out of the depths of our sin
and say to Him, 'Save me from going down to the
pit, for I have found a Ransom. And my Ransom
is Thyself, O Thou priceless Son of God!' And,
thus, when it is all finished, both God and man,
both angels and saints, shall all unite in this great
doxology of indebtedness to Jesus Christ, and shall
say: 'Worthy is the Lamb that was slain to receive

power, and riches, and wisdom, and strength, and honour, and glory, and blessing.' And we who are the saved from among men, and by that time the saved from all our corruptions and all our abominations, we will add this, and will say for ourselves: 'Unto Him that loved us, and washed us from our sins in His own blood, to Him be glory and dominion for ever and ever. Amen.'

Students of divinity! Happiest and most enviable of all our young men! Paul's Epistles are the true divinity for you. They contain God's finest wheat for you. They are full of honey and the honeycomb out of His Rock for you. 'Study down,' therefore, Paul's Epistles, as we are told Thomas Goodwin studied them down. And your love for Paul's Epistles, and for such expositions of Paul's Epistles as Luther on the Galatians, and Goodwin on the Ephesians, will be a sure prophecy to you of the power and the fruitfulness of your future preaching. Be you—if you will take a word of advice from me—be you sleepless students day and night of Paul's Epistles, and of his only true successors: the first Reformers, and the Puritans of England, and the Covenanted Presbyterians of Scotland. Take the deep substance of Paul's Epistles and put all that deep substance into Newman's English, or at least into Spurgeon's English, and that will make you perfect preachers to the best of your future people. For do not doubt but that God who watches what books you read in your student days, and what divinity you delight in, will both own and bless the provision you are already beginning to make for His poor in Zion. At the same time, make up

your mind that there will be people in all your
congregations who will not away with your preaching of Paul's gospel. They can make nothing of
Paul. Like John Bunyan at one time, they greatly
enjoy well-written and well-delivered lectures on
the historical parts of the Bible. They praise the
preachers whom William Law denounces — the
preachers who preach on Euroclydon and on the
times when the gospels were writ. And they will
let you explore and preach anything you like but
the corruptions of their own hearts, and the want
and worth of Jesus Christ to save them. But never
you mind. Go you on, going deeper and deeper
both into Paul and into yourself every returning
Sabbath day, and those deserters of your ministry
will all return to it when the scales fall off their
eyes. Aye, like Paul himself they will return to
support and to defend and perchance some of
them to occupy the pulpit that at one time they
so hated and persecuted and fled from. If they
are ordained to eternal life, they will yet be heard
repeating Bunyan's great apostrophe and saying,
O blessed Paul! O ever dear and ever blessed
Paul! Aye, and to your amazement they will add
this: O dear and blessed minister who first taught
us to read Paul's Epistles, and to understand them,
and to enjoy them, and to enjoy nothing else like
them in all the world. Amen.

VI

'Another thing was my dancing.'

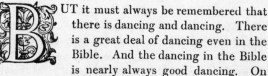UT it must always be remembered that there is dancing and dancing. There is a great deal of dancing even in the Bible. And the dancing in the Bible is nearly always good dancing. On the shore of the Red Sea Miriam the prophetess, the sister of Moses and Aaron, took a timbrel in her hand, and all the women went out after her with timbrels and with dances. And David was so full of holy joy at the homebringing of the Ark that he leaped and danced on the very street to the terrible scandal of his cold-hearted queen. And then in the New Testament the return of the prodigal son was celebrated with such an outburst of jubilation that the whole house was filled with feasting and with music and with dancing. As much as to say that there will be feasting and music and dancing in heaven, or something far better, when we return home to our Father's house to go no more out. And then Bunyan boldly declares that in vision one Sabbath morning he saw our Lord actually leaping and dancing around His empty grave, because He had gotten the victory for us over sin, and death, and hell. There is no doubt some very bad dancing recorded in the Bible, but

by far the most part of it is good, as good as the worship of God is good, as good as the overpowering joyfulness of the saints of God is good.

And then there is both good and bad dancing in the *Pilgrim's Progress* also. 'Come,' said Mrs. Lightmind, 'put this kind of talk away. I was yesterday at Madam Wanton's where we were all as merry as the maids. For who do you think should be there but I and Mrs. Love-the-flesh and three or four more, with Mr. Lechery, Mrs. Filth, and some others. So we had music and dancing, and what else was meet to fill up the pleasure. And I dare say, my Lady herself is an admirably-bred gentlewoman, and Mr. Lechery is as pretty a fellow.' And then we have this other dancing-party further on in the same book. 'Now Christiana, if need was, could play upon the viol, and her daughter Mercy upon the lute. So since they were so merry disposed, she played them a lesson, and Mr. Ready-to-halt would dance. So he took Mr. Despondency's daughter, named Miss Much-afraid, by the hand, and to dancing they went on the road. True, he could not dance without one crutch in his hand; but, I promise you, he footed it well; also the girl was to be commended, for she answered the music handsomely. As for Mr. Despondency, the music was too much for him; he was for feeding rather than dancing, for that he was almost starved. So Christiana gave him some of her bottle of spirits for his present relief, and then prepared him something to eat, and in a little the old gentleman came to himself, and began to be finely revived.' So that, you see, there are more kinds of dancing than one. It all depends on whose house it is in which you dance, and in whose company, and to what music, and especially who is your partner.

Another thing of Bunyan's at that time of his life was his bellringing. I must give you his bellringing at length and in his own words. For it wholly spoils John Bunyan to put him into any other man's words but his own. 'Now, you must know, that before this I had taken much delight in bellringing, but my conscience beginning to be tender, I thought such practice was but vain, and therefore forced myself to leave it, yet my mind hankered. Wherefore, I should go to the steeple door and look on, though I durst not ring. But I thought this did not become religion neither, yet I forced myself, and would look on still. But quickly after, I began to think—How if one of the bells should fall! Then I chose to stand under a main beam that lay overthwart the steeple, thinking there I might stand sure. But then I should think again, should the bell fall with a swing it might first hit the wall, and then rebounding upon me, might kill me for all that beam. This made me stand in the steeple door; and now, thought I, I am safe enough, for if a bell should then fall, I can slip out behind these thick walls, and so be preserved notwithstanding. So after this I would go to see them ring, but would not go further than the steeple door. But, then, it came into my heart —How if the steeple itself should fall! And this thought—it may fall for ought I know, when I stood and looked on, did continually so shake my mind that I durst not stand at the steeple door any longer, but was forced to flee, for fear the steeple should fall on my head.'

Now from all that it comes out as clear as day that it was neither his bellringing nor his dancing in themselves that so tortured and terrified Bunyan. It was his old and evil associations with these amusements that so greatly distressed him now. It was the cruel way that his conscience took him by the throat as often as he returned to these now condemned indulgences. Bunyan's conscience was now so scrupulous that she would not allow him so much as to touch one of his former bell-ropes, nor to lift so much as a foot in one of his former dances. And thus it is that our proper lesson out of Bunyan to-night is neither concerning bell-ringing, nor dancing, nor anything of that kind. Our proper lesson to-night is our own consciences; and the things, be they bells or dances, or what else, that lacerate and exasperate our consciences, and turn them into our fiercest accusers, and into our most relentless judges, and into our most cruel jailors.

'We are fearfully and wonderfully made,' says the Psalmist. And in nothing are we more fearfully and more wonderfully made than just in the matter of our conscience. For our conscience is set supreme and sovereign over all that is within us, and over all that we do without us. Our conscience is more than our conscience; our conscience may almost be said to be our God. So much so, that whatever our conscience commands us to do or not to do we must instantly obey her voice on pain of her heavy hand falling upon us and the still heavier hand of God Himself. So absolutely is our conscience the true and very voice of God to us that even when for any reason her voice is in anything dubious or doubtful, as it sometimes is, even to go

against the dubiety and the doubt is to go against
the clear command of God Himself. 'He that
doubteth is damned if he eat.' Our conscience and
God and our own immortal souls must always have
the benefit of the doubt, and never once our sup-
posed interests or our affections or our appetites.
All Hebrew and Greek and Latin and English, both
ethic and religion, are full of that. I could fill the
whole of this discourse with the proofs and the
illustrations of that. There may be no wrong to
you in bell-ringing or in dancing, but there would
have been mortal wrong to Bunyan had he gone
on with these condemned indulgences after his
conscience had once said No! For to him that
esteemeth anything to be unclean, to him it is
unclean. And how terrible the voice and the hand
of conscience can be when she has been outraged
and exasperated—of that the whole Bible and the
whole of our best literature in all languages is full.
And no literature is more full of that than our own
Shakespeare. And a plain evangelical preacher
has this :

> O conscience ! who can stand against thy power !
> Endure thy stripes or agonies one hour !
> Stone, gout, strappado, racks, whatever is
> Dreadful to sense are only toys to this.
> No pleasures, riches, honour, friends, can tell
> How to give ease to this : 'tis like to hell.

And then when the day of grace comes, as to the
part that conscience performs in conversion, Dr.
Newman sings :

> Thus the Apostles tamed the pagan breast,
> They argued not, but preach'd, and conscience did the rest.

Bunyan began life with what Paul describes as a conscience seared with a red-hot iron. Now this would sometimes happen to Bunyan in his tinker days and in his father's workshop. By some accident he would let fall a piece of red-hot iron on his hand or on his arm. And after a time of great agony the soft and tender flesh would be burned and seared into a hard and an unfeeling scar. And it would abide a hard and an unfeeling scar all his after days. Till afterwards he would often strike the scar with a sharp knife or with a red-hot rod, and would say like our Lord, So is the kingdom of heaven. The whole world was full of parables to Bunyan: his father's workshop and all. He never opened his eyes that he did not, like our Lord, see the kingdom of heaven. So is it with sin, he would say. Sin turns the tender side of the soul into a seared scar. Till the sinner goes on in his sin without so much as a single twinge of conscience. So it was with Bunyan himself, all through his early days in the army and in the tinker's stall. Till that never-to-be-forgotten Sabbath when the time of his merciful visitation had come at last. And then by the hand of the Holy Ghost Himself, the seared scar fell off Bunyan's conscience, and the dark scales fell off his eyes. And ever after that day of salvation to Bunyan his conscience entered on her rightful office in Bunyan's bosom, and she performed her office better and better down to the end of his obedient life. The first time you commit a certain sin your conscience will seize you by the throat and will hale you to judgment. But if you go on committing that sin in spite of your conscience her protest and her

warning will grow weaker and weaker till you will
take your fill of your sin without much remon-
strance from your conscience.   The time was when
you could not sleep, such was the accusation of your
conscience, but now she lies quietly on your pillow
beside you and takes your sin as a matter of course.
And when it comes to that—unless God visits you
and your conscience as He visited Bunyan—you are
a lost man.   You will die in your sin ; and then
your conscience will awaken from her sleep and will
be in your bosom and on your bed in hell, the
worm that dieth not, and the fire that is not
quenched.

But as God would have it with Bunyan and as
we read on in his masterly narrative we come to this
remarkable and remarkably expressed paragraph :
' But all this time, as to the act of sinning, I never
was so tender as now.   I durst not take a pin or a
stick, though but so big as a straw, for my conscience now was sore, and would smart at every
touch.   I could not now tell how to speak my
words for fear I should misplace them.   Oh ! how
gingerly did I then go in all I said and did !   I
found myself as on a miry bog that shook if I did
but stir ; and I was as if I were there left of God,
and man, and all good things.'   Have you ever had
any experience of a tenderness of conscience like
that ?   Let me take a case in illustration.   And that
not in bellringing, nor in dancing, but if only for a
variety let me take say novel-reading.   The time
was with myself when I could not so much as open
certain romances without my conscience becoming
like John Bunyan's 82nd paragraph.   I was brought
up to love and honour the Covenanters.   I had

early drunk in all I could lay my hands upon about those true makers of Scotland and of much more than Scotland. And I had gathered somehow and somewhere that a certain famous man in Edinburgh had laughed at the Covenanters in his novels, and had led the people of Edinburgh to laugh at them. And even when the time came that I could read those romances for myself, my conscience would not let me do that with entire comfort. And to-day I confess that I have a more tender heart than ever toward the Covenanters; and over against that I have a certain scrupulosity and a certain severity of conscience toward Sir Walter Scott that I cannot wholly get over. So much so that I never pass his monument in Princes Street that I do not wish that I could take off my hat with a more complete reverence and gratitude and love than I have ever attained to. I am quite well aware that I have lost not a little through my life-long grudge of conscience and heart against the great novelist. But then this is to be said in balance and in compensation of that: I get out of the Covenanters for my deepest needs more and more of what that wizard with all his genius cannot give me because he does not have it himself. I know what a master Sir Walter Scott is in some great departments of life and literature, and it is my daily lament that the great Covenanters did not take time to write English like his. But bad English and all, they are beyond all price to me. And you will agree with me when you have read, say, Rutherford, and Guthrie, and Durham, and Fraser, as often as I have read them. I have been led into that line of reflection through the truth, and the force, and the English of John Bunyan's 33rd and 82nd paragraphs.

Take another illustration from another side of our daily life. Many men among us have an uneasy conscience, aye, many among us have a very angry conscience, over their self-condemned habit of taking intoxicating drink in these days. The awful ravages that intoxicating drink is making among our Scottish people, the fearful state of our Edinburgh slums, and all owing to intoxicating drink—these things come home to the consciences of many men who still resist and silence their consciences. 'I thought it did not become religion,' says Bunyan. And, again, 'I was a full year before I could give it up.' And, again, 'Now, all the time my conscience would smart at every touch.' Yes; there are thousands of men in Scotland to-day who feel exactly like Bunyan. They feel in their consciences that, in the present distress, they ought at once to give up all consumption of intoxicating drink at their tables, and all indulgence in it themselves. But, then, they like it and their guests like it; and interest and habit and fashion and appetite are so strong that they browbeat and silence conscience. 'All our lives long,' says Christina Rossetti, 'we shall be bound to refrain our soul, and to keep it low; but what then? For the books we now forbear to read, we shall one day be endued with wisdom and knowledge. For the music we will not listen to, we shall join in the song of the redeemed. For the pictures from which we turn away, we shall gaze unabashed on the Beatific vision. For the companionships we shun, we shall be welcomed into angelic society, and into the

communion of triumphant saints. For all the
amusements we avoid, we shall keep the supreme
jubilee. And for all the pleasures we miss, we
shall abide, and shall for evermore abide, in the
rapture of heaven.'

VII

'I came where there were three or four poor women, sitting at a door in the sun, and talking about the things of God.'

BUT upon a day the good providence of God did cast me to Bedford, to work on my calling; and, in one of the streets of that town, I came where there were three or four poor women, sitting at a door in the sun, and talking about the things of God; and being now willing to hear them discourse, I drew near to hear what they said. But I may say, I heard, but I understood not; for they were far above, out of my reach. Methought they spake as if joy did make them speak; they spake with such pleasantness of Scripture language, and with such appearance of grace in all they said, that they were to me as if they had found a new world, as if they were a people that dwelt alone, and were not to be reckoned amongst their neighbours.'

What is that wonderful thing we call genius? And what is that other wonderful thing we call style? For when John Bunyan touches any subject whatsoever with his genius and with his style, the thing he so touches is at once made both classical and immortal. As here. We read these few simple-looking lines about those three or four poor women, and we at once know them far better than if we had lived next door to them all our days. We overhear and we understand every syllable of their godly conversation far better than if we had sat on the same doorstep beside them. We see down into the very bottom of their hearts, and we honour and love them from the very bottom of our hearts. What a gift is genius! And what a talent is style!

The husbands of those four poor women were away at their work, their children were off to school, their beds were all made, and their floors were all swept, and they all came out as if one spirit had moved them, and they met and sat down on a doorstep together to enjoy for a little the forenoon sun. And they plunged immediately into their inexhaustible and ever-fresh subject: God and their own souls. And even when the young tinker came along with his satchel of tools on his shoulder and stopped and leaned against the doorpost beside them they did not much mind him, but went on with the things of God that so possessed them. I have been thinking a great deal about that great night in the third of John, said one; and she went on to tell some of her thoughts to the other three. And as she went on, the young tinker standing beside her had never before heard that there was a third of John. Not one syllable did he understand more than if she had been speaking in Hebrew. Another said that all the time she was doing up the house that morning her Scripture had been a passage out of Paul, and at the name of Paul she kissed her hand to him as if he had been standing beside her. 'But God,' she repeated out of Paul,

'who is rich in mercy, for His great love wherewith
He loved us, even when we were dead in sins, hath
quickened us together with Christ.' And then one
who had a sweet trembling voice made her con-
tribution to the conversation in a few selected
verses out of the 51st Psalm. 'Therefore I should
often make it my business to be going again and
again into the company of these poor people, for I
could not stay away. And the more I went
amongst them the more I did question my condition.'

Another day as he was again passing by, behold
the same poor women were still occupied with the
same things of God. 'Since last we met,' said one
'my constant song has been that faith is the gift of
God.' And another answered her with the man
who said, 'Lord, I believe, help Thou mine unbelief.' And then the third woman took her New
Testament out of her pocket, it also was so old that
it was ready to fall piece from piece if she did but
turn it over. But she soon found the Epistle she
was looking for, and she read it till the Apostle
himself could not have read it better, so did she
contemn and slight and abhor her own righteousness as filthy and insufficient to do her any good.
'By these things,' adds Bunyan, 'my mind was now
so turned that it lay like a horse-leech at the vein,
and was still crying give, give. Yea, my mind was
now so fixed on Eternity, and on the things of the
kingdom of heaven, that neither pleasures, nor
profits, nor persuasions, nor threats could loosen it,
or make it let go its hold.'

Now for an illustration and a parallel to all that,
take this which was going forward in the Highlands

of Scotland at the same moment and that in a man of great spiritual genius and great spiritual sensibility. ' Being in T. H. his house, a godly man, his conversation did me much good. As likewise his prayers did me much good. As likewise the marvellous light he threw on Scripture at family worship, manifesting an order and a depth in the Scriptures that I had never seen before. Which did so astonish me as to make me see somewhat of a Godhead in the Scriptures. Lastly, his cheerful demeanour and that, as I saw, from a deep inward joy. Before that I had sometimes thought that a true saint was but a fancy. But truly I thought mine eyes now saw a true saint here and a man of a true New Testament spirit till I was persuaded that there was a holiness attainable by man. Surely I received much good from the conversation and the example of Mr. T. H.' And just as I am penning these lines a friend who has come in has occasion to tell me something similar about himself. Like John Bunyan, he tells me, he was a brisk talker about religion. Till one day a woman, like one of those women whose talk was so blessed to Bunyan, took him somehow into her confidence, and began to tell him some of the things that God had done for her soul. But as she went on his conscience spoke out till he was compelled to say to her that she wholly mistook him, for he was not a Christian like her. When his own words about himself so startled and alarmed him that he took no rest till he was a Christian like her. And now he is nothing short of a John Bunyan in his own way, as he works night and day among the poorest and the neediest people of our poor and needy city.

Now from all these cases, and from many more that will come to every thinking mind, we learn this impressive lesson, that it is one of God's most frequent ways to make use of godly conversation to the awakening and to the undeceiving of those who have hitherto had nothing but a name to live. And more than that; He makes use of godly and close-coming conversation, not only for the awakening and the undeceiving of others, but for the deeper awakening and the deeper undeceiving of those who are His own people already. 'I would be very glad,' writes Teresa, 'that we five should meet together from time to time for the undeceiving of one another, and to confer together how we are to reform ourselves so as to give His Majesty some satisfaction in us. For,' she continues, 'no man knows himself so well as other men know him. And no man is so frank and so true toward himself as a wise and a firm friend is, or ought to be. Our preachers,' she continues, 'ought to do all that for us. But as a matter of fact, everybody knows that they do not much help their hearers to the knowledge of themselves. They do not come close enough to us. They do not tell us plainly enough what we are. They do not call a spade a spade. They preach, but it is so as not to alarm us too much, or to offend us in any way. Just look around you and see,' she continues; 'do you know any man whose life has been much amended by the preaching he has heard? Yes; let us five friends meet together regularly with this one determination, to speak plainly to one another before it is too late.' So far Santa Teresa. And I have sometimes had her idea in my own mind. I have sometimes thought myself of trying to start a secret clerical club of five or six men who were in dead earnest about their own souls. Not a club for questions of theological science, or for questions of Old or New Testament criticism, or even for pulpit and pastoral efficiency. But for questions that are arising within us all every day concerning our own corrupt hearts. A club for deep and searching and self-undeceiving and God-pleasing work within ourselves; work exactly like that which that great saint and great genius tried in vain to start in Spain. But I am afraid that I have postponed my proposal till it is too late. At any rate the club has lost Dr. Laidlaw who would have been our convener and our chairman. He is taking the chair now where an altogether other kind of questions are being discussed, and where in God's light he is now seeing light. But perhaps some of his former students, or some of yourselves, will take up and will carry out my too-late intention, and will start in your own presbytery some such club of the soul.

From this page of John Bunyan we learn this also, what and where is the true Church of Christ on the earth. The true test of a true Church as of a true tree is its fruit. Those three or four poor women were the true tests and the true seals of the true Church of Christ in Bedford. It is of next to no consequence how the Church of Christ is governed, whether by popes, or by cardinals, or by bishops, or by presbyters, or by managers: a true Church is known not by its form of government but by its fruits; by the walk and the conversation of its members. It is of no consequence at all where a

Church hails from, or by what name it likes to be known among men; whether Rome, or Moscow, or Geneva, or Canterbury, or Edinburgh. The one thing of any real consequence for a Church is this: What do her people, and especially what do her poor women talk about when they meet and sit down in the sun? 'Have you forgot the close, and the milk-house, and the stable, and the barn, where God did visit your souls?' asks Bunyan of his first readers. That is the true communion roll which has a people upon it like that. Depend upon it, in God's sight that is the true Church of Rome, and of England, and of Scotland, and He knows no other Church. That is the true Church of Christ and He will acknowledge no other. Do you have any such poor women in your Church? How many such do you know in your Church? Do you know one? What is her name and what is her address? In what street is her doorstep? Send me her name, for I fear she is very lonely. And I would like to introduce her to one or two women like herself whom I have discovered, and with whom she could hold a conversation now and then about the deep things of God.

And then there is this. A woman is known by her companions as well as a man. But then a woman is not so able to go far afield to choose her companions, as a man is able to do. No. But she can always choose her books. And the best books are in our day within the reach of our poorest women, if they only knew the names of the best books and in what bookseller's shop to find them. John Bunyan's immortal books especially are to be had for next to nothing. *Grace Abounding* is to

be had by anybody for three or four pence. I
remember when it was not to be had in all our
town for love or money. I was told to my great
delight the other day that a Glasgow gentleman
had given the Tract Society a generous gift of
money to enable them to offer a 5000 edition of the
Pilgrim's Progress to the poor men and women of
Scotland—a beautiful edition to be sold at four-
pence each copy. The poorest godly woman in
Scotland can thus have the best of companionships,
even John Bunyan himself, to talk to her as she sits
in the sun.

To come back to where we began and so close.
' Upon a day the good providence of God did cast
me to Bedford, to work on my calling.' Now, have
you any such providential day in your autobiography ?
When was it ? Where was it ? How did it come
about ? And how did it end ? Was it your over-
hearing a godly conversation like Bunyan, or was it
your being in a godly man's house like Brea ? Or
was it hearing a sermon like one of the sermons the
London merchant heard during his tour in Scotland ?
Was it on the majesty of God, like Robert Blair's
sermon in St. Andrews ? Or was it on the loveli-
ness of Christ, like the sermon of that little fair
man Samuel Rutherford ? Or was it like the
sermon of that proper old man at Irvine, who
showed that London merchant his own heart ?
That was a good providence indeed to Bunyan.
That was one of the very best providences that was
ever cast upon him. What was your very best
providence ? And how has it ended ? Has it
ended by uniting you for ever to that blessed
companionship so celebrated by the Hebrew pro-

phet?—'Then they that feared the LORD spake often one to another; and the LORD hearkened, and heard it, and a book of remembrance was written before Him for them that feared the LORD, and that thought upon His name. And they shall be Mine, saith the LORD of Hosts, in that day when I make up My jewels; and I will spare them, as a man spareth his own son that serveth him.'

VIII

'I found that ancient Christian to be a good man, but a stranger to much combat with the devil.'

OUNG Bunyan was far more fortunate with the ancient women of his acquaintance than he was with the ancient men. The three or four ancient women who sat one day at a door in the sun and talked together in young Bunyan's hearing about the things of God were nothing less than so many mothers in Israel to this fatherless and motherless lad. But this ancient Christian man gave young Bunyan but cold comfort when he told him all his anxious and sorrowful story. He was a good man, Bunyan admits, but he had not gone very deep into his own heart, nor had the tempter troubled him very much either about his heart or his life. For some reason or other the enemy of human souls did not give much attention to this ancient Christian. And thus it was that the old man had no understanding whatever of young Bunyan's much-tried and much-tempted case. When he was consulted the stupid old creature gave it as his decided opinion that the young tinker had already committed the unpardonable sin, and so was past hope. Bunyan does not say it in as many words, but I feel sure that he knocked at the door of some of those ancient and much-experienced women on his weary way home that dark day.

Compared with those three or four ancient women, and compared even with this young inquirer, that ancient Christian man had lived a sheltered, a peaceful, and an easy life. Ancient, as by this time he was; and neophyte, as Bunyan still was; Bunyan's depreciatory description of himself at that period does not need to be much altered to make it exactly applicable to his old friend. For if this ancient Christian had indeed been born again, the thought of that did not much occupy the old man's mind. Neither knew he aught of the treachery and the deceitfulness of his own heart. And as for his secret thoughts, he took no notice of them at all. The truth is, born again as he undoubtedly was, and old man as he now was, the shell was still on his ancient head, he was still but a babe at the breast.

Now you will stop me at this point and will say to me that such a stupid old creature as that could not surely be a really Christian man at all. But don't be so severe. Don't be so exacting in your demands on old Christian men. Don't be so ready to excommunicate and to reprobate old men or young men either who may not have had all the length and breadth and height and depth of your spiritual experience. Young Bunyan was not so harsh in his judgments as you are. It is true that this ancient Christian man was as blind as any Bedfordshire mole to all Bunyan's extraordinary experiences. But Bunyan never so much as once suggests that the innocent old man was other than a true Christian according to his type and according

to his attainments. At the same time, he feels
bound to admit that this ancient and not untrue
Christian was a total stranger to anything that
could be called a combat with the devil and with
the sin of his own heart. Now, how are we to
account for the existence of that man, and of so
many men like him among ourselves also? Especially when we see that some other men's hearts and
lives among us are all combat together. All combat
together, and without a single day's discharge all
their life from this fearful inward war.

Well to begin with, the commander of an army
selects and allots and places his soldiers as pleases
himself. He appoints his men their duties, and
their dangers, and their opportunities, as seems
good, and wise, and safe, in his own eyes. And
thus it is that some soldiers are always set in the
hottest front of the hottest battle, while some other
soldiers are always to be found in the rear, till they
are rather so many camp-followers than real
soldiers. Some so-called soldiers never rise above
being raw recruits all their days, while some others
are always at the head of some forlorn hope
or other, somewhere or other. Some so-called
soldiers are so many drawing-room ornaments
rather than real soldiers: they are always to be
seen on a street parade before a crowd of
admiring boys; while some other soldiers are not
fit to be seen with their torn uniforms, and their
gaping wounds, and their clotted blood, and their
broken swords. And so is it in the army of Jesus
Christ the Captain of our salvation. Let some of
His good soldiers be described in one sentence of
a fine book about them: 'Who through faith sub-

dued kingdoms,' we read, 'wrought righteousness, obtained promises, stopped the mouths of lions, quenched the violence of fire, out of weakness were made strong, waxed valiant in fight, turned to flight the armies of the aliens; others were tortured not accepting deliverance, they were stoned, they were sawn asunder, were tempted, were slain with the sword; being destitute, afflicted, tormented; of whom the world was not worthy.' John Bunyan was always far more at home with such torn and dismembered heroes as these, than he was with that ancient Christian in Bedford who had never been half a mile away from his own chimney corner.

Many country clowns and city loungers have taken the King's shilling who will never all their days really earn it. They have just passed the standard for height and weight and scarcely that; their eyes and their ears and their teeth and the beating of their hearts have barely got their certificate. You will sometimes see an undersized, ill-knit, narrow-chested, wax-complexioned stripling wearing the King's uniform, till you cannot help wondering how he ever passed his examination, and what the King's army is to make of him. And the sight of him calls to mind many so-called soldiers of Jesus Christ among us. They will, no doubt, be of some use, sometime and somewhere; but it will not be in much combat with the devil and with their own hearts that they will ever win their spurs. The old enemy altogether ignores them. He absolutely despises them. He leaves them all their days in an unbroken peace, while he sets on some other men with all his hellish fury, and that too without ceasing. 'Fight neither with small nor great, save only with the King of Israel,' said the King of Syria. And these are sometimes the devil's exact orders to his soldiers also. 'Fight you to the death with that dangerous young tinker,' said the devil, pointing to young John Bunyan. 'Bring me his head in a charger, and I will give you an increase of rations, and a red-ribbon for your shoulder-knot.' Now, after hearing that, if any of you have the curiosity to know how that combat went on and how it ended in the case of John Bunyan, you may read all that in his fine chapters on Greatheart and Standfast, as also in his *Grace Abounding* and in his *Holy War*. Alexander the Great had always under his pillow, both in the palace and in the field, a small silver casket which contained nothing but his lifelong copy of Homer. And all of you who are always in the high places of the field have, I warrant you, the Psalms, and the Romans, and the Revelation, and the *Grace Abounding* always within reach of your camp-bed. But on the other hand, there are many ancient Christians among us who never once slept with their clothes on and their sword beside them all their days. And when you speak to them about having their Homers within reach they do not know what you are saying : they never spent a shilling on a Homer all their days. 'Add to this,' says M. Bremond in his masterly and most delightful book, *The Mystery of Newman*, 'add to this, a multitude of good people resign themselves to a life without any combat in it at all. They are not bad Christians ; but they are satisfied with a cold and dry religion. The spiritual battles of the soul do not trouble them.' And then he quotes this passage from the great preacher himself: 'They are most excellent men, in their way, but they do not walk in a lofty path. There is nothing at all unearthly about them. They do not take time to contemplate, and to prepare for, the world to come. They do not wait on God all the day. They weary of watching for Him. They do not feel that they are in a world with a height above it, and with a depth beneath it. They have no difficulties in their religion; they think everything plain and easy.' In short, they are total strangers, as John Bunyan would say, to much combat with the devil, and with the sinfulness of their own hearts.

Now, the deepest of the Apostles gives us the whole explanation of all that superficiality and shallowness in one word of his, when he says that the law of God had never once really entered the minds and the hearts and the imaginations and the consciences of those self-complacent men. With the greatest of the Apostles everything turns on the entrance or the non-entrance of God's holy law. Speaking for himself, the whole difference between Saul the Pharisee, and Paul the greatest of God's saints, was simply this, that the holy law of God had now pierced to the dividing asunder of his soul and his spirit, and of his joints and his marrow: the holy law of God, in every commandment of it, was now a discerner of every thought and every intent of Paul's half-sanctified heart. And the whole difference between this stupid old man and the future author of the *Grace Abounding* was the same thing, the law had entered the young man's heart to all its depth, whereas it had scarcely so much as

grazed the surface of the old man's skin. As our
great Highland preachers were wont to say, there
had never been any real 'law-work' in that ancient
man's heart; while, on the other hand, every paragraph of poor Bunyan's autobiography brings out
some new combat of his with the devil and with
his own inward evil. Some new combat about sin
and about the forgiveness of sin. Some new combat about faith, both as it justifies the ungodly and
as it sanctifies the godly. Some new combat about
the Bible, and about the Apocrypha; everlasting
combats indeed. Bunyan, all his days, was the
King of Israel over again. You would have thought
that the prince of darkness had no man in all England in his evil eye in those days but the future
author of the *Pilgrim's Progress*, and the *Holy
War*, and the *Grace Abounding*. Whereas Bunyan's
ancient friend was as innocent of all those combats
as any of yourselves. I say yourselves: for there
are crowds of this ancient Christian's spiritual off-
spring among yourselves. Speak to them about
the entrance of the law, and they will go about
saying that you do not preach the Gospel. Speak
to them about the exceeding sinfulness of heart-
sin, and you might as well speak to them in
Hebrew. Speak in their hearing about the depth
and the difficulty of this or that divine truth; or
speak in their hearing about the discoveries made
by the Scripture scholarship of our day, and they
will advertise you far and near for an infidel.
'Here, therefore, I had but cold comfort; but,
talking a little more with him, I found him,
though a good man, a stranger to much combat
of any kind.' In Paul's all-explaining words,

the law of truth and love and holiness had got little or no entrance into his ancient head and heart.

Now, young Bunyan's great mistake, which he here writes out for our warning was this, that he took his intricate case to the wrong counsellor. He should have sought out some of those ancient women of Bedford into whose sinful hearts the holy law of God was entering deeper and deeper every day, and they would soon have resolved his whole case for him. 'A soldier who has been in the wars can best tell another soldier how to fight,' says Jacob Behmen in his *Way to Christ*. Now if any of you have like John Bunyan been early chosen and enlisted and appointed to enter on a life-long combat with the devil and with your own heart, take good care what counsellor you consult about that matter. And especially take good care what preachers you sit under and what authors you read. There are plenty of good men and able men and learned men in our pulpits to-day; but you will get but cold comfort from the best and the ablest of them unless, like John Bunyan and you, they are in a constant and an increasing combat themselves with John Bunyan's enemy and yours. But even if your combat is appointed you in a place where you have no choice of preachers, you can always choose your authors. Luther would be a first-rate author for you, if you could lay your hands on him, and Jacob Behmen, Luther's great disciple. But thank God you do not need to go outside your own tongue to read abundantly the same wonderful workings of the Spirit of God. For in your own richest of tongues, you have the

immortal and inexhaustible Bunyan himself, and
you have his great contemporaries—such as Baxter,
and Owen, and Goodwin, and Sibbs in England;
and Rutherford, and Brea, and Halyburton in Scotland; and after them Boston, and Chalmers, and
M'Cheyne, and many more. 'O, but we have
heard to weariness all these old-fashioned names
and obsolete men!' you will say to me. 'Are you
never to recommend to us some of the up-to-date
authors!' you will say to me. So the slovens,
and the camp-followers, and the cowards, and the
deserters no doubt said to the great soldier who
had never anything newer than Homer under
his pillow. But our Homeric books are not run
upon in Mudie's or in the *Times* bookshop. Only
things called books, that sell by their thousands
to-day, and line our trunks to-morrow. And
hence our ignorance, and our cowardice, and
our continual desertions from the great combats
of the soul.

Take a closing word to the point out of Luther,
that great combatant of the devil. He is speaking
to the young preachers of his day. 'No,' he says,
'I did not learn to preach Christ all at once. It
was my temptations and my corruptions that best
prepared me for my pulpit. The devil has been
my best professor of exegetical and experimental
divinity. Before that great schoolmaster took me
in hand, I was a sucking child and not a grown
man. It was my combats with sin and with Satan
that made me a true minister of the New Testament. It is always a great grace to me, and to my
people, for me to be able to say to them: I *know*
this text to be true! I know it *for certain* to be

true! Without incessant combat, and pain, and sweat, and blood, no ignorant stripling of a student ever yet became a powerful preacher.' So says one of the most powerful preachers that ever entered the Pauline pulpit.

IX

'As for secret thoughts, I took no notice of them.'

R. EDISON, that eminent American man of science, was once asked whether he ever expected with all his inventiveness to be able to advertise an instrument to enable a man to see down into his neighbour's secret thoughts. And the answer of that most original man was to this effect: 'Even if I could construct such a terrible instrument, God forbid that I should ever publish it to the world. For,' he said, 'did we all see down into the secret thoughts of one another about one another, human life would no longer be bearable on the earth. There would not be two friends left to trust one another, and to love one another, in the whole world. Family life itself would instantly fly into pieces. Human society, in all its combinations, would at once become dissolved. For all men would flee to the rocks, and to the mountains, and would cry to them, "Fall on us and hide us and all our secret thoughts from before the faces of all men."'

Now though our Almighty Maker, the Great Inventor, has not intrusted us with an instrument wherewith to see down into our neighbour's secret thoughts about us, He has done far better than

that. For He has committed to our keeping and
to our constant use an infallible instrument for
seeing down into our own secret thoughts about
ourselves, and about our neighbours, and about
everything else. And that secret window is so
wonderfully constructed, and is so filled in all its
frames with such wonderful glass, that every pane
of it is as dark as midnight to every eye but the
Eye of the Great Inventor and our own eye. And
thus it is that my God and Saviour and I myself
are the sole spectators of all that goes on in my
mind and in my heart and down among my secret
thoughts. 'O Lord, Thou hast searched me and
known me. Thou knowest my downsitting and
mine uprising. Thou understandest my thoughts
afar off.'

Well then that being so, to go back to that little
company of four poor women and one poor tinker
on that eventful forenoon in Bedford, they all had
that same secret window in themselves, and they all
had it opening down into their own secret thoughts.
Only, up till now, there had been this great difference between them. Those four wise women
scarce ever gave a glance into any other window
but their own. Whereas that born fool of a tinker
never looked into his own inward window at all.
In his own ashamed and remorseful words written
long afterwards he says : 'As for my secret thoughts,
I had taken no notice of them at all. Neither had
I the very least understanding of Satan's suggestions and temptations, nor how those suggestions
and temptations were to be withstood and resisted.'
Now, this large congregation in Edinburgh this
evening is exactly like that little company in Bed-

ford that forenoon. There are some people here who are exactly like those four poor women. There are those here whose inward eyes are so occupied with their own secret thoughts that they have neither time nor taste to think much about anything else in this world. But on the other hand, it is much to be feared that there are not a few people among us who are exactly like that blind and besotted tinker. They think about everybody but themselves. They watch everybody but themselves. They suspect injury from everybody but themselves. Their ears are open to the faults of everybody but themselves. Their eyes wander over the whole city looking into everybody's window but their own. John Bunyan describes them in this exact description of himself, 'As for my secret thoughts, I took no notice of them at all.'

Now, my brethren, in the measure that we take notice of our secret thoughts some most important results will most certainly follow to us as well as to those four poor and pious women.

And first, a great and a growing contrition of heart will follow, a great and a growing humiliation of heart will follow, and a great and a growing horror of heart will follow. ' If thou hast thought evil in thine heart,' says a wise man, ' then lay thy hand upon thy mouth.' And thus it was that the hands of those four wise women were never off their mouths night nor day. Now what do you say to that? Who among you will join with Agur and with those four wise women in laying your hands on your mouths? And that because of the indescribable evil of so many of your secret thoughts? Because of the indescribable vanity and folly and

lawlessness and disorderliness of your secret
thoughts, even when they are not so absolutely
evil. Yes, Mr. Edison, stand to your resolution.
Keep that terrible instrument of yours to yourself.
Over here we do not need it. For our great
Inventor has been beforehand with you. He has
long ere now produced and perfected a secret
instrument for our own exclusive use. And as
often as we honestly make use of that secret instrument upon ourselves we have no wish left to see
down into any man's secret thoughts but our own.
If our neighbour's secret thoughts toward us are
ever as selfish, and as mean, and as treacherous,
and as envious, and as malicious, and as murderous
as our secret thoughts so often are toward him,—
No, sir, we do not need your fearful invention.
For to us every hour of the day and every watch
of the night the word of God is quick and
powerful and sharper than any two-edged sword,
piercing even to the dividing asunder of soul
and spirit, and of the joints and marrow, and is a
discerner of the thoughts and intents of the heart.
When Thomas Fuller was under examination by
Oliver Cromwell's Puritan triers, they proposed
this test to him: Whether he had ever had any
experience of a work of grace in his own heart?
To which question Fuller was able to answer that
he could appeal to the Searcher of hearts that
he had for long made conscience toward God of his
very thoughts. 'With that answer,' says Calamy,
'the triers were quite satisfied,' as, indeed, they
might well be. Now can you take an appeal to
the Great Trier and say as much as honest Thomas
Fuller said? For if so then your conscience holds

no sinecure amid the multitude of your secret thoughts within you.

And a second result of your taking notice of your secret thoughts will be this: *Obsta principiis.* That is to say, you will learn to strangle your sins in their very birth. You will learn to detect and to detest and to denounce and to deliver over to instant death your most secret thoughts as soon as they show the least taint of original sin. Luther, like Paul his master, was a great noticer of his own sinful thoughts. Preaching one of his plain-spoken sermons he said that he was not always able to keep unclean birds from circling and screaming round his head. But, God helping him, they should not alight and roost and breed and bring forth their abominable young ones under his hat. And Thomas A'Kempis has this classical passage to the very same effect : *Cogitatio, imaginatio, delectatio, assentio.* That is to say, there is first the bare thought of the sin. Then there is an imaginative anticipation of it. Then with that the sinner's heart enters into the speculative enjoyment of it. And then immediately after that the stupid sinner has sold himself for nought. Resist therefore the very first beginnings of sin, even in thought.

But comfort my people, saith your God. Well, in fulfilment of that command, one of John Bunyan's ablest and best and most heart-comforting contemporaries has this comforting passage. 'The bulk,' he says, 'of the unregenerate part in the most of Christian men, is far greater than the bulk of the truly regenerate and sanctified part. So much is this the case that if a Christian man were to go to measure himself by the bulk of sin in his secret thoughts he might well despair of himself. But he is to make a careful measurement of himself, not by the multitude, or the frequency, or the urgency, of his sinful thoughts, but, rather, by the entertainment they receive at his hands when they arise within him. If his sinful thoughts are welcomed, and are encouraged, and are hospitably entertained, he may well despair. But, on the other hand, if his sinful thoughts, as they arise, are instantly hated, and are instantly repudiated, and are instantly cast out of his mind and his heart, then that man may honestly take comfort and say with another of God's people, Now, then, it is no more I that do it, but sin that dwelleth in me. For I delight in the law of God after the inward man.' Watch, then, what manner of thoughts arise incessantly in your most inward mind and heart. And at the same time watch with all your inward eyes what reception, and what entertainment, they receive at the hands of your inward man.

And then God's people are to be comforted in this way also. Let them watch well the good thoughts that arise in their hearts from time to time. As also watch well the reception and the welcome and the kind of entertainment those good thoughts get when they so arise. Such good thoughts as these: their kind thoughts towards other people; their tender-hearted and charitable thoughts towards other people; their sympathising and friendly thoughts towards other people; their forgiving and their forgetting thoughts towards their enemies; their meek and lowly-minded thoughts about themselves, and their generous and

magnanimous thoughts about their neighbours, and
especially about their rivals, and those in the same
line of life with themselves. But above all let
them watch and acknowledge and cherish all their
secret and spontaneous and loving and adoring
thoughts about Jesus Christ. For, far above all
else, it is as a man thinks about Jesus Christ in his
secret thoughts so is that man in the sight of God.
The time was when John Bunyan never thought
whether there was a Jesus Christ or no. But that
dreadful time is for ever past with many of you.
Nowadays some days you scarcely think about anything else; at least not with your whole mind and
heart. For instance is not this the simple truth?
You never waken in the morning nowadays that
your first thought is not of Jesus Christ. 'When I
awake,' you say, 'I am still with Thee.'

> 'Dark and cheerless is the morn,'—you sing—
>   'Unaccompanied by Thee;
> Joyless is the day's return
>   Till Thy mercy's beams I see.'

And you put on Christ all the time you are putting
on your morning clothes. Before you venture to
open your letters or your newspapers you first fill
your hearts with strengthening and with supporting
and with calming thoughts of Jesus Christ. And
so on all the day, till those who sit beside you all
the day and those who lie beside you all the night
would be amazed to be told who they have had all
the time in the same house with them.

And then before closing there is this: It was
not of their neighbour's things nor was it of their
own things that those three or four poor women
talked that day as they sat in the sun; it was all

the time of 'the things of God.' That is to say,
their own miserable state by nature, the suggestions
and the temptations of Satan, the wretchedness of
their own hearts, the filthiness and the raggedness
of their own righteousness, these things and such
things as these were among the things of God of
which they talked that day. All these things; and
then the new birth, and God's visitation of their
souls with His love in the Lord Jesus, with all His
comforts and all His promises in Christ. All these
things were among the things of God talked about
on that doorstep in Bedford that day. Take a great
comfort out of that also, all you sin-harassed and
sick-hearted people of God. For your God is such
a God that all your secret sinfulness, and all your
untold pain and shame on account of your secret
sinfulness, all that is actually counted up among the
things of God. It is something not unlike this.
All the diseases and all the pains and all the pollutions of his patient are the things of his physician.
All the guilt and all the condemnation of the
accused man are the things of his advocate. All
the debts and all the imprisonments of his client
are the things of his surety. And much more all
the sin and all the misery of the people of God are
the things of their God and of His Christ. In the
covenant of grace all these things are now much
more God's things than they are your things.
Take this home with you then as your crowning
comfort this evening of comfort; this crowning
comfort, that it was nothing less than the very
things of God of which those four wise and
well-taught women spake when they went so
far below and then so far above the tinker's

reach as yet. 'Thus, therefore, when I had heard and considered what they said, I left them, and went about my employment again. But their talk and discourse went with me. Also my heart would tarry with them; for I was greatly affected with their words; both because, by these words of theirs, I was convinced that I wanted the true tokens of a truly godly man; and, also, because by their words I was convinced of the happy and blessed condition of him that was such an one as they were, who thus sat in the sun and talked together of the things of God.' 'Search me, O God, and know my heart; try me, and know my thoughts. And see if there be any wicked way in me, and lead me in the way everlasting.'

X

' At this time I sat under the ministry of holy Mr. Gifford, whose doctrine, by God's grace, was much for my stability.'

I MUST first tell you something about holy Mr. Gifford himself. Well, John Gifford was the very minister for John Bunyan; for in everything but literary genius John Gifford had been a John Bunyan himself, only unspeakably worse. John Gifford had at one time been a Royalist officer in the great Civil War; and like so many officers and men on that bad side he was a man of a very bad life. In the course of the conflict he fell into the hands of his enemies, and for some transgression of the laws of war he was condemned to death. But by the devotion and the determination of his sister he managed to outwit his jailor and to escape from his prison. After some hairbreadth escapes Gifford was enabled somehow to set up as a doctor in the town of Bedford, where he continued his old life of debauchery and was notorious far and near for his hatred and ill-usage of the Puritan people. But one night after losing all his money at cards—'as God would have it,' as Bunyan was wont to say— Gifford was led to open a book of the famous Puritan Robert Bolton, when something that he read in that book took such a hold of him that he lay in agony of conscience for several weeks afterwards. 'At last,' as his old kirk-session record still extant has it, 'God did so plentifully discover to him the forgiveness of his sins for the sake of Christ that all his life after he lost not the light of God's countenance, save only about two days before he died.' No sooner did John Gifford become a changed man than, like Saul of Tarsus, he openly joined himself to those whom he had hitherto persecuted, and ultimately he became their beloved pastor. The three or four poor women whom Bunyan one day saw sitting at a door in the sun and talking about the things of God were all members of John Gifford's Free Church congregation. And in long after days John Bunyan immortalised John Gifford as his Evangelist in the *Pilgrim's Progress*. Such then was holy Mr. Gifford, whose doctrine, by God's grace, was so much for John Bunyan's stability.

The first thing that John Bunyan tells us about John Gifford was the way he conducted his young communicants' class. Not that young Bunyan was actually an enrolled member of that class as yet. But Mr. Gifford did as your ministers sometimes do in imitation of him. He invited all the young people of his congregation to attend his class for young communicants, even though they were not intending to sit down at the approaching table. You hear your ministers making that same intimation and giving that same invitation before every communion, and there are always some wise and foreseeing parents and guardians who send their young people to such great opportunities. I cannot tell you to a certainty how Mr. Gifford succeeded with his other young people, but his

success with young Bunyan was almost too terrible.
Either Gifford must have been a terrible teacher,
or else his tinker-student must have made terrible
conscience of all that he heard in the class, as well
as of all that went on in his own heart during those
pre-communion days and nights; for he tells his
experience of those days and nights in a narrative
far too terrible for me to repeat to you to-night.
You will find it for yourselves, if you are interested
in such things, in paragraphs 77 to 88 of his *Grace
Abounding to the Chief of Sinners.* In a conversation
he once held with me about his ministry, Dr.
Moody Stuart said to me that if he had ever had
any success to speak of in his long pastorate, it had
mostly been with young communicants, and with
fathers when they came to speak to him about
baptism for their children. Dr. Moody Stuart was
the most pungent man I ever knew, but I doubt
if any even of his young communicants ever came
through those eleven paragraphs in *Grace Abounding.*
It takes two to make an experience like that. It
takes a Gifford or a Moody Stuart and it takes a
young John Bunyan. Are our young communicants'
classes conducted nowadays with anything of the
labour and the earnestness of John Gifford's classes
and Dr. Moody Stuart's? If there were a young
John Bunyan in our classes would he put our
names into his autobiography with anything of the
love and the honour and the everlasting gratitude
that John Bunyan puts John Gifford into his *Grace
Abounding?* And yet the most faithful of ministers
may do their very best in their classes, and with too
little lasting result. A minister may be a very
Gifford in his class, and yet he may have to weep

over crowds of his young communicants in after
days.   I suppose after John Bunyan succeeded
John Gifford as pastor of that little Puritan congregation he was not one whit behind Gifford himself
in his fidelity to the souls of his young communicants.   And yet I find him making this sad entry
in his *Grace Abounding* toward the end of his life.
'If any of those who were awakened by my
ministry did after fall back, as sometimes too many
did, I can truly say their loss hath been more to
me than if one of my own children, begotten of my
body, had been going to its grave.   I think, verily,
I may speak it without an offence to my Lord,
nothing hath gone so near me as that, unless it
was the fear of the loss of my own soul.   I have
counted as if I had goodly buildings and lordships
in those places where my spiritual children were
born.   My heart hath been so wrapped up in the
glory of this excellent work that I counted myself
more blessed and honoured of God than if He had
made me Emperor of the Christian world, or the
Lord of all the glory of the earth.'

John Gifford's pulpit was quite as much blessed
to young Bunyan as was his communicants' class.
And Bunyan long afterwards went back upon and
signalised these four features of John Gifford's
pulpit-work—its Scriptural character, its doctrinal
character, its experimental character, and its evangelical character.   I was not bold enough to give
you the terrible paragraphs in which John Bunyan
tells the terrible results that John Gifford's classes
had upon him.   But I have no hesitation in reading his hundred and twentieth paragraph to you,
in which he tells us in his own inimitable way how

his minister taught him to read his New Testament;
and, especially, how he taught him to employ his
eyes upon Jesus Christ in his New Testament.
Both in his class and in his pulpit John Gifford
was very happy to have such a great hand in the
opening of John Bunyan's splendid eyes. We do
not all have eyes like John Bunyan's eyes. But
we all have our own eyes for our employment of
which on our New Testament and on Jesus Christ
and on everything else we shall all one day have
to give an account. And we are happy in having
a specimen of John Bunyan's account in his hundred
and twentieth paragraph. 'Under the ministry of
holy Mr. Gifford, O how my soul was led on from
truth to truth! Even from the birth and cradle of
the Son of God, to His ascension and second coming
from heaven to judge the world. There was not
one part of the Gospel of the Lord Jesus 'but I
was orderly led into it. Methought I was as if I
had seen Him born, as if I had seen Him grow up,
as if I had seen Him walk through this world from
His cradle to His cross; to which also, when He
came, I saw how gently He gave Himself to be
hanged and nailed upon it for my sins and my
wicked doings. Also, as I mused on this His
progress, that Scripture dropped on my spirit, He
was ordained for the slaughter.' What a contrast
to the time when young Bunyan could not away
with the Scriptures. And when he said, 'What
is the Bible? Give me a ballad, a newsbook,
George on horseback or *Bevis of Southampton*. Give
me some book that teaches curious arts, or that
tells old fables; but for the Holy Scriptures I
cared not,' what a happy service John Gifford did

to John Bunyan, and to us, and to all the world!
What a happy class, and what a happy pulpit!

And, then, all his after days, John Bunyan—
tinker, preacher, great writer, and great saint of
God — went back upon John Gifford's doctrinal
preaching with an ever-increasing gratitude. A
great preacher and a great writer of the last
generation has this in his famous autobiography:
'When I was fifteen, a great change of thought
took place in me. I fell under the influences of a
definite creed, and received into my intellect impressions of dogma, which, through God's mercy,
have never been effaced or obscured.' Now, John
Bunyan, our great preacher and great writer, had
the very same experience in his early days. 'At
this time, also, I sat under the ministry of holy
Mr. Gifford, whose doctrine, by God's grace, was
much for my stability. His doctrine was as season-
able to my soul as the former and the latter rain
in their season. Wherefore I found my soul,
through grace, very apt to drink in his doctrine.'
Both John Gifford's day and John Bunyan's day
were the greatest days of doctrinal preaching the
Church of Christ has seen since Paul's day. Whereas your day and mine is the weakest in doctrine
that the Church of Christ has ever had to come
through. But the day of sound and deep doctrine
in religion must come back again. All real knowledge takes the form of doctrine. A doctrine is
a truth that is so sure that it can be taught and
can be trusted to. Every branch of human knowledge, to be called knowledge, takes the form and
takes the name of doctrine. Take any branch of
human knowledge you choose: medicine, law, com-

merce, statesmanship, war; all the great sciences,
and all the great arts, have their stability deep
down in their respective doctrines. And our states-
men, and our business men, and our scientific men,
and our artistic men are all trusted and are all
honoured and are all rewarded just in the measure
that they master the foundation doctrines of their
several professions and services, and then go on to
put those doctrines into practice. And it cannot
surely continue to be, that the one thing needful
for all men to know should be left to stand without
a foundation in men's understandings, as well as
without a hold over their hearts and their lives.
The real truth is that the doctrines of the evangelical pulpit are the only sure and stable and un-
changeable and everlasting doctrines on which the
mind and the heart and the conscience of mortal
man can ever rest. All other doctrines, whether
of philosophy, or of science, or of art, have been
the slow and the gradual discovery of human
observation and experiment. But the doctrines of
grace are of another kind, and they come from
another world. Unless they are the greatest delu-
sion and the greatest snare the doctrines of grace
are the very wisdom of God, and the very power
of God, to the salvation of sinful and suffering men.
And in the Word of God those doctrines stand
revealed from heaven in all their fullness and in
all their assurance of grace and truth, and in a fullness to which no man is ever to add or is ever to
take away. When the Son of God finished His
redeeming work on earth, and when God the
Father so revealed His Son in Paul as to enable
the greatest of the Apostles to cast Christ and His

life and His work into evangelical doctrine, that
canon of divine truth was closed for all time. And
thus it was that the men of the first century, the
Romans, and the Corinthians, and the Galatians,
and the Ephesians, and the Colossians had as
developed and as rich and as sure a word of
doctrine as we have. And we have just what they
had and we need no more. We, like them, are
complete in Christ. So much so that, as a matter
of indisputable fact, every real reformation of the
Christian religion, all down the centuries, as well
as every individual conversion and sanctification,
has come about, not by any new discovery of
doctrine, but by a believing return and an entire
surrender to the doctrines and the precepts and
the counsels and the comforts of the New Testament. Paul was the greatest of Christian preachers
and he was also the humblest of men, and this is
how he writes to the Galatians and to us about his
doctrine of Christ: 'I marvel that you are so soon
removed from Him that called you into the grace
of Christ unto another gospel: which is not another.
[He means that there is nothing else on the face
of the earth for one moment to be called a gospel.]
For I certify you, brethren, that the gospel which
is preached by me is not after men. For I neither
received it of men, neither was I taught it, but
by the revelation of Jesus Christ.' 'Progress in
Christianity,' says Bishop Gore, 'is always reversion
to an original and a perfect type.' So it is. And
Paul is that original and perfect type in doctrine,
just as Jesus Christ is that perfect and original
type in life, and in character, and in walk, and in
conversation.

XI

'And now I began to look into the Bible with new eyes: and, especially, the Epistles of the Apostle Paul were sweet and pleasant to me.'

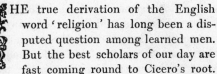HE true derivation of the English word 'religion' has long been a disputed question among learned men. But the best scholars of our day are fast coming round to Cicero's root. That great genius in language held that the Latin word *religio* originally meant the continual reading and re-reading of the sacred books. To Tully, as to David, the truly religious man is he whose delight is in the law of the Lord, and in His law doth he meditate day and night. And he shall be like a tree planted by the rivers of water, that bringeth forth his fruit in his season: his leaf also shall not wither; and all that he doeth shall prosper. That is to say, true religion, even in its etymology, stands firm and fruitful in the continual reading of the word of God, till that word dwells richly in the assiduous reader's mind and heart. Cicero's etymology continually comes to my mind as often as I open Bunyan's impressive paragraphs on the Bible. And that true etymology comes even more to my mind as often as I open Halyburton's autobiography everywhere. But it is with Bunyan and his new eyes and his new Bible that we have specially to do to-night.

From the beginning to the end of his *Grace Abounding*, Bunyan describes to us the successive eyes with which he read his Bible from first to last. When Bunyan began first to read his Bible it was with the eyes of a child. As a child he greatly delighted in the enthralling stories of the Bible. The garden of Eden, Cain and Abel, Noah and his ark, Abraham and Isaac and Jacob and Joseph, and all their adventures, Moses and his floating cradle among the bulrushes of the Nile, the gigantic labours of Samson, and the pious prowess of David, and so on. Then, through the native strength and the native originality of his mind, though he never went to school to the Fathers or to the early Councils, he began to look into his Bible with the eyes of a student. All our well-read divinity students know those most interesting passages in *Grace Abounding* on the Apocrypha and on the Canon, and such like. And then after that the eyes of a sinner intent on seeking his own salvation were given of God to Bunyan. And it is most helpful to ourselves when we are intent on seeking our own salvation, to see what special parts of the Bible brought salvation to John Bunyan, who writes himself down on his title-page as the chief of sinners. And then long afterwards we see him employing his eyes on his Bible as a Puritan preacher. All true preachers are greatly interested in watching what texts Bunyan chose to preach upon as he went deeper and deeper into his texts, and as he became more and more spiritual, and more and more evangelical, and more and more experimental, in his preaching. And, as we go on through his wonderful book we rejoice to trace how the eyes of a true saint are more and more given him of God; the eyes of his understanding being enlightened that he might know the hope of God's calling, and what the riches of His inheritance in the saints.

After Bunyan had once got his new eyes, this was the way he immediately began to read his Bible and especially his New Testament. 'Methought I was as if I had seen Him born; as if I had seen Him grow up; as if I had seen Him walk through this world from His cradle to His cross; to which, also, when He came, I saw how gently He gave Himself to be hanged and nailed upon it, for my sins and wicked doings. Also, as I mused upon this His progress, that scripture dropped upon my spirit, He was ordained for the slaughter.' Let us all learn to read our New Testament in that way. For reading in that way is not only a sure evidence to us that we have got new eyes from God, but as we go on to read in that way our eyes will become more and more new every day. Scale after scale will fall from off our eyes till we shall see deeper and deeper into the word of God every time we open it. This is what has been called reading with 'the eye on the object,' which is the only true and fruitful way of reading the Bible and everything else.

'Especially the Epistles of the Apostle Paul were sweet and pleasant to me.' If Dr. Thomas Goodwin is right when he says that reconciliation is the main argument of the Bible, then that argument comes to its consummation and its crown in Paul's Epistles. And that was Paul's own conviction and assurance about his Epistles and about his whole

apostleship.   For he claims in every Epistle of his
that to him above all other men had been committed the word of reconciliation.   Now if that is
so, then Bunyan is entirely right in his immense
indebtedness to Paul, and in his immense enjoyment of Paul.   And we also are right if Paul's
reconciliation-Epistles are immensely sweet and
pleasant to us.   And in the pulpit they only are
the true successors of Paul who say more and more
with Paul every new Sabbath day, 'Now, then, we
are ambassadors for Christ, as though God did
beseech you by us : we pray you in Christ's stead,
be ye reconciled to God.'   But you are not
preachers of reconciliation like Paul and Bunyan.
You are only retired and private readers of Paul's
Epistles of reconciliation.   Only, are you even
that ?   Have you got your new eyes from God
even yet ?   When you sit down at night for a little
heart-sweetening reading after another heart-
embittering day to what part of your Bible do you
turn your eyes ?   Luther said that since he was
always sinning so he was always reading the Romans
and the Galatians.   Now since you are always sinning
what are you always reading ?   We are all confiding friends here, and I will not ask you such home-
coming questions as that, without answering for
myself.   Well, for myself, I often sweeten my
heart, at the end of the day, with this passage out
of Paul : 'Being justified freely by His grace,
through the redemption that is in Christ Jesus,
whom God hath set forth to be a propitiation
through faith in His blood.'   Now, if you know
anything in all the world more sweet to the sin-
embittered heart than that, I would like you to

tell me where I can find it. Many of your new
eyes have been fastened, like mine, upon this also :
' To him that worketh not, but believeth on Him
that justifieth the ungodly, his faith is counted for
righteousness.' And on this : ' Who was delivered
for our offences, and was raised again for our justification.' And on this : ' Where sin abounded,
grace did much more abound.' And then, what
consolation and what sweetness there is in the
seventh and eighth chapters of the Romans,
especially when we read those two chapters together at the same down-sitting. Only, do you
ever do that ? Speak out, and say.

' Indeed, I was then never out of the Bible.'
Just so. When once any man has really got his
new eyes from God, and when once he has fairly
gone into his Bible with his new eyes, that man
will never again be long out of his Bible. His
daily life will not let him be long out of his Bible.
And especially his evil heart will not let him be
long out of his Bible. His house may be full of
books, and not bad books either ; but his Bible is
the only book of them all that wholly answers to
his life around him and especially to his life within
him. But let me throw in this parenthetically at
this point. Rich and full as John Bunyan is, on
the splendid service his Bible did him, our own
Halyburton is richer and fuller far. And Jacob
Behmen tells an anxious inquirer to cast himself
once every hour into the depths of his Bible : aye
every half-hour ; and he will find himself to be
straightway penetrated with the divine glory, and
will taste a sweetness that no tongue can express.
' Thou wouldst then love thy cross more than all

the goods and all the joys of this world'—so Jacob
Behmen assures his disciple.

'I was then never out of the Bible.' Have you
ever had a time in your whole life of which you
could so speak? When was it? Was it when you
first got your new eyes from God? And when it
seemed to you as if your new eyes were far too new
and far too good for you to throw them away upon
anything but your Bible? Or was it when some
great sin of yours threatened to find you out? Or
again, was it in some great shipwreck of desire and
hope when all your other books on which you had
fed your desire and your hope had suddenly become
so much dust and ashes in your mouth? Was it
then that you began to find such a sweetness and
such a solace in your Bible, that like Bunyan you
were never out of it? And when, like Jacob
Behmen's obedient disciple, you plunged yourself
back into your Bible every half-hour? A time of
a great bereavement also sends some people back
in a hurry to their deserted Bible. When their life
was full of all manner of prosperity, when their
days and nights were full of family affections and
family interests, when their head was anointed
every day with fresh oil, and when their cup was
always running over, in those days they could not
away with Paul's Epistles or anything else of that
so heavenly kind. But when they sat solitary, and
when no man cared for their soul, then their Bible
began to come to its own again in their broken
hearts. Then like Bunyan 'it was marvellous to
them to find the fitness of God's word to their case.
The wonderful rightness of the timing of it, the
power, the sweetness, the light, and the glory that

all come with it.' And then the forsaken soul rose
up out of the dust of death, and said: 'I will go,
and will return to my first Husband, for then it was
better with me than now.'

'And, now, I began to look into the Bible with
new eyes, and read as I never did before. And,
especially, the Epistles of the Apostle Paul were
sweet and pleasant to me. And, indeed, I was
then never out of the Bible, either by reading or
meditation.' Delightful! Delightful! But what
is this? For I turn the leaf, and I find this: 'I am
convinced that I am an ignorant sot; and that I
want those blessed gifts that other good people
have : the blessed gifts of spiritual knowledge and
spiritual understanding. For I am tossed continually between the devil and my own ignorance, and
am so perplexed, especially at some times, that I
cannot tell what to do.' Now, are you not—some
of you—secretly glad to hear that? Does that not
immensely comfort you? I am sure it does. At
any rate, it immensely comforts me. To know
that John Bunyan with all his new eyes and with
all his rapturous love for Paul's Epistles, yet at
some times felt himself to be a sot of a man ; and
to be tossed about by the devil and by his own
ignorance of divine things—does that not comfort
you? At any rate, I say, I for one get great
comfort and great hope out of all that, as well as
out of such corresponding Scriptures as these : 'I
am dust and ashes,' said Abraham ; 'I am a worm,
and no man,' said a psalmist ; 'I am a beast before
God,' said another psalmist ; 'I was shapen in
iniquity,' said the greatest and best of all the
psalmists ; 'I am a man of unclean lips, and all my

righteousnesses are but so many filthy rags,' said
the most evangelical of all the prophets; 'I am
more brutish than any man,' said one of the wisest
of men; 'I abhor myself,' said Job; 'I am sold
under sin,' said Paul; 'None but the devil could
equal me in pollution of mind and heart,' said
Bunyan. And, again, 'I am an ignorant sot, tossed
about by the devil at his will.' And so on—in
every sincere and genuine saint of God who is
undergoing a great sanctification for a great service
on earth and in heaven. Dear, sin-tormented
people of God! Do not be too much cast down!
You are in good company. You are in the best of
company. Angels envy you and your company.
They would exchange all their glory for such an
experience and for such a prospect as yours.
Meantime, take these sweet and pleasant passages
out of Paul, and take them home with you: 'There
is therefore now no condemnation to them which
are in Christ Jesus. And if children, then heirs:
heirs of God, and joint-heirs with Christ. If so be
that we suffer with Him, that we may be also
glorified together. And we know that all things
work together for good to them that love God.
Who shall separate us from the love of Christ?
Nay, in all these things we are more than con-
querors, through Him that loved us. Nor height,
nor depth, nor any other creature shall be able to
separate us from the love of God, which is in Christ
Jesus, our Lord.' Wherefore, comfort your hearts
with these words, and with a thousand more words
like these, in Paul's so sweet and so pleasant
Epistles.

XII

'Now began I to labour to call again time that was past.

'AND now began I to labour to call again time that was past, wishing a thousand times, twice told, that the day was yet to come when I should be tempted to such and such a sin! Concluding with great indignation how I would rather have been torn in pieces than have been found a consenter thereto. But, alas! these thoughts, and wishings, and resolvings, were now too late to help me. Oh! thought I, that it was with me as in months past, as in the days when God preserved me! Upon another time I was somewhat inclining to a consumption, insomuch that I thought I could not live. Now began I afresh to give myself to a serious consideration after my state and condition for the future. But I had no sooner begun to do that, than there came flocking into my mind an innumerable company of my sins and transgressions; amongst which these were at this time most to my affliction, namely, my deadness, my dullness, and my coldness in holy duties; my wanderings of heart, my wearisomeness in all good things, my want of love to God, to His ways, and to His people. At the apprehension of these things my sickness was doubled upon me; for, now, I was sick in my inward man, and my soul was clogged with guilt. Now was I very greatly pinched between these two considerations :—Live I may not. Die I dare not. Now I sunk and fell in my spirit, and was about giving up all for lost. But, as I was walking up and down the house, as a man in a most woful state, that word of God took hold of my heart—Ye are justified freely by His Grace, through the redemption that is in Christ Jesus. And, O, what a turn that made upon me! Now was I as one awakened out of a troublesome dream; and, listening to this heavenly sentence, I was as if I heard it thus expounded to me: 'Sinner, thou thinkest that, because of thy sins and infirmities, I cannot save thy soul; but, behold My Son is by Me; and upon Him I look, and not on thee; and I will deal with thee according as I am pleased with Him.' At this I was greatly lightened in my mind, and was made to understand that God could justify a sinner at any time. It was but His looking upon Christ, and then imputing His benefits to us, and the work was forthwith done. Now was I got on high; now I saw myself within the arms of grace and mercy; and, though I was before afraid to think of a dying hour, yet now I cried, Let me die! Now death was lovely and beautiful in my eyes; for I saw that we shall never live indeed till we be gone to the other world. At this time I saw more in these words—Heirs of God, than ever I shall be able to express while I live in this world. Heirs of God! God Himself the Inheritance and the Portion of His saints!'

So far John Bunyan in his *Grace Abounding*. And now for some of the lessons to ourselves out of

all that.   As we see in a thousand Scripture cases,
and as we see in John Bunyan's case, and as too
many of us see only too well in our own case, a
very bitter remorse is the first result of our going
back on our past life of sin.   I do not need to
labour to prove that for it is written on every page
of Holy Scripture.   *Grace Abounding* is full of it,
and our own awakened consciences are equally full
of it.   But blessed be God both Holy Scripture,
and Bunyan's autobiography, and our own experience, all have this testimony also to give on this
subject ; this blessed testimony that by the grace
of God, and by our own godly sincerity in calling
to mind and in keeping in mind our past sins, some
most blessed fruits are to be reaped even out of our
past life.   Speaking of the sinful past of the Church
of Israel, God said in never-to-be-forgotten words :
' I will give her her vineyards from thence, and the
valley of Achor for a door of hope.   And I will say
to them which were not my people, Thou art my
people, and they shall say, Thou art my God.'   And
all that is there said of the awakened and returning
Church is said of every awakened and returning
sinner, as I shall now proceed to show.

In whatever way and from whatever quarter it
comes to us there is no more becoming and no
more blessed mind in any man in this world than
a penitential mind.   Every several and individual
man among us has his own special reasons for
possessing a penitential mind.   But no mortal man
can look down into his own heart and back into his
own life without immediately and henceforth having
his head made waters and his eyes a fountain of
tears.   No mortal man, with his eyes opened can

set his past life before his present face without
having all John Bunyan's remorses and repentances
awakened within him. Aye and many men among
us will have many very bitter remorses, and many
very black despairs awakened within them that the
young tinker miraculously escaped. On such a
matter as this I like to fortify myself and to gratify
you with the words of some of the great Puritan
divines when I can find the appropriate words in
any of those unequalled masters in these matters.
'God,' says one of those experts in the matters of
God and the soul, 'God gives a penitential mind
not only presently after the sins are committed, but
He continues and increases that mind long after
those sins have for many years been confessed and
pardoned, both in our own consciences and in
heaven. In the secret experience of the soul the
old guilt with a new contrition on account of it
will return again and again. Thus Job for the sins
of his youth, for which, questionless, he had often
humbled himself, and of which he had every assurance of pardon; yet God did, from time to time,
write bitter things against His servant, many years
after, and made him still to possess his old sins, as
himself speaks. In our presumption and stupidity
we think that the lapse of years somehow wears out
both the guilt of our long past sins, as well as
weakens God's demand for a broken heart on
account of them. But that is not so. That is very
far from being so. Great sins forgiven must never
be for a single day forgotten.' And this way of
God's working gives us some of the most golden
passages of our whole golden Bibles; as every
penitent reader of the Bible knows in his happy

experience. As thus: ' I will establish my covenant
with thee; and thou shalt know that I am the
Lord; that thou mayest remember, and be confounded, and never open thy mouth any more
because of thy shame, when I am pacified toward
thee for all that thou hast done, saith the Lord
God.' And again, in the same prophet: 'Then
will I sprinkle clean water upon you, and ye shall
be clean: from all your filthiness, and from all your
idols, will I cleanse you. . . . Then shall ye remember your own evil ways, and your doings that
were not good, and shall loathe yourselves, in your
own sight, for your iniquities and for your abominations.' And thus it is brought about that an
always-remembered past is a perfect storehouse of
penitential and evangelical graces to every forgiven
and accepted sinner. Every such sinner goes back
continually and brings up out of his past the one
sacrifice that best pleases God; that is to say, an
ever-broken and an ever-contrite heart. In paragraph after paragraph of this profoundly spiritual
and thrillingly experimental book, John Bunyan
testifies to us how he ' laboured' to call again time
that was past, and then in his most rapturous words
he tells us also how great was his reward for all
that labour. Like Israel of old, he got his vineyards from thence, and the valley of Achor for a
door of hope.

Then again, though you would not think it at
first sight, an often-visited past, as a matter of fact,
comes to be a great impulse and a great assistance
to justifying faith. Before faith begins its work in
the soul a bad past causes an absolutely paralysing
terror in the soul. But after God's gift of faith to

the soul and after faith has begun its divine work
in the soul nothing helps faith forward like self-
despair and a great and a growing and a godly
sorrow.   Faith thrives best in a heart wholly empty
and for ever empty of all self-righteousness and all
self-defence and all self-help and all self-hope.   And
nothing so prostrates the sinner before the cross of
Christ and before the throne of grace as an oft-
visited past; oft visited and always taken again to
heart.   Look at the great experimental psalms;
look at the great experimental hymns; look at the
great experimental autobiographies, with *Grace
Abounding* standing at their head, and they will all
tell you that nothing so casts the soul upon Christ
alone for salvation as a sinful and an oft-visited
past.   The great experimental divine to whom I
have already referred, tells us that he always
preached his best sermon after a turn on the
Sabbath morning up and down among the sins
of his past life.   And I, for one, wholly believe
him.

Again, evangelical humility is by far the most
becoming, as it is by far the most Christ-like, of all
our evangelical and spiritual graces.   And the most
inward and the most spiritual and the most ex-
quisitely beautiful humility comes up into the
sinner's heart and life out of his evil past, aggra-
vated as his evil past is by his still evil present.
It was his ever-present remembrance of his past
life that made the Apostle Paul such a pattern of
Christian humility.   Paul bore in his deepest soul
the painful scars of his past life down to his dying
day.   And it was that, far more than the thorn in
his flesh, that made him so like his Master in his

Master's favourite grace of humility and meekness of heart. And even after he was Paul the aged he came back on the sins of his youth with a deeper pain and with a more burning shame than ever before. His past life sank into his spirit more and more the older he became and the holier and the more heavenly-minded he became. And wherever you find a proud and a puffed-up man, a man jealous of his good name and his high place among his fellows; wherever you find a noisy, disputatious, self-asserting, egotistical man, that temper of his does not prove that he has not a bad past, but it proves to demonstration that he never visits his bad past. And on the other hand, wherever you find a man whose mouth is in the dust, however you praise him, or however you blame him, you may be quite sure where the loom works that weaves the garment of humility with which he is always found to be clothed.

Then again such are the enriching vineyards that God gives us from thence that from our own past lives we learn this also: to be sympathetic, and patient, and kind, and hopeful toward the sinners who are sinning all around us to-day, as we ourselves at one time sinned. We recollect the strength of our own temptations, as also the feeble fight we made against them. Like John Bunyan we wish a thousand times twice told that the days of our temptations were yet to come. And the poignancy of that too late wish makes us watch over and warn and help in every possible way, those men around us whose hour and power of temptation are so strong upon them at the present moment. Our Lord Himself was made the merci-

ful and faithful High Priest that He is by being
tempted in all points like as we are.   And,

> He still remembers in the skies
> His tears and agonies and cries.

And his best servants are like their merciful Master
in that.   In the skies of their pardon and their
peace they still remember the days of their temptations and their transgressions.   And having been
forgiven their ten thousand talents they take their
fellow-sinner by the hand and tell him what God
has done to redeem and to deliver their own lost
souls.   And thus it is that when you see a hard
man, and an implacable man, and a cruel man, and
a man without sympathy and fellow-feeling, and a
man who takes his fellow-sinner by the throat,
depend upon it that man's ten thousand talents are
still standing against him and the tormentors'
scourging hands are still awaiting him.   The great
experimental divine that I have drawn upon twice
to-night already has this also: 'Our Master,' he
says, 'gives His servants a lady's hand for binding
up burdened consciences and broken hearts, by
the way He unburdens their own consciences, and
binds up their own broken hearts.'   Till they are
able to open and to hold out doors of hope to all
other men, even as Christ opened and held out a
door of hope to them.

Now this is the last Sabbath night of an old and
an evil year.   And therefore it is the best night in
all the year in which to labour to call again the
past year and all the years that are past.   Every
man and every woman here to-night, aye, and every
child, has their own past known to God and to

themselves alone. And God, to whom we all
belong, and to whom all our past and all our
present and all our future belongs—He comes to
us to-night requiring of us that which is past
between Him and us. He demands that we shall
go over and tell both to Him and to ourselves just
what our past life has been. What our childhood
was and our youth; what were the many doors of
His goodness and His grace that He opened to us
as our lives opened : our home life, our school life,
our college life, our office life, our workshop life.
What company we chose and frequented, and what
marks for good or for evil our company made upon
us; the first good book we remember reading, and
the good effect it had upon us; our first bad
book, and the bad effect it had upon us; the first
corrupting word that fell on our young heart, and
the first remorse we felt for our first sin. John
Bunyan was brought up to curse and to swear, even
as a child ; to break the Sabbath day ; and to rise in
the morning and to lie down at night, without God
in the world. But as soon as he came to himself he
laboured all his after days, to call again those times
that were past ; wishing a thousand times, twice
told, that those days of temptation were yet to
come. Take an hour or two of the same godly
labour to-night. For this is fit and fruitful labour
for the evening of the Lord's own day. And He
will come Himself and will help you with that
labour and will reward you with great wages for it.
O all men and women with such a past! Will you
cast all this of Holy Scripture and of *Grace Abounding* behind your back? Will you go on into
another year risking and defying all God's anger

when He offers you to-night all His grace? Surely
you will not so destroy yourselves! Would this
not be for ever a grand night to you to look back
upon if the handwriting that stands so black
against you was to-night for ever blotted out, and
all your past life of sin cast to-night into the
depths of the sea? Why should not this be said
over you also before you sleep to-night; even
this; 'I will sprinkle clean water upon you also, and
you shall be clean: from all your filthiness, and
from all your idols, will I cleanse you. A new
heart also will I give you, and a new spirit will I
put within you; and I will take the stony heart out
of your flesh, and I will give you an heart of flesh.
And, from this night, you shall be my people, and I
will be your God'? O! labour to-night before you
sleep that all that may be true of you, and that it
may all belong to you from this night forward and
for ever. And, then, this will be a night to be
remembered by John Bunyan, and by you, and by
me, both on earth and in heaven. Amen.

XIII

' Especially this word Faith put me to it.'

'ESPECIALLY this word *Faith* put me to it. For I could not help it, but sometimes must question, whether I had any Faith or no. But I was loth to conclude that I had no Faith; for, if I do so, thought I, then I shall count myself a castaway indeed.' Now, who can tell but there may be some people here this evening who are just at John Bunyan's stage in their salvation? They, like him, are never out of their Bibles. But, as they read Paul's Epistles, they are greatly put to it by this word *Faith*, which rises up and meets them at every turn. Now if there are any such here I shall do my best to speak to them and to their case for a little to-night.

Well then what exactly is this thing *faith*, of which the whole New Testament speaks so often and says so much? What is this thing faith, which nonplussed John Bunyan so often and which nonplusses ourselves so often? Take it, to begin with, as the Shorter Catechism so scripturally and so succinctly has it: 'Faith in Jesus Christ is a saving grace, whereby we receive and rest upon Him alone for salvation, as He is offered to us in the Gospel.' Keep that fine Catechism answer well in

mind, and take occasion from time to time to turn
that answer over word by word in your mind and
in your heart, and every time you so turn it over
act upon it immediately, perform it immediately,
practise it immediately, make it your own immediately; that is to say, every hour of every day
receive and rest upon Jesus Christ as He is every
hour of every day offered to you in the Gospel.

Ever since my student days Bishop O'Brien's
answer to the question as to what faith is has
remained with me and has often been very helpful
to me : 'They who know what is meant by faith
in a promise, know what is meant by faith in the
Gospel ; they who know what is meant by faith in
a remedy, know what is meant by faith in the
blood of the Redeemer ; they who know what is
meant by faith in a physician, faith in an advocate,
faith in a friend, know, too, what the Scriptures
mean to express when they speak of faith in the
Lord Jesus Christ.'   The Bishop of Ossory's
Nature and Effects of Faith was a classic with us in
our day both for its rich evangelical substance and
for its fine English style.

And then just to keep in mind some of the Scripture synonyms and equivalents for faith, that is a
great help both to the young inquirer and to the
advanced believer.   As thus : Faith is just believing ; it is just assenting and consenting ; it is just
confiding and relying, and staying oneself upon.
Again, it is rising up ; it is coming ; it is walking ;
it is running ; it is fleeing ; it is laying hold on ; it
is receiving, and it is resting on.   Again, it is seeing ; it is hearing ; it is understanding, and it is
meditating on.   Again, it is tasting ; it is eating ;

it is drinking, and drinking abundantly. Again, it is washing in a fountain ; it is putting on fine linen ; it is putting on Christ to justification of life ; and so on, all through the Scriptures. The Old Testament saints were eminent believers and they were always saying and singing their wonderful faith in language like this : ' The Lord, He is my God, and He is become my salvation. The Lord is my rock, and my fortress, and my high tower, and my deliverer : in Him will I trust. Behold, God is my salvation : I will trust, and I will not be afraid what man can do to me. O my soul, hope thou in God ; who is the health of my countenance, and my God.' And then when like Bunyan we open Paul's Epistles, faith is the gift of God. Faith is the fruit of the Spirit. It is a shield. It is a breastplate. It is a battle, which always ends in a victory. Without faith it is impossible to please God. The just shall live by faith. The sinner is justified by faith, and the saint is sanctified by faith. We have access by faith into this grace wherein we stand, we stand fast by faith, and having done all, we stand. And, to crown all, Christ dwells in our hearts by faith. But the only adequate specimen of Paul upon faith is all the Epistles we have from the Apostle's pen. Indeed you must never be out of Paul's Epistles if you would know all the things that faith performs in the salvation of sinners, and in the sanctification of saints, and in the glory of God   And then a Latin father and a preacher of the school of Paul has this : ' Give me a passionate man, a hot-headed man, and one that is headstrong and unmanageable ; and with faith as a grain of mustard seed, I will, by degrees, make that man as quiet as a lamb. Then give me a covetous man, an avaricious man, a miserly man; and with a little faith working like leaven in his heart, I will yet make him a perfect spendthrift for the Church of Christ and for the poor. Then give me one who is mortally afraid of pain; and one who all his days is in bondage through fear of death; and let the spirit of faith once enter and take its seat in his heart and in his imagination, and he shall, in a short time, despise all your crosses and flames and even the bull of Phalaris itself. Then show me a man with an unclean heart and I will undertake, by his faith in Christ, to make him whiter than the snow, till he will not know himself to be the same man.'

The grand difficulty, said Bunyan, in the way of my faith is just *myself*. Myself to me, he said, as a fallen and an unsanctified man, is more than all things else. Myself is more to me than God Himself, and Christ Himself, and the Holy Ghost Himself. Put myself in one scale, and all the Godhead in another scale, and it is all as nothing, over against myself. And it is because the nature and the operations of faith reverse all that for me for ever, that, to the day of my death, I so resist the approaches of faith to me and its full dominion in me. It is because faith so humbles me and so slays me and so utterly annihilates me that I find it so impossible for me to live the life of faith. It is because faith every day of my life and in every part of my life makes me nothing and far less than nothing, while it makes Another everything and far more than everything. That was the rub with Halyburton also, who when he was in any

spiritual strait, 'betook himself to any shift but
Christ. Anything,' he said, 'rather than faith and
Christ.' And that was the same rub with Bunyan.
That was the reason why he was so put to it
both with the word *Faith* and with the thing. It
was because he had to go wholly and for ever out
of himself for his salvation. It was because he had
to depend wholly and for ever on Another; and, to
add to his difficulty, that Other was one he had
never seen, but by that faith which all through so
put him to it. And he had to depend on that
unseen Another for hourly pardon, for hourly
peace, and for everything else worth having, on
earth and in heaven, in time and in eternity. He
had to count all his best things to be but dung compared with Christ, and all his best deeds to be but
filthy rags, beside the robe of Christ's righteousness. And worst of all he had to take all his sins
and all his sinfulness; all the vilest and all the
wickedest things he had ever done, or had ever
desired to do, and he had to lay them all on the
substituted head of the Son of God. He had to
go to Calvary every day and every hour and
immediately after every sinful thought and word
and deed, and he had to lay them all on the Son of
God, nailed to the Cross, and there made a curse
for him and for his sin. No wonder that that word
Faith so terribly put Bunyan to it! And no
wonder that we so revolt from that same word ourselves! No wonder it is so hard for us who are so
proud and so unbroken men, simply and like little
children to receive the atonement! But when
Bunyan humbled himself to receive that substitution of Another in his room: or, rather, when he

was humbled of God to receive it : no wonder that
being the passionate and eloquent man he was he
broke forth in this rapturous strain : ' Oh, methinks it makes my heart to bleed to think that
the very Son of God bled to death for me, and for
my wicked doings ! O, Thou Loving One ! O,
Thou Blessed One ! How much I owe Thee !
Now was my heart filled with comfort and with
hope. Yea, I was so taken that day with the love
and the mercy of God to me, that I could not contain it all till I went home. I could have spoken
of God's mercy to me to the very crows that sat
upon the ploughed lands before me, had they been
capable to have understood me. To speak as then
I thought, had I had a thousand gallons of blood
within my veins, I could freely have spilt it all at
the feet of my Lord and Saviour.' After all that I
am prepared to receive this so apposite paragraph
in Walter Marshall's Bunyan-like life : Upon con-
sulting several eminent divines, and giving one of
them an account of the state of his soul, and
particularising his sins which lay upon his conscience, the divine told him that he had forgotten
to mention the greatest of all his sins, namely, the
master sin of unbelief, in not believing on the Lord
Jesus Christ, for the remission of all his sins, and
for the sanctification of his heart and his life.
Hereupon Marshall set himself to studying and
preaching Christ, till he attained to eminent holiness, and to great peace of conscience. His last
words on his death-bed were these words out of his
favourite Apostle : ' The gift of God is eternal life,
through Jesus Christ our Lord.'

And now that we have seen something of what

true faith is, let us ask before we close who and what a true believer is. Well, a true believer, says a master in these high matters, is one 'who has given over all other lives but that of faith.' Ever since I first came on that stroke of experimental and spiritual insight it has dwelt in my mind in a most illuminating and suggestive way. But true and good and most suggestive as that definition of a true believer is, at the same time, standing on my own experience and observation, I will take the liberty of turning that definition round the other way, and will state it to you in this way: A true believer is one who has been given over by all other lives but the life of faith. For all the true believers I know or have ever heard of clung to all their other lives as long as they could. And it was only after all their other lives had shaken them off that they betook themselves to the life of faith. Take some of the greatest believers in the Bible. Take that saint and psalmist of such wonderful spiritual genius, Asaph. In his priceless seventy-third psalm Asaph tells us his own painful experience in this matter of all his lives giving him over. He frankly tells us, for one thing, how consumed he was with envy at the men who were in greater prosperity than he was himself. Their great prosperity was his continual torment. He felt as if he had nothing left to live for, so torn with envy was he and so miserable. And all that went on till he took all that up to the sanctuary where faith in God was preached and sung and celebrated continually. And it was when he was standing one day in the heavenly light of the sanctuary, that the spirit of faith came down upon him till, like

Bunyan, he could not contain himself till he went home, but sang this psalm on the spot till all the other worshippers heard him:

> Nevertheless, continually,
>   O Lord, I am with Thee:
> Thou dost me hold by my right hand,
>   And still upholdest me.
> My flesh and heart doth faint and fail,
>   But God doth fail me never:
> For of my heart God is the strength
>   And portion for ever.

And so it was with the prophet Habakkuk. You all have his noble song by heart: 'Although the fig-tree shall not blossom, neither shall fruit be in the vines: the labour of the olive shall fail, and the fields shall yield no meat; the flock shall be cut off from the fold, and there shall be no herd in the stalls: yet will I rejoice in the Lord, I will joy in the God of my salvation.' And in this also as in everything else of an experimental kind Paul comes in to crown them all. And then ourselves. Many of us now here are true believers, just in the measure that this life and that other life of ours have given us over. God would never get us at all unless He made first this life of ours and then that to give us over. I would tell out all your spiritual life as well as all my own were I to enter into those particular lives of ours that He has made to cast us off and to give us over to the life of faith. God makes all manner of losses and crosses and disappointments and bereavements to come to us in order to shut us up to the life of faith and to Himself. Till He makes this song to be sung over us as well as over all the desolate and downcast in Israel:

On eagles' wings they mount, they soar,
  Their wings are faith and love,
Till past the cloudy regions here,
  They rise to heav'n above.

The true believer then, the truest and the best
and the most blessed believer, is just the man who
has absolutely no other life left him to live but the
life of faith. Christ and his faith in Christ: that,
now, sums up his whole life. Till to him also
to live is Christ, and to die is gain. Properly
speaking, he has no book now left him but his
Bible; and he is scarce ever out of his Bible,
either by reading or by meditation, day nor night.
And that goes on with him till his faith is to him
nothing less than the substance of things hoped
for, and the evidence of things not seen as yet.

One moment more: for I find this among my
notes on this word faith; and I will give it, not
to the congregation but to the divinity students
present. I find this among my notes, after I think
my sixth or seventh reading, and that pencil in
hand, of Dr. Thomas Goodwin's golden volume on
The Object and Acts of Justifying Faith. This is
my note: 'Let any divinity student or young
preacher master Goodwin's eighth volume by
repeated and by student-like readings, and he will
be set up in his own soul and in his pulpit on that
word faith for the rest of his life.' God bless the
divinity students with this great gift of saving
faith. Till they preach faith to their believing
people with that full assurance and that full
authority which a personal experience of it alone
can give.

XIV

'The guilt of sin did help me much.'

HEN we set ourselves to study John
Bunyan scripturally and experiment-
ally and sympathetically, and to
study in the same way some other
men of his spiritual insight and
spiritual depth and spiritual power, we find that
they all agree in this: that their great sinfulness
greatly helped them; first, to their own salvation,
and then to their efficiency and their success as
preachers of the Gospel. Let us do our best
then to look into this somewhat deep matter
to-night: that is to say, into some of the clearly
ascertained ways in which their great sin and their
great guilt did so much help Bunyan and some
other Bunyan-like men.

And to begin with, John Bunyan tells us that his
great guilt immensely helped him to read his Bible
aright. The Bible was written for the salvation of
guilty sinners alone; and no man, learned nor
simple, has ever read the Bible aright, or ever will
read it aright, unless he always comes to it as a
guilty sinner. And John Bunyan himself was all
his days the very man for whom the Bible was
written. For all his days and down to the end of
his days he became more and more the chief of

sinners. No man in the whole of England in that
day was better fitted to read the Bible and to
understand it and to appreciate it than was that
ungodly tinker of Bedford, that man of untutored
genius called John Bunyan. And the deeper and
the more spiritual his experience of his sinfulness
became the better a reader of the Bible he became.
Till he became as sure that the Bible was the very
word of God to him as he was sure of his own
existence. Indeed in his own believing and bold
way, Bunyan held that both David and Paul had
been specially raised up, and had been specially
tempted and tried and brought low, in order to pen
their psalms and their epistles for his sake ; far less
for their own sakes than for his sake. For he saw
himself as in a divine glass every time he opened
a penitential psalm or returned to study an experimental epistle. Till as time went on he felt
absolutely sure that He who had made him had
had the Bible specially written for him in all its
message of salvation by the blood of the Son of
God. 'I was driven by those fomentations of error
that were abroad in my day,' he says, 'to a far
deeper search of the Scriptures ; and was, through
their testimony, not only enlightened, but greatly
confirmed and comforted. And, besides that, the
guilt of my sin did help me much, both to understand the Scriptures, and continually to close with
Christ.'

And from that John Bunyan's sin and guilt went
on to help him much both in his prayers and in his
praises. No man ever prayed without ceasing, as
Paul tells all men to do, who did not also sin
without ceasing, as Paul did himself. Luther, who

was Paul's best successor, was wont to say that
since he was always sinning so he was always
confessing sin and was always praying for its
pardon. Many men have prayed without ceasing
for this thing and for that thing at certain seasons
in their lives, but their sinfulness makes some men
pray at every season, and day and night, and more
and more the longer they live. And so it was with
Bunyan's singing of God's praises also both in the
church and at family worship, and in the way he
filled up his time when he was walking to and fro
in pursuit of his calling. And let God be most
warmly thanked that He has so bountifully provided both prayers and psalms and hymns for the
chief of sinners. As for instance, the penitential
and the Pauline Psalms, the Olney Hymns, the
Wesley Hymns, the Bonar Hymns, and many more
hymns of that most excellent sort for the chief of
sinners.

And then most happily for his people John
Bunyan's abiding and increasing sinfulness greatly
helped him to preach the Gospel in all its freeness
and in all its fullness when he became a minister.
Vanity Fair long ago had a caricature of Mr. Gladstone, under which these words were written: 'If
he were a worse man he would be a better
statesman.' 'I hae nae doot,' said an old woman
in Glasgow to her elder who was canvassing his
district for signatures to a call which was being
subscribed to a young minister: 'I hae nae doot but
that the lad is all you say he is, but it's clear to me
that he disna ken that he's fallen yet, an' he's no
the minister for me.' The radiant youth had
preached an eloquent college discourse on 'The

Dignity of Human Nature,' which had captivated the raw elder but had exasperated the old saint. You are not unfamiliar in this house with the great name of Thomas Halyburton, Professor of Divinity in the University of St. Andrews. To some ministers standing beside his deathbed, Halyburton raised himself up and said: 'I am in circumstances now that justify me in suggesting to you all this word of advice. Be diligent in composing your sermons. But above all be diligent in scanning your own evil hearts. And then make use of the discoveries you get there to enable you to dive down into the consciences of your people, to unmask the hypocrites among them, and to separate the precious from the vile. I loved to preach in that way,' he added, 'and since I lay down here I have not changed my mind about my preaching.' And, as is the influence of sinfulness on preaching, so is it in the matter of hearing preaching and understanding it and valuing it. Many of yourselves now hearing me have—I will not say too little sin—but I will say far too little conscience of sin to make you good hearers of good preaching. Your minister is your very best friend when in his despair of you he prays and waits for something to happen to you that will come both to his help and to your help in the matter of your salvation. I will not be bold enough to put into plain words what I sometimes ask for some of you. But when your sin and your guilt do at last come to help forward your salvation, then you will understand and will defend and will justify me for asking for you what I dare not now name. Up till now the holy law of God has not entered your heart.

And till that all-essential experience comes home to you no preacher worth calling a preacher will have any acceptance or any success with some of you. It is a terrible truth, but it is as true as the Gospel is true, that it is only through his great sin that any sinner will ever come to his great salvation. It is only in the measure of the burden and the bitterness and the curse of his sin that any sinner will ever repent and believe to everlasting life. ' I am not come to call the righteous, but sinners to repentance. The whole have no need of a physician, but they that are sick,' said the Saviour and the Healer of sinners.

And then Bunyan's great sin and great guilt greatly helped him to understand and to console the great sinners who crowded round his pulpit. They crowded round his pulpit till he had sometimes to be carried shoulder high into his pulpit. And it was largely his terrible sense of sin that made him so popular. How far away some of our most popular modern preachers are from us when our hearts are sick and our consciences are laden with sin! How far away we are from them! They seem to know nothing of the disease, and how then can they apply the proper remedy? They cannot. They never felt this awful kind of pain, and no wonder they are no hands at administering the right alleviation of such pain. They never ran up between the walls called salvation with a great burden on their back, and how can they guide us up to the place where stands a cross? They cannot. They never needed to wash in the Fountain opened for sin and uncleanness, and how can they be expected to be good at giving a sinner a hand to

help him down into that Fountain? Did you ever
read John Bunyan's exquisite Preface to his *Grace
Abounding*? If you have the book at home you
might read the preface to-night in support and in
supplement of what I am now saying, if your interest in what I am now saying lasts till you get
home. When you read and understand and love
that remarkable piece, the great writer of it will
tell you what a heavy price he had to pay before he
was fully taught of God how to unburden loaded
consciences, and how to bind up broken hearts, and
how to cheer the sin-sad children of God. As John
Bunyan's friend Thomas Goodwin says, ' His own
sinfulness, and his own suffering, combine to give a
minister a lady's hand for the binding up of broken
hearts.'

Now in all that of the guilt of his sin helping him
so much, John Bunyan is neither so original, nor is
he so exceptional, as you might think he is. By no
means. He is only one among many if you know
where to find them, and if you have any interest
and any pleasure in finding them. I have found
some of them for you, and I will not wind up
to-night till I have introduced you to some of them.
Some of them are old authorities and old favourites
with some of you. And you will not weary to hear
them again on this great matter of how sin and
guilt are sometimes employed for a sinner's great
help in entering on and in living out the divine life.
And first, hear Hooker himself on Peter's great fall.
In his *Learned Sermon of the Nature of Pride* that
great father of the English Church says this: ' I am
not afraid to affirm it boldly, with St. Augustine,
that puffed up men receive a benefit at the hands

of God, and are assisted by His grace, when with
His grace they are not assisted, but are permitted,
and that grievously, to transgress. Ask the very
soul of Peter, and it shall undoubtedly make you
this answer : My eager protestations, made in the
glory of my ghostly strength, I am ashamed of ;
but those crystal tears, wherewith my sin and weakness were bewailed, have procured my endless joy :
my strength hath been my ruin, and my fall hath
been my stay.' And hear Hooker's still greater
contemporary,—

> O benefit of ill ! now I find true
> That better is by evil still made better ;
> And ruin'd love, when it is built anew,
> Grows fairer than at first, more strong, far greater.
> So I return rebuk'd to my content,
> And gain by ill thrice more than I have spent.

Or as our own fellow-townsman almost too boldly
has it,—

> O Lord, if too obdurate I,
> Choose Thou before my spirit die,
> A piercing pain, a killing sin,
> And to my dead heart run them in.

And hear Halyburton again on his death-bed ; ' I
was fond enough of books, but I must say that what
the Lord let me see of my own ill heart, and what
was necessary against it, that was more steadable
to me than all my books.' And again : ' The Lord
did humble me, and did prove me, and did let me
see what all was in my heart, even a great deal
more of wickedness than I had suspected. And
the Lord hereby instructed me that this is not my
rest, and made me value heaven far more than otherwise I would have done. Thus was I made a gainer
by my losses, and a more upright man by my falls,

to the praise of His glorious grace.' And our old
Highland friend Fraser, that truly great theologian
and truly great saint, has this which I have had by
heart ever since I first read it some forty years ago :
' I find advantages by my sins,' he says. ' " Peccare
nocet, peccavisse vero juvat." I may say, as Mr.
Fox said (not George ; George as a preacher was
like Mr. Gladstone as a statesman): As Mr. Fox
said, My sins, in a manner, have done me more good
than my graces. For, by my sins I am made more
humble, more watchful, and more revengeful
against myself. I am made to see a greater need
to depend upon God, and to love Him the more
who continues such kindness to me, notwithstanding my manifold provocations. I find that true also
which Thomas Shepard saith, My sin loses some of
its strength by every new fall of mine.' My
brethren, know and honour and love the names
of those great men of God. They are the only true
theologians, and they are the very princes of
preachers.

But none of them all can beat Bunyan. ' Oh,
the remembrance of my great sins ! They bring
afresh into my mind the remembrance of my great
help, and my great support from heaven, and the
great grace that God extended to such a wretch as I.
Great sins do draw out great grace. And where
guilt is most terrible and fierce, there the mercy of
God in Christ appears most high and mighty.' And,
after enumerating the ' seven abominations ' that he
still finds in his heart, he bears this experimental
witness : ' Yet,' he says, ' the wisdom of God doth
order them for my good. For (1) they make me
abhor myself; (2) they keep me from trusting my

heart; (3) they convince me of the insufficiency of
all inherent righteousness; (4) they show me the
necessity of fleeing to Jesus; (5) they press me to
pray unto God; (6) they show me the need I have
to watch and be sober; (7) they provoke me to
look to God, through Christ, to help me, and to
carry me through this world.'

Dr. Du Bose, in some of his books, is about the
best writer of the present day to my taste. Dr.
Du Bose is one of the most up-to-date, as you
would say, of all our living divines. And as to the
subject in hand, namely, the serviceableness of sin
in the work of salvation, this is a specimen of what
the divinity students are taught in the University
of the South. 'The distinction,' says Dr. Du Bose,
'which our Lord and the New Testament con-
sistently make, is not that some men are sinners,
and some are not. But that some men are so
content to be sinners that they know not that they
are sinners. While other men are so convinced and
convicted of their own unholiness that they are con-
scious of nothing else in themselves but their sin.
Blessed are we, even that we are sinners, if we know
our sin; if through knowledge of the curse of sin
we have been brought to know the blessedness of
holiness. For beings like ourselves, the consummate
joy of holiness would be incomprehensible and
impossible save through a corresponding and an
equal sense of sin, and sorrow for sin. All our true
joy, in what we are to be, is born of our true
sorrow for what we now are.' But all the greatest
authorities in the world, ancient and modern,
apostolical and evangelical, Anglican and Puritan,
will not convince the man who is not, by his own

experience, absolutely convinced of all that already. And the man who is absolutely convinced of all that already, he does not need the men of authority whom I have now laid before him. He does not need them: no, but he immensely enjoys them; and makes them, more and more, his favourite authors. Who are your favourite authors?

Since I finished the writing of these lines I stumbled last night upon this in Jonathan Edwards that prince in our Puritan Israel: 'Our sin and our misery, by this divine contrivance of redemption, are made the occasion of our greater blessedness. By our sin we had deserved everlasting misery; but, by the divine wisdom and grace, our sin and our misery are made the occasion of our being everlastingly blessed. The saved sinner shall be far more holy and far more blessed than he would have been if he had never sinned at all. His great sin is made the occasion of his far greater salvation. For, where sin abounded, grace did much more abound. That, as sin hath reigned unto death, even so might grace reign, through righteousness, unto eternal life, by Jesus Christ our Lord.'

XV

'The right way to take off guilt.'

JOHN BUNYAN tells us that he came to see that the very worst way to take off his guilt was to let it die away of itself: to let it die away of itself till at last it died out of his heart and conscience altogether. We all know that fatal way of taking off guilt, and indeed the most of us take that fatal way. But there are other fatal ways that we sometimes take with our guilt besides that so fatal way of the mere lapse of time. Jacob thought to take off his guilt by heaping up presents of reparation upon Esau. David in his silence and in his guile toward God made the redress of marriage to Bathsheba. And Zacchæus restored fourfold to the impoverished widows and orphans of Jericho. Codes of penance also and systems of self-punishment have been invented and vows have been sworn of the most stringent self-denials and self-crucifixions. We ourselves, some of us, have fallen on our faces in a sweat of blood. We have watered our couches with our tears. And we have thought to quiet our consciences with the most solemnly sworn covenants of future obedience. But that so promising method of pacification broke down also till it left us far more miserable men

than we were before. Amendment for the future
we took to be sufficient atonement for the past.
But the hours of temptation soon tore our most
solemn covenants into rags, till we came to the
prophet's discovery that our hearts are deceitful
above all things, and desperately wicked.

But let us all attend to this out of Bunyan's
autobiography and let us all remember it: 'Though
I was thus troubled, and tossed, and afflicted, with
the sight, and the sense, and the terror of my sin;
yet, I was afraid to let this sight and sense of my
sin go quite off my mind. For I found that, unless
guilt of conscience was taken off the right way,
that is to say, by the blood of Christ, a man grew
rather worse, than better, for the loss of his trouble
of mind. Wherefore if my guilt lay hard upon me,
then I should cry that the blood of Christ should
take it off. And, if my guilt was going off, without the blood of Christ, then I should also strive to
bring my guilt back again upon my heart and my
conscience.'

The blood of Christ: the sin-atoning and peace-
speaking blood of Christ. I do not know, my
Brethren, how it may be with you in this awful
matter of the blood of Christ. There may be some of
you who are not without some difficulty in receiving
and in holding by the fact and the doctrine of the
Atonement. But for my part, my insurmountable
difficulty would be if there were no absolute fact,
and no sure and certain doctrine, of the Atonement.
Whether or no God could at once and for ever forgive my sin without the Atonement I cannot tell.
I am not one of His counsellors. But one thing I
do know and can tell. When I take counsel with

my own soul about my sin, I both see and know
that, to all eternity, I never could forgive myself,
or endure myself, but for the all-satisfying and all-
obliterating atonement for all my sin that has been
made by the Son of God.   Neither lapse of time,
nor attempts at redress and reparation, nor penances,
nor self-denials, nor floods of tears, nor sweats of
blood, nor solemnly sworn covenants, no, nor all
these things taken together, could ever take away
the awful load of my sin.   But when Jesus Christ,
the Son of God, is 'made sin' by my sin : when both
the fault and the stain and the guilt of my sin are
all taken away from me by His blood, then a peace
that simply passes all my understanding, as a
matter of fact and of sure experience, takes possession of my heart and my conscience.   And when I
again fall into fresh sin and fresh guilt, and that is
with every breath I draw, and when I again receive
the Atonement, that great peace again returns to
me.   I quite willingly allow you that I cannot fully
understand all the divine mysteries that enter into
the Atonement.   I frankly admit to you that I cannot
wade out into all the unfathomable depths of the
Atonement.   Enough for me that Almighty God fully
understands and fully approves of the Atonement,
and that both He and His Son and His Spirit, all
Three together go down to the very bottom of it.
Enough for me that the Judge of all the earth has
proclaimed Himself to be well pleased with His
Son's finished work, and with any and every sinner
who receives and rests upon His crucified Son for
his salvation.   This, then, be you sure is the right
way, and the only right way, to take off your guilt
and mine.   And till you can show me a better way,

I for my part am to take Paul's way, and Luther's way, and John Bunyan's way, and William Cowper's way, and I am to sing with him in this way :

> Dear dying Lamb! Thy precious blood
>   Shall never lose its power
> Till all the ransomed Church of God
>   Be saved to sin no more.
>
> E'er since by faith I saw the stream
>   Thy flowing wounds supply,
> Redeeming love has been my theme,
>   And shall be till I die.

So right, and so alone right, is this redemption-way of taking off guilt, and so absolutely convinced of this is John Bunyan that according to the *Pilgrim's Progress* even Christ Himself cannot take away a sinner's guilt short of His cross and His sepulchre. Spurgeon somewhere blames Bunyan for making Christian carry his burden of guilt so far and so long. For even after Goodwill had admitted Christian into the Strait Gate, and had pointed him into the Narrow Way, he still sent that pilgrim on his upward way with his burden on his back. As thus : 'Then I saw in my dream that Christian asked the keeper of the gate if he could not help him off with his burden that was upon his back. For as yet he had not got rid thereof, nor could he by any means get it off without help. But Goodwill told him : As to thy burden, be content to bear it until thou comest to the place of deliverance. For, there, it will fall off thy back of itself.' Then, still with his burden on his back, Christian comes to the House of the Interpreter, and is entertained by the Interpreter in a way we will never forget : 'Then I saw in my dream that the highway up which Christian was to go was fenced on either side with a wall, and that wall is called Salvation. Up this way, then, did burdened Christian run. But not without great difficulty, because of the load that was upon his back. He ran thus till he came to a place somewhat ascending. And upon that place stood a cross, and a little below, in the bottom, a sepulchre. So I saw in my dream that just as Christian came up with the cross, his burden loosed off his shoulder, and fell from off his back, and began to tumble, and so continued to do till it came to the mouth of the sepulchre, where it fell in, and I saw it no more. Then was Christian glad, and lightsome, and said with a merry heart, He hath given me rest by His sorrow, and life by His death. He looked at the cross therefore, and looked again, even till the springs that were in his head sent the waters down his cheeks. And then he went on singing:

> Blest cross! Blest sepulchre! Blest rather be
> The Man that there was put to shame for me.'

That is the Gospel of our Salvation in a puritan allegory. And we have the same Gospel in apostolical doctrine in that greatest of the Epistles where it is written: 'Being justified freely by His grace through the redemption that is in Christ Jesus, whom God hath set forth to be a propitiation through faith in His blood.' Now, we must have faith in absolutely everything connected with Christ. We must have faith in his Godhead, and in His Manhood, in His coming in our flesh, in His whole life on our earth, in His death, in His rising from the dead, and in His ascension home to heaven again, and we must have faith in all His heavenly offices both toward God and toward man. But always as we are guilty and condemned sinners, it is to faith in His blood that we are invited and commanded. We are justified, not by our faith in His being made flesh, but by our faith in His being made sin. Not by His being made our example, but by His being made our propitiation. We are justified, and we are accepted, not by anything in the Father, or in the Son, or in the Holy Ghost, but by our faith alone, and that in the blood of Christ alone. If the Apostle Paul had any insight given him into the mystery of Christ, that is it. The greatest of Christ's apostles has nothing to preach to us compared with the sin-atoning blood of Christ. That is Paul's one Gospel, first and last, both to himself and to us. The bare thought of any other Gospel being preached to sinners puts Paul beside himself with scorn and with contempt and with indignation.

Now, having I hope seen somewhat clearly the right way to take off guilt, let us also see the right way to keep it off. John Bunyan, like all other great authors, is his own best annotator and interpreter. And when we raise this question with him; this question as to how he kept off both his old guilt and his new guilt, this is his clear answer made both to Prudence and to ourselves: 'When I think of what I saw and came through at the cross, that will do it. And when I look upon my broidered coat, that will do it. And when my thoughts wax warm about the place to which I am going, that will do it. Things and thoughts like these will keep off sin, and will thus keep guilt off my conscience.' And, then, this was our own Halyburton's way. 'Here,' he says, 'in my opinion, is one of the greatest secrets of practical godliness, and one of the highest attainments in a close walk with God. That is to say, to know how to come, daily and hourly, to the fountain opened for sin and for uncleanness. Never to be for long; or, indeed, ever at all, away for a moment from that fountain: that is the only sure way to keep off guilt.' Now to these two masters I will only venture to add this,—singing and saying to yourselves, day and night, the great evangelical and experimental psalms and hymns will greatly help to keep off returning and recurring guilt. Especially the hymns in the hymn-book collected under the heads of Faith and Penitence, Love and Gratitude, Joy and Peace.

Another good and indeed indispensable lesson is to get your new guilt taken off immediately. Even before it is well on get it taken off on the spot. If it is a sinful word that you have spoken, before that sinful word has lighted on your neighbour's ear, before it has had time to enter your neighbour's heart, and before the recording angel has had time to get his pen into his inkhorn, be you beforehand with him. Be you back at the cross in the twinkling of an eye. Be you prostrate in soul before the mercy-seat. And so with all your other sins that so easily beset you, and that so continually load your conscience with new guilt. God is said greatly to love certain of our adverbs. And no adverb more than the adverb immediately; unless it be the kindred evangelical adverbs vicariously and believingly. Well, then, as soon as you again fall

into any sin, go to God alone about it; and go
vicariously, and believingly, and immediately.

And then for the absolutely greatest sinner
hiding in this house of God to-night there is
this tremendous but most glorious lesson. It is not
only the blood of Christ, and the blood of the
Lamb, it is this: 'The Church of GOD, which He
hath purchased with HIS OWN BLOOD.' The BLOOD
OF GOD: the tremendous bareness, so to speak, and
the tremendous boldness of the words: the astound-
ing and overwhelming grace of the words, will
surely bring them home to every specially guilty
conscience and to every specially corrupt heart.
Times and occasions without number, when every
other scripture has threatened to fail myself, this
supreme scripture has been a house of refuge and
a high and heavenly tower to me. The BLOOD OF
GOD has a specially inward and a specially personal
and a specially experimental evidence to me, and
I recommend that most wonderful of all the
scriptures to them that need it; I recommend it
to them with all my heart.

> His blood can make the foulest clean,
> His blood avails for me :

so sings Charles Wesley. ' Let it be counted folly,
or phrenzy, or fury, or whatsoever,' says Richard
Hooker, in what is, perhaps, the greatest sermon
in the English language, ' it is our wisdom and our
comfort. We care for no other knowledge in the
world but this : that man hath sinned and God
hath suffered : that God hath made Himself the
sin of men, and that men are made the righteousness of God.'

And then there is this so opportune and timeous lesson. You are on the search for a new minister who shall preach to you, and to your children, the right way to take off guilt, and to keep it off. Well, long ago, your fathers in this congregation were on the same scent, as Thomas Boston says of himself. And their spiritual scent took them north to Stewart of Cromarty. Now, if I once saw you settled with a minister like Stewart of Cromarty, I could depart in peace; so far, at any rate, as you are concerned. But tell us something about that elect-minister of our fathers, you will say. Well, Hugh Miller, who had such a sure scent both for evangelical doctrine and for English style in a sermon, he will tell you best all about Stewart. But take this home with you to-night out of one of Stewart's Cromarty sermons. 'Blood was sprinkled on the doorposts in Egypt; blood was sprinkled on the Book of the Law; blood was sprinkled on all the Tabernacle and on all the vessels of ministry; blood was sprinkled on the horns of the altar; blood was sprinkled from age to age within the veil; the priests were all sprinkled with blood; and the same blood was sprinkled upon all the worshipping people. And all this proclaimed continually that remission of sin in Israel was only to be obtained through the shedding and the sprinkling of blood. I implore you then,' the great preacher continued, 'to seek your forgiveness through that New Testament blood to which all that Old Testament blood pointed.' That was Stewart of Cromarty's way of preaching the right way to take off guilt and to keep it off.

And, O God, may that be the way of every

future preacher who shall ever stand and minister to Thy people and to their children in this pulpit, which has, by Thy grace, from the beginning been above all things an apostolical and an evangelical pulpit!   Amen.

XVI

' A thousand pounds for a tear. '

R. WETEYES is one of John Bunyan's most speaking likenesses in his splendid gallery of spiritual portraits. Luther's artist friend, Albert Durer, in a noble act of penitence put his own head and face on his famous portrait of the prodigal son. And in like manner, John Bunyan has put his own broken heart into the breast of Mr. Weteyes of the town of Mansoul. In his masterpiece portrait of Mr. Fearing, and in his companion portrait of Mr. Weteyes, we have John Bunyan's own personal experience and his clear testimony concerning the true place of penitential tears in the spiritual life of a penitent sinner.

The scientific students of tears tell us that they have discovered and have distinguished four outstanding kinds of tears. Namely natural tears, and diabolical tears, and human tears, and divine tears. Natural tears, according to those teachers, are all those tears that proceed from constitution, and from temperament, and from age, and from sex, and from all suchlike causes. And such tears as proceed from these and from all suchlike causes they assert have no real value at all; they have no religious value at all, nor any real importance whatsoever. Human tears again are such tears as flow

at the loss of temporal goods, at the breaking up of
earthly friendships and attachments, and at desolat-
ing bereavements; as also, sometimes, simply at
pathetic occurrences and moving narrations. We all
shed, and we see other people shedding, whole
rivers of such humane tears every day. And such
tears are not without a real value to us and to
others if we make a right use of them. But the
tears that those great authorities call divine tears
are very different from the very best of all such
natural and human tears. For divine tears, as
their fine name indicates, are the immediate gift of
God. And the tears that God gives are pre-
eminently if not exclusively shed for sin. Divine
tears are all those tears that we shed on account of
the existence and the prevalence of sin. On
account of the dominion of sin, and the pain of sin,
and the guilt of sin, and the shame of sin, and the
curse of sin, and especially because of all that in
our own sin. The truly penitent sinner often sheds
divine tears as he meditates upon and somewhat
realises what his sin has cost his Saviour. Every
true penitent sheds divine tears every day also for
all the pain and all the sorrow and all the sin that
he has brought upon other people through his own
past sin as well as through his own present sinfulness. All these are the divine tears that the Holy
Ghost alone can give to us and that the true penitents among us alone can shed. And all such tears
are acceptable before God in the measure that
they come up before Him in and through the
intercessions and the tears of the Man of Sorrows.

At this point it will both instruct us and impress
us if we call to mind some of those Bible saints

who were specially blest with the grace of tears.
Those penitent saints whose divine tears were put
into God's bottle and in His bottle have been preserved to this day. 'All the night make I my bed
to swim,' says the Weteyes of the Old Testament;
'I water my couch with my tears.' And again:
'My tears have been my meat day and night.'
And again: 'I have eaten ashes like bread, and I
have mingled my drink with my weeping.' And
again: 'Thou feedest Thy people with the bread
of tears, and Thou givest them tears to drink in
great measure.' And the prophet Jeremias, whom
the Jews took to have come back to them again
in the person of our Lord, he has filled his two
books with utterances like these: 'Oh that my
head were waters, and mine eyes a fountain of tears.
Mine eyes shall weep sore, and my soul shall weep
in secret places because the Lord's people are
carried away captive. Let mine eyes run down
with tears night and day, and let them not cease,
for the daughter of my people is stricken with a
very sore blow.' And so Ezra, and Daniel, and
Hosea, and Micah continually. And we never can
forget that New Testament woman who by the
grace given to her washed her Saviour's feet with
her tears and wiped them with the hairs of her
head. Nor can we ever forget Peter in the garden
of the high priest, nor Paul in his pastorate and
in his whole apostleship. And to pass by whole
generations of weeping penitents, we come to our
present so penitent author. And we see him in
the person of his own Christian standing and looking at the Cross till the springs that were in his
head sent the waters down his cheeks. 'Of all

tears,' he tells us, 'they are by far the best that spring up within us at the moment when we are being sprinkled with the blood of Christ. And of all our joys they are the sweetest that are mixed with our mourning over the sufferings of Christ for our sins.' But Bunyan is at his best in his Mr. Weteyes. 'For you must know that this Mr. Weteyes was a poor man, and a man of a broken spirit, and one that could speak well to a petition. And for this cause he was often sent up from the town of Mansoul to intercede with the King. When he would fall down, and would utter himself in this way. Oh, my Lord, he would say, what I truly am I know not myself, nor whether my name of Weteyes be feigned or true. Especially when I begin to think what some have said, and that is, that this name of Weteyes was given me because Mr. Repentance was my father. But good men have sometimes bad children ; and sinners do sometimes beget hypocrites. My mother also called me by this name of mine from my cradle. But whether she said so because of the moistness of my brain, or because of the softness of my heart, I never could make out. Be that as it may, I see much impurity in mine own tears, and great stains in the bottom of my prayers. But, I pray thee (and all the time the gentleman wept) that thou wouldest not remember against us our transgressions, nor take offence at the unqualifiedness of thy servants.' Now with all that, and with whole volumes more like that, it is no wonder that among all the angels that stand around the throne,—

> This is the angel of the earth
> And she is always weeping.

And at this point Jeremy Taylor comes in with this. Our tears for sin, he says, are so unlike the tears of the great saints ; our divinest tears are so slow in coming, and they are so soon staunched and dried up again, that the great masters of the devotional life have invented ' suppletory arts and spiritual stratagems' so as to secure to us both timeous and sufficient tears. And one of those ' suppletory arts,' of which Taylor himself was such a past master, is the great art of penitential preaching. Now that great art never flourished more nor ever bore better fruit than just in the days of Taylor and Bunyan in England and in those same days in Scotland. But that great divine art is almost a lost art in our day both in Scotland and in England. Real penitential preaching, close and bold preaching coming right home to the conscience, preaching like Thomas Boston's to terrify the godly in their too easy and too presuming way with God and with themselves, preaching fitted to keep a sinner once penitent always penitent, preaching that makes the holy law of God to enter deeper and deeper every day into the deceitful and corrupt and wicked heart ; life-searching, heart-searching, conscience-searching preaching, so far as can be gathered from the sermons that are published and belauded and widely sold among us is all but a lost art. There is great intellectual power in the preaching of our day, there never was more ; there is great Biblical and other scholarship, great eloquence, and great earnestness, of a kind ; but preaching to the heart and to the conscience is a neglected, if not an altogether lost art. And the pity is, our best people are quite well pleased to

have it so. They get what they want; and hence
their hardness, and their dryness, and their self-
complacency in the matter of divine tears; in the
matter of that sacrifice which so pleases God when
He can get it at the hands of His people.

At the same time if the pulpits of your preachers
are all but silent on the great penitential texts and
topics, you have the penitential books of a far
deeper and a far more spiritual day; as many of
you as pine for such instruction and such direction. Though I have been labouring after it all
my days among you, I bitterly feel that I have
sinfully failed in preaching to you with the art, and
with the power, and with the alternate commanding-
ness and winningness of the great preachers of the
penitential pulpit. At the same time, you cannot
deny this that I have always told you about those
great and true preachers and have pressed their
priceless books upon you. *The Way to Christ, The
Imitation of Christ, The Unregenerate Man, The
Indwelling Sin, The Mortification of Sin, The Saving
Interest, The Saint's Rest, The Holy Living and
Dying, The Private Devotions, The Serious Call, The
Christian Perfection, The Religious Affections*, and so
on; and the great spiritual autobiographies. If
any one among you seriously wishes to have himself exercised in some of the 'suppletory arts and
spiritual stratagems' of repentance unto life and
divine tears, these books, and a lifetime of suchlike books, are confidently recommended to the
purchase, and to the constant perusal, of that truly
wise man.

I have no books, penitential or other, said the
author of *The Way to Christ*, but I have myself.

And one who early fell in love with her own salvation, and who kept true to her first love, and whom Behmen would have loved to have had for a daughter, she reports herself from the Valley of Humiliation in these inimitable terms : 'This place, methinks, suits well with my spirit. For I love to be in such places where there is no rattling with coaches, and no rumbling with wheels. Methinks, one may here, without much molestation, be thinking what he was, whence he came, what he has done, and to what his King has called him. Here one may think and break at heart, and may melt in one's spirit until one's eyes become like the fishpools of Heshbon.' 'Here one may think and break at heart.' As much as to say that all our hearts would be broken, and all our eyes would be fountains of tears, if we would only think on the topics on which Mercy thought so much and so sweetly and so profitably. Thinking, then, just thinking, is another sure stratagem to be confidently recommended to all those who have neither the money to buy penitential books, nor have the help they so much need but in vain look for from their ministers' pulpits.

'More tears,' said McCheyne to himself when he was inquiring what was wanting in order to secure more success in missionary work. 'More tears,' he said, for the lost estate of this whole world, and more tears for the 'unqualifiedness,' as Mr. Weteyes called it, of those who go out to do missionary work. Let both home ministers and foreign missionaries also shed far more tears, said McCheyne. 'Tears gain everything,' says Santa Teresa, in her so tearful autobiography. And then the restoration

Psalmist strikes in to comfort both Teresa and McCheyne and says to them : 'They that sow in tears shall reap in joy. He that goeth forth and weepeth, bearing precious seed, shall doubtless come again with rejoicing, bringing his sheaves with him.'

Let us all close with seeking to say each one his own Amen to this penitential prayer of the great Weteyes of the English Church : 'Thou knowest, O Lord, that I have great heaviness, and continual sorrow in my heart, for the way I have sinned against Thee. But, with all that, I am a burden to myself in that I cannot sorrow more. I beseech Thee, then, for a contrite heart, and for tears of blood for my great sins. Woe is me, for the sinfulness of my life, and for the hardness of my heart, and the dryness of my eyes. I can sin ; but, of myself, I cannot repent. I am dried up like a potsherd. Woe, woe is me. Turn, O Lord, the hard rock into a pool. Give tears : give a fountain of tears. Give the grace of tears. Tears, such as Thou didst give to David, and to Jeremiah, and to Peter, and to Mary Magdalene. Give me some of the tears of the Man of Sorrows. And blessed be His Name, who so wept and so bled for me ! Blessed be His name for ever by me ! Even the Name of the Man of Sorrows and acquainted with grief for me. Amen.'

XVII

' The enmity that is in me to God.'

ALVIN says that the first table of the
law, spiritually considered, holds by
far the higher rank of the two ; but
the second table, he says, is far
better adapted for making a scrutiny
into our sinful hearts. And Stier takes the same
view when he says that the second table is far
better fitted than the first to carry conviction to our
coarse-grained consciences. Now since that is so,
let us commence to-night with our enmity to our
neighbours. And when conviction is carried home
to our evil hearts in the matter of our enmity to
our neighbours, then after that we shall the better
come to the far more spiritual scrutiny of our enmity
to God.

But to begin with, what exactly is this evil thing
here called enmity ? Enmity is estrangement. It
is alienation. It is dislike. It is antipathy. It
is animosity. It is ill-will. It is deep hostility of
heart. As the saying is, it is to be at daggers-
drawn with a man. Now, let us take those synonyms
of enmity, and let us boldly and honestly make use
of them for a somewhat thorough scrutiny of ourselves in this sad matter of enmity.

Well, then, who and what man is he from whom
we are so estranged and so alienated? Let us
name him to ourselves. From having been at one
time good friends, or at least from having been at
one time innocent and well-disposed neighbours,
why are we now so estranged and so alienated?
What was the original cause of this sinful estrangement and alienation? What was it in him, if it
was in him? But more likely, what was it in us?
A good and honest heart always begins a scrutiny
like this with suspecting itself. My brethren,
you will make yourselves good and honest hearts
just by the way you set yourselves to find out
in yourselves the whole cause of your sinful
estrangement and alienation from so-and-so, naming
him to yourselves as you commence your scrutiny
of yourselves concerning him.

Again, why do you so bitterly dislike so-and-so?
What is it in him that makes you so to dislike him?
Is there really anything in him fully to account for
your bitter feelings towards him? Make sure that
it is not something in yourself. Is your dislike of
him wholly honourable and creditable to you; or is
it wholly the reverse? Imagine to yourself something that would turn your dislike to him into
liking for him. Tell yourself what it is that would
wholly turn your heart round to him. And that
will throw a great light on yourself, and on your
self-seeking heart.

Again, against what man do you harbour a secret
and a rancorous ill-will? Put your finger on the
name of the man concerning whom you like to hear
evil tidings; on the name of the man concerning
whom you hate to hear any good. How has that

horrible state of mind arisen within you? Explain
to yourself why it is that you have sunk to such a
depth of wickedness as that. And at that point
play the man. Look in your own evil face and
tell yourself to your face that you have found yourself out. Say to yourself that you are that most
hateful thing on the whole earth, a malicious-
minded man. Cut open and spread out the black
inside of your heart before God, and give Him no
rest as long as an atom of that black heart dwells
within you. Tell Jesus Christ in secret and unceasing prayer that since His name and His office
are what they are, it is His proper and promised
business to kill and cast out the devil who
harbours and burrows and spits hell-fire in your
heart. And tell Him that you look to Him to do it.
And to do it as quickly as possible, lest you die a
devil yourself.

Then again, why have you nursed and suckled
and secretly fed your ill-will till you could kill such
and such a man? Aye, and would do it too if
you were not such a coward. You have not the
courage of your evil feelings else you would dispatch
him on his way home some dark night. As it is
it would make you the best of company at the
breakfast table to-morrow morning if you read in
the paper that some other enemy of his had done
your work for you. But among the weapons of
civilisation cowards employ an anonymous pen
where brave men employ an open dagger.
Whether you go to that depth with yourselves or
no, that was the way John Calvin scrutinised himself concerning his neighbour. And especially
concerning his neighbour in the sixth and ninth

commandments. Now you are all sound Calvinists
in the doctrines of election, and redemption, and
the final perseverance of the saints. Up then and
be sound Calvinists henceforth in your scrutiny of
yourselves, in your detection of yourselves, in your
detestation of yourselves, and in your condemnation
of yourselves. 'Condemn yourselves,' said Calvin's
master, 'and God will justify you. But cover yourselves up, and excuse yourselves, and defend yourselves, and God will expose and condemn you, and
that without appeal.'

In still further scrutiny of our enmity to our
neighbour, take our ecclesiastical divisions and
alienations. Now, do I love and honour and wish
well to the ministers and the members of other
churches, as I wish well to those of my own
church? Or do I grieve over their prosperity,
and does it rejoice my heart to hear of their
adversity? Let every one of us scrutinise himself and then honestly answer that. Our Lord's
last prayer was offered to His Father concerning
those rancorous animosities and hatreds and mutual
persecutions which He foresaw would so lacerate
the Church which is His body. Now how do you
stand toward that great prayer of His? And
is your heart and life advancing or frustrating that
intercession of His? Does any minister, especially,
deny this enmity? Then he is not a good heathen
yet, not to say a good Christian. For even the
ministers of heathendom all examined themselves
and said to themselves, Know thyself. Calvin also
had many a sore scrutiny of himself in respect of
the church divisions of his day.

And since we are among churches, how do you

feel toward those men who have left your church and gone over to another church? But perhaps your hearts are too lukewarm to your own church to care very much about who comes to it or who leaves it. Only there are others among us who have the temptations that always accompany a real love and a real loyalty to their own church. Ministers, especially. Why, a minister will remember the people who deserted him and his ministry thirty, forty years ago. The wound those deserters gave to his proud heart is not healed to this day. And again on the other hand, the minister who receives those deserters with such effusiveness and with such open arms never has a thought to spare for the solace of his brother whose loss has been his gain. And I do not know that a minister's elation of heart when he receives such deserters is one whit less sinful in the sight of God than is his neighbour's enmity of heart at him and at them. Let a minister in prosperity as well as in adversity severely scrutinise himself.

But you are not ministers, and you cannot be expected to understand or to sympathise with all their special temptations. But you are tradesmen, and shopkeepers, and lawyers, and advocates, and schoolmasters, and so on. And the same proud and selfish heart beats out its enmities in your bosom as in your minister's bosom. And you also must learn to make your daily temptations in your shop and in your office so many calls and so many opportunities for a scrutiny of yourselves. Resentful merchants will remember the customers who left their shop with quite as long a memory as ministers will remember their ungrateful and runaway people. You will see shopkeepers scowling at you on the street and in the church after ten, after twenty years.

Then, again, you will sometimes see Mr. Worldly-wiseman leaving a poor and struggling congregation, and joining a rich and an influential congregation, in the hope of finding a ladder there by the help of which he may climb up to the ambition of his heart. You see through him quite well; everybody sees through him. And you are tempted to despise him and to hate him. But, though he deserves to be despised, you must not dwell too much on his motives and his meanness. For your heart only too easily falls into a state of real enmity towards such men. Place-hunting, and especially in the Church of Christ, is very hateful. But your heart is not a safe home for much hatred. You must watch, and take good care, not to hate any man; no, not even in the interests of religion, nor in the interests of Church purity, nor in any other interest whatsoever.

In all this, I may not have come within a thousand miles of my own special enmity, and yours. So unsearchable, so past finding out, is the sinful heart. So endless are the corruptions, and the malignities, and the enmities of the human heart, that it must be left to each spiritually minded man to scrutinise himself without ceasing, making use, as every spiritually minded man will do, of the unceasing calls and opportunities to that scrutiny which his God and Saviour and Sanctifier supplies to him. You will see that all I have done is to point out some of the more outstanding and more glaring instances of enmity, leaving it to each

several man to go into his own hidden heart and
to scrutinise himself there, by the help of the holy
Word of God and the holy Spirit of God.

Now I very much doubt, my brethren, whether
any man of us all has sufficient fineness of mind by
nature, and sufficient spirituality of mind by grace,
to enable him to enter truly and fully on the
subject of his own enmity to God. Many who
would quite frankly admit their enmity to certain
men would honestly and loudly deny that they
had any enmity to God. And I do not feel that I
am able to-night to enter into all the scriptural
proofs and experimental evidences of that universal
and awful enmity. The Scriptures are full of the
proofs and the evidences of our enmity to God.
And what is, to my mind, by far the deepest and
the truest theological literature of the Church,
both doctrinal and experimental, is also full of it.
And what is more to me than all that, my own
scrutiny of my own heart over a long and a heart-
searching life is full of it. But all that does not
make me feel able to-night to enter fully with you
on your enmity to God and my enmity to Him.
The subject is so dreadful, the fact is so fearful,
that the proper handling of it is beyond me to-
night. If I entered on it, by my unskilful handling
of it, I would be sure to arouse denial and contra-
diction in some men's minds, and that would cause
more harm to them and to the truth than any good
I could hope to do. A man must have that enmity
in himself : he must have discovered that enmity
deep down and widespread in his own heart, and
he must daily lament and bewail its existence in
himself, before I could preach with any profit to

him about it. I do not say that any of us have
such enmity to God as we have to some men; such
enmity as that we would destroy Him out of existence if we could. And yet I am not sure. Let
each man scrutinise his own heart about that.
But no man can possibly deny his deep distaste
sometimes, aye oftentimes, for spiritual duties and
spiritual exercises; for secret prayer, for secret meditation, for secret self-examination, for secret communion with God, and for the pure spirituality and
the pure divinity of all such exercises. And what is
all that but distaste, and dislike, and weariness, and
averseness, and almost enmity, to God Himself?
Now to him who bitterly and with a broken heart
feels all that in himself, and who hates his own
ungodly and atheistic heart like hell, I will close
with one word of encouragement to that man.
And I take that word of encouragement out of a
great forerunner of his in the depths of the divine
life—the little read but invaluable Halyburton.
'I looked on it,' says the Professor, 'as part of my
duty to-day to search into my spiritual state. And
after earnest application to God for His Holy Spirit,
who alone searches the heart of man, I pitched
upon this evidence of the progress of His work of
grace within me. I found in myself a real and true
approbation of the holy law of God, in both its
tables, and an approbation of the holiness of God
in all His law. I am now satisfied with the holiness and the justice and the spirituality of the law
of God. The carnal heart is enmity against God,
and is not subject to the law of God, neither,
indeed, can be. But, blessed be God, the enmity
that I once had to the law of God is now wholly

and for ever removed.' So writes that great man of God in his priceless diary.

And till you come to that, take home with you to-night the paragraph of to-night out of John Bunyan. It is paragraph 115. I will read it again : 'I remember that, one day, as I was travelling into the country, and was musing on the wickedness and blasphemy of my heart, and was considering the enmity that was in me to God, this scripture came to my mind : "He hath made peace by the blood of His Cross." By which scripture I was made to see, both again, and again, and again, that day, that God and my soul were made friends by this blood. Yea, I saw that the justice of God and my sinful soul could now embrace and kiss each other through this blood. That was a good day to me ; I hope I shall not forget it.'

XVIII

' One day, as I was passing in the field, having some dashes on my conscience, this fell upon my soul: Thy Righteousness is in Heaven.'

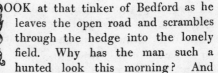OOK at that tinker of Bedford as he leaves the open road and scrambles through the hedge into the lonely field. Why has the man such a hunted look this morning? And why does he turn his back so sullenly on his own house and on all the walks of his fellow-townsmen? Look well at him as he sets out to pursue his calling this morning with his satchel of tools on his shoulder and takes his solitary way across the lonely fields and through the dark and silent woods. What is the matter this morning with John Bunyan who was wont to frequent the roads and the streets of Bedford and to salute so genially every man he met? It is his conscience. It is his dashed conscience. He does not tell us what exactly it was that had so dashed his conscience and had so darkened his heart that morning. And thus it is that we are left to guess for ourselves what it may have been. Well, it may have been this. He may have dashed his wife's heart that morning at breakfast by his cruel words to her. Or he may have dashed the heart of his blind child by his unkind

impatience with her, till he left both his wife and
his child in tears together. Or he may have lost
his temper and let loose his tongue on some
apprentice or some fellow-workman of his. Or
again he may have been guilty of some great outbreak of ill-will against some other tinker in the
town. Or again it may have been some of his
'seven abominations' that had so broken out that
morning as to leave his conscience one mass of
remorse and wounds and blood. I have my own
guess what it was, but I cannot be absolutely sure.
At any rate, there he is stumbling through the
ploughed field, laden to the earth with that mill-
stone of a satchel, and nigh unto death with those
great dashes on his conscience.

And then there was this also. As he stumbled
on among the deep furrows of that lonely field that
terrible breakdown of his religious life at home
that morning set him a-questioning as to the reality
of his conversion, and as to the truth of all his
professions of religion. 'I must have been deceiving myself all along,' he said to himself. 'And I
must have been deceiving my minister and all the
devout people of Bedford all along. For no man
that had ever been truly born again could ever so
misbehave himself, both to God and man, as I have
again misbehaved myself this morning. No. I see
now that I am a reprobate and a castaway as I so
richly deserve to be.' But the miserable man had
scarcely said that to himself when suddenly this
sentence fell from God on his soul: 'Thy Righteousness is in Heaven.' Hear himself about it.
'Now, methought, withal, I saw, with the eyes of
my soul, Jesus Christ at God's Right Hand. There,

I say, I saw my Righteousness; so that, wherever I was, or whatever I was a-doing, God could not say of me that He wanted my Righteousness; for, there IT was just beside Him. I also saw, moreover, that it was not my good frame of heart that made my Righteousness better; nor yet my bad frame of heart that made my Righteousness worse. For, my Righteousness was JESUS CHRIST HIMSELF: the same yesterday, to-day, and for ever. Now did my chains fall off my legs indeed. I was loosed from all my affliction and iron. My temptations also fled away. And now I went home that night rejoicing in the grace and in the love of God. O methought, Christ! Christ! There was nothing but Christ that was before my eyes. Because I could now look from myself to Him; and should reckon that all those graces of God, that now were but green on me, were yet but like those crack-groats and fourpence-halfpennies that rich men carry in their purses, when their gold is in their trunks at home! O yes: I saw that my gold was in my trunk at home! Even in Christ, my Lord and Saviour! Now Christ was all to me. He was all my Wisdom, all my Righteousness, all my Sanctification, and all my Redemption. Now could I see myself in heaven, and on earth, and both at once. In heaven by my Christ, by my Head, by my Righteousness, and by my Life: though on earth by my body or person.'

Now is there any man in this house this evening with a dashed conscience? What have you been doing, Sir? When was it, and where was it? Was it at breakfast this morning, or was it at dinner this afternoon? Was it an outburst of bitter anger and

bad temper? Or was it your enmity at some innocent and unsuspecting man? Have you struck
again at your neighbour with your wicked tongue
or with your wicked pen? After all that both
God and man have done for your soul have you
gone back again as a dog to his vomit, and as a
sow that is washed to her wallowing in the mire?
No wonder then, that your conscience is dashed
to pieces to-night. No wonder that you are avoid-
ing the eyes of good men. No wonder that you
are in such shame and despair. But God delights
in mercy to miserable men like you. And He has
been beforehand with His mercy to you. For,
among other things, He has had *Grace Abounding*
written for you. And as God's much experienced
servant hands down his golden book to you, he says
to you, and to all his readers: ' My children, Grace
be with you, Amen. I have sent you here enclosed
a drop of that honey which I have taken out of the
carcase of a lion. I have eaten thereof myself
also, and I have been much refreshed thereby.
This book of mine is something of a relation of
the work of God upon my own soul; even from the
very first till now. Wherein you may see my cast-
ings down, and my raisings up. For He woundeth,
and His hands make whole. It is written in the
Scriptures that the father to the children shall
make known the truth of God. Yea, it was for
this reason that I lay so long at Sinai, to see the
fire, and the cloud, and the darkness, and the
tempest, that I might fear the Lord all the days
of my life on earth, and so tell of God's wonderful
works to the ears of my children.'

Now the one sure lesson for you out of all that

of John Bunyan is this: God, who justifies the
ungodly, and Jesus Christ, who is the sinner's
Righteousness, are both the very same in this
house this evening as they were in that Bedford
field that forenoon. The only difference is that
you have taken John Bunyan's place before God.
John Bunyan is no longer in Bedford with such
dashes on his conscience. He is now for ever with
Christ and for ever like Christ. He is now where
his Righteousness and his Sanctification have always
been. And you are in his identical place in this
house this Sabbath evening. Like him that forenoon your conscience is sorely dashed with your
sins ; sorely dashed with the re-awakened remembrance of old sins, as well as with the fresh dashes
of new sins. When suddenly this same sentence
falls on your soul: O chief of sinners! Do not
despair, for thy Righteousness is in heaven! Now
after that heavenly voice has fallen on your soul,
all that you have got to do to-night is to *believe* it
so as not to make God a liar about it. All that you
have got to do to-night is to look up, and to keep
on looking up, till like John Bunyan you clearly
see with the eyes of your soul Jesus Christ at
God's right hand, and there representing you, and
appearing for you, and transacting for you. All
you have got to do to-night, and every day and
every night till you die, is to see continually, and
to believe continually, and to assure yourself continually, that it is not your good frame of heart
that makes your Righteousness better, nor your bad
frame of heart that makes your Righteousness
worse. Now, if you believe and receive that and
continue to believe and receive that—and you have

the same right and title and command to believe
that as Paul and Luther and Hooker and Bunyan
had—then your chains also will fall off your legs.
You will be loosed from all your affliction and iron.
And all your temptations to be a boor and a brute
at home and abroad will more and more flee away,
till you will find yourself exclaiming continually
with John Bunyan, O Christ! O Christ! O Christ!
And till there will be nothing but Jesus Christ
before your eyes.　You are frightened to have your
name coupled with the names of such saints as
Paul and Luther and Hooker and Bunyan.　And
no wonder.　But all the difference between those
four great saints and you is this: they are all men
of great spiritual genius, and you are in your own
eyes a cheap and a commonplace sinner.　And that
is quite true.　But then you have Paul himself to
comfort you and to encourage you in that respect
in a great passage of his where he says: 'Not many
wise men, not many noble, not many mighty are
called.　But base things of the world, and things
which are despised, hath God chosen.　And therefore of Him are you also in Christ Jesus—if you
will only consent to have it so—who of God is
made unto you, not Righteousness alone, but
Wisdom, and Sanctification, and Redemption also.
That, according as it is written, he that glorieth,
let him glory in the Lord.'

What a glorious 'device' is the gospel of our
justification,—William Guthrie is always exclaiming
in his *Saving Interest*.　That Almighty God should
devise and should discover to us such a way in order
to show forth His holiness and His justice and His
grace; and all working together into such a deep

plot of divine wisdom! Yes, indeed, what a deep
device! And how like God Himself in every
respect! That, to begin with, He should place us
sinful men under a law of His which is so holy,
and which is so spiritual in its holiness, that no
mortal man can, by any possibility, obey it so as to
attain to eternal life by the obedience of it. A law
so spiritual and so holy that we only break it the
more hopelessly the more deeply we enter into it.
And then that God should make His own Son,
Jesus Christ, under that same holy and spiritual
law, and that He should magnify the universally
broken law, and make it honourable; should obey
it and fulfil it in every thought and word and deed
of His down to every jot and tittle of it. And
should, both by His obedience and by His blood,
finish for us what Paul by the Holy Ghost always
calls the 'Righteousness of God.' And then that
Jesus Christ should be made to us our immediate
and everlasting Righteousness—what a 'device' of
combined holiness and justice and grace is that!
No wonder that Bunyan never ceased exclaiming:
O Christ! O Christ! O Christ! And no wonder
that Christiana exclaimed after Greatheart had
expounded Christ's righteousness to her: 'O this
is brave!' she exclaimed. 'Good Mercy, let us
labour to keep this well in mind. And do you
also, all my children, remember it all your days on
earth.'

But with all that some of you will still say that
you cannot believe it and receive it so as at all
times to stay and rest your whole soul upon it.
You cannot believe it, that the very next moment
after some fresh outbreak of your deep-seated

sinfulness you should have no more to do but just
to look up to heaven and say: The Lord Jesus
Christ, up there, is my complete Righteousness!
You are concerned, for one thing, for God's honour,
and for the honour and for the authority of His
holy law. And at other times you cannot be too
much concerned about all that. But not now.
Look up on the spot and claim Christ as your all-
justifying righteousness, and leave God's honour
and the honour of His holy law in His own hands.
You may depend upon it that both God and His
Son have looked well to all that long before they
had the gospel of your free and full and immediate
and everlasting forgiveness preached to you. And
more than that, as a matter of sure fact and of
indisputable experience, God has had His great
device of an imputed Righteousness vindicated by
two thousand years of the holiest men on the face
of the earth. No; you need not take fear for God
and His holy law. For neither you nor any other
divinely forgiven man will ever be found sinning
that grace may abound. No; but you will always
find yourself, in the hour and in the opportunity of
temptation, instinctively and indignantly protesting
and saying, God forbid! Shall I, who am dead to
sin, live any longer therein? Just put this immense
matter upon an immediate experiment. The next
time you fall, inwardly or outwardly, look up that
moment to your Righteousness in heaven; and see
if that sight will not, in the end, wholly sanctify
you as well as wholly justify you. It will; it most
certainly will; if Paul is right in his Romans, and
if Bunyan is right in his *Grace Abounding*, and if
Hooker is right in his immortal sermon. Paul's

Romans you all know, and Hooker's sermon you have all heard of, and Bunyan's experience you are every Sabbath evening coming more and more to know. But Luther, Paul's best gospel scholar, you only know by name as yet. Take, then, this taste of the great Reformer before you go home. He is writing to an Augustinian monk, and he says: 'I should be very glad, my dear Spentein, to know what is the state of your soul. Are you not clean tired of working out your own righteousness? In our day pride seduces many, and especially those who labour, with all their might, to make themselves righteous. When you were living with me, you were in that fatal error, and so was I. And I am still struggling against that so fatal error. I have not even yet entirely triumphed over it. O, my dear brother, learn to know Christ, and Him crucified! Learn this new song, and sing it unceasingly to Christ: "Thou, O Lord Jesus Christ, art my Righteousness, and I am Thy sin. Thou hast taken what was mine, and hast, in room of it, given me what was Thine. What Thou wast not Thou didst become, in order that I might become and might remain, what, at one time, I was not." Sing and say that to Christ continually. Beware, O my brother, of ever pretending to such purity of heart and life as no longer to confess thyself a sinner; for Christ dwells only with sinners. If our labours and our afflictions could have given us peace of conscience why should Christ have died for us? Dear Spentein, you will find no peace save in Christ. And Christ is always opening His arms to you; He is always taking all your sins upon Himself, and giving you all His Righteousness.'

Learn that by heart, my brethren ; as also this :
' One day, as I was passing in the field, and that,
too, with some dashes on my conscience, fearing
lest yet all was not right, suddenly this sentence
fell upon my soul : Thy Righteousness is in Heaven.'

XIX

'The most fit book for a wounded conscience.'

BEFORE I had gone thus far out of these my temptations, I did greatly long to see some ancient godly man's experience, who had writ some hundred of years before I was born. For, those who had writ in our days I thought (but I desire them now to pardon me) that they had writ only that which others felt, or else had, through the strength of their wits and parts, studied to answer such objections as they perceived others were perplexed with, without going down themselves into the deep. Well, after many such longings in my mind, the God in whose hands are all our days and ways, did cast into my hand one day a book of Martin Luther; it was his *Comment on the Galatians*—it also was so old that it was ready to fall piece from piece if I did but turn it over. Now I was pleased much that such an old book had fallen into my hands; the which, when I had but a little way perused, I found my condition, in his experience, so largely and so profoundly handled, as if his book had been written out of my own heart. But of particulars here I intend nothing. Only this, methinks, I must let fall before all men, I do prefer this book of Martin

Luther upon the Galatians (excepting the Holy Bible) before all the books that ever I have seen, as most fit for a wounded conscience.'

Now, since very few of you can possibly have access to Luther's *Comment on the Galatians*, I propose to give up the whole of this evening hour to that great Reformation book. I shall stand aside to-night and I shall let Martin Luther speak to you as he spoke to John Bunyan.

Take first, then, what Luther taught and what Bunyan felt and experienced about SIN. 'SIN in Holy Scripture,' says Luther, 'signifies far less the outward act, than the sinful spirit that lives and works deep down in the bottom of the sinner's heart. According to the universal teaching of Holy Scripture, the sinful heart is the true seat, and the real source, of all our evil. And, then, more than that, Holy Scripture looks on our UNBELIEF as being the real spring of all our evil, both inward and outward. "The Holy Ghost shall convince the world of sin," says our Lord, "because they believe not on Me." According to Holy Scripture faith alone justifies, and unbelief alone condemns.' Therefore, says Luther, wherever you find a sin, the unbelief of the heart is always at the root of that sin. And then, like all Scripture, and like all spiritual experience, Luther adds that 'our unbelief and our sin are so deeply rooted in our depraved hearts that they are never wholly eradicated in this life. Even the best saints are continually falling into sin through unbelief and an evil heart. Abraham fell, Isaac fell, Jacob fell. And so on, all down the Holy Scriptures. And all these sins of God's saints are recorded in the Holy

Scriptures in order that we may take comfort and may not despair. If Jacob, and Aaron, and David, and Peter fell, and rose again, so may we rise again like them. They rose again by repentance, and by faith, and by prayer, and so may we,' says Luther. Now, I can imagine John Bunyan walking in the fields, with some dashes in his conscience, and with these strong passages out of Luther taking possession of his heart for the first time.

There is nothing on which Luther is more Pauline and more powerful than on the LAW, and on our right use of the LAW. 'Understand,' he is continually saying, 'that Moses is not intended to be your saviour. You will never save yourself by the deeds of the LAW. The LAW is intended to have the very opposite result. For the divine intention of the LAW is, to begin with, to show us ourselves. Its first function is to reveal to us our hopeless sinfulness and our estate of condemnation. Nay, not only does the Law reveal to us our hopeless sinfulness, it mightily increases our sinfulness, and it mightily deepens and darkens our despair.' The Law enters, says Luther's master in divinity, in order that the offence may abound. Moses with his Law is most terrible to us, Luther is always saying. There never was the like of Moses for terrifying our consciences and tyrannising over our hearts, he is always threatening and thundering against us. Moses and his Law never have had one single word of comfort, or of hope, to say to any poor sinner. Let every well-taught Christian man, then, learn to reason with the Law in this way, says Luther. 'Let every well-taught Christian man dispute with the Law, and say to it: O thou

so severe and so inflexible Law! thou wouldst fain
set up thy seat of judgment in my guilty conscience! Thou wouldst fain summon up all thy
witnesses against me! Thou wouldst fain sentence
me as I deserve! But keep thee to thy proper office.
Lay all thy terrors upon my sinful heart, and upon
my evil life. But come not near my tender conscience. For thou must know that Christ, thy
Master and mine, has Himself died for me. He
has Himself settled all my accounts for me. And
in Him I have, and I am righteously entitled to
have, peace of conscience and a quiet mind. He
has led me wholly out of thy jurisdiction, and He
has placed me down in an estate of salvation, in
which estate there is no condemnation. I am now
the subject of a kingdom in which there is nothing
but forgiveness, and peace, and joy, and health,
and love, and everlasting life. Tell the Law that
if it has anything in any way to say to thee now,
it must say all that to thee through Christ. Say to
it that thou art now stone dead to every one and to
everything but Christ.' That Gospel doctrine concerning the Law was very marrow and fatness to
Bunyan's soul. And then after he had thoroughly
mastered all that out of Paul and out of Luther
Bunyan puts it all to us in his own dramatic way,
when he shows us Christian going out of the right
road and wandering astray under the thunders and
the earthquakes of Sinai, till Evangelist found him
and spoke to him with such a severe countenance
concerning his all but fatal error.

Out of a thousand passages about CHRIST in
Luther's writings Bunyan would read this a thousand times. 'Christ, then, is no Moses. Christ

does not speak from Sinai. No weapons in His hands are seen, nor voice of terror heard. Christ is not a hard master who will compel the uttermost farthing. Christ comes to all sinners full of grace and mercy; both able and willing to save. Christ is nothing but infinite grace and goodness. Be sure that you always paint Christ to yourself in His true and correct colours. It is the very top and complete crown of Christian truth to be able to define and describe Christ aright, and that especially in the season of sin and guilt and condemnation. Hold fast, at all times, by Paul's description and definition of Christ. Now Paul's true description and definition is this: He loved me, and gave Himself for me. For myself,' says this true Pauline preacher and true pastor of souls; 'for myself, I have much difficulty in always holding this divine definition of Christ which Paul gives to all believers. When I was a young man,' says Luther, 'I was so drowned in unscriptural and anti-evangelical error that my heart trembled at the very name of Christ, for I was taught to think of Him as an angry judge; whereas He is our Redeemer and our Saviour. Christ is joy and sweetness to every trembling and broken heart. Christ is the true and faithful lover of all those who are in trouble and anguish because of sin. He is the merciful High Priest of all miserable and fearful sinners. Let us learn to practise this distinction; and not in sacred words only, but in life and in experience, and with a warm inward feeling. For where Christ is rightly understood and held by, there must needs be joy of heart and peace of conscience. And that because He is our reconciliation, and our righteousness, and our peace, and our life, and our whole and complete salvation. *In brief*, whatsoever the afflicted conscience desires, that it finds in Christ abundantly and continually.' In brief, says Luther; but instead of being brief he dwells upon Christ in that way at all length and in every sermon and comment of his. Spurgeon was like Luther his forerunner when he said that what his faultfinders complained of concerning his sermons was quite true; wherever he took his texts it did not matter, he straightway made across country to Jesus Christ. Spurgeon could not be brief when he came to Christ, and neither could Luther, and neither could Bunyan. 'O methought, Christ! Christ! There was nothing and no one now but Christ before my eyes!'

You all know what a supreme and what a universal place FAITH holds in the Bible, and especially in the New Testament, and especially in Paul's Epistles. Well, faith holds an equally supreme and universal place in all Luther's writings. And rightly so. For there is nothing in all the world so necessary to us as faith, and there is nothing so little understood by us. 'Especially that word *faith* put me to it,' says Bunyan. And it was Luther who first and fully cleared up this supreme matter of faith to Bunyan. I take this passage on faith not from his Comment on the Galatians, but from his Christian Liberty, which is the finest thing that Luther ever wrote, and one of the foundation documents of our evangelical divinity : 'Now since these promises of God are such words of holiness, and truth, and righteousness, and liberty, and peace, and are so full of universal goodness, the soul which cleaves to them with a firm faith is so united to them as to be penetrated and saturated with all their sweetness. For if the mere finger-touch of Christ's clothes was so healing, how much more does that most spiritual touch of pure faith communicate to the soul all that stands in the divine word concerning Christ. In this way therefore the soul through faith alone is from the Word of God justified, sanctified, endued with truth and peace and liberty, and filled full with every good thing. There is this incomparable virtue in faith also, that it unites the soul to Christ as the wife is united to her husband; by which " mystery," as the Apostle teaches, Christ and the soul are made one for ever. Now if they are made one for ever, and if the most perfect of all marriages is accomplished between them (for our human marriages are but feeble types of this one great marriage), then whatsoever Christ possesses, all that the believing soul may take to itself and hold as its own; just as whatever belongs to the soul Christ takes to Himself and holds as His own. Now Christ, our husband, is full of grace, and life, and salvation; and the soul is full of sin, and death, and condemnation. But let faith step in, and then our sin and our death and our hell itself will all belong to Christ; and all His grace and life and salvation will all belong to us. In all this the delightful sight is seen of our victory, and salvation, and redemption. When our Bridegroom, by the wedding ring of faith, takes the sins of the soul and makes them all His own, then must all our sin and death and hell be swallowed up in the stupendous conflict our Husband holds with all our enemies. For His righteousness rises far above all our sins;

and His life is now far more powerful than is our
last enemy; and His great salvation is the con-
quest of our very hell itself. My Beloved is mine,
the soul sings, and I am His. Thanks be to God
who giveth us the victory through our Lord Jesus
Christ.' I wish I could put into your believing
hands the whole of Luther's incomparable treatise
Concerning Christian Liberty. And especially I wish
I could put into your hands those fine pages, those
truly exquisite pages, on faith as it is the fulfilling
of the whole law of God.

But I must not withhold from you this great
passage about GRACE which one was reading aloud
in a prayer-meeting in London at a quarter to
seven one evening when John Wesley, on hearing
it, had his eyes opened, and immediately entered
into light and life. ' Grace has this distinction,'
writes Luther, 'that it signifies the favour and the
affection of God, through which He pours Christ
and His Spirit into our hearts. And though our
sinfulness remains in us more or less all our life on
earth, nevertheless grace does so much for us that
we are regarded as fully and entirely justified
before God. For His grace does not divide itself,
and parcel itself out, but it receives us at once and
wholly into the divine favour for the sake of Christ.
You can understand, therefore, the seventh chapter
of the Romans, where Paul so reproaches himself
as a sinner, and yet in the eighth chapter goes on
to say that there is no condemnation to them which
are in Christ Jesus. On account of our indwelling
sin we are still sinners; but because of our faith
and trust in Christ, God is favourable to us, and
will act toward us according to our faith in Christ

till our sin is completely mortified from within us.'
Returning to the Galatians we find Luther saying;
'There is nothing in all the world more precious
than this doctrine of grace. For they who understand this doctrine know that sin, and death, and
all our other afflictions and calamities, as well of
the body as of the soul, do work together for good.
Moreover, they know that God is then most near
to them, when they think Him furthest off. And
that He is then most full of mercy and of love
to them, when they think Him to be most offended
and most angry with them. Also, they know that
by grace they have an everlasting righteousness
laid up for them in heaven, even when they feel in
themselves the most terrible terrors of sin and
death and hell. But this cunning knowledge is
not learned,' says Luther, 'without many and great
temptations.'

Hazlitt says that the only specimen of Burke is
all that he ever wrote. And so I will say of
Luther on the topics I have just touched. At the
same time, I must sum up this shamefully meagre
specimen of Luther's riches, and I will do so with
quoting to you one or two of the things he says
about the right use of some of the Pronouns.
Commenting on Paul's words—Jesus Christ, which
gave Himself for our sins, Luther says: 'Weigh
well every word of Paul, and especially weigh well
this pronoun *our*. For thou wilt easily believe that
Jesus Christ gave Himself for the sins of Peter
and Paul; but it is a different thing to believe that
He gave Himself for thine invincible, infinite, and
horrible sins. But be sure to exercise thyself
diligently in this pronoun *our*; and this single

syllable, being rightly believed, will swallow up all thy sins. Only, to do this when we are in the conflict with unbelief, is, of all things, the most hard and difficult. I speak this by experience,' says Luther. And, again, on Paul's further words —The Son of God, who loved me, and gave Himself for me, Luther asks: ' But who is this *me*? It is even I, Martin Luther, a wretched and a condemned sinner. This word *me* is full of saving faith,' he says. ' He who will utter aright this little word *me* shall be a good advocate and disputer against all the accusations of the law, and of his own conscience. For Christ delivered up for *me* neither sheep, nor ox, nor gold, nor silver, but Himself, and that entirely and wholly for *me*. Yes even for *me*, who am such a wretched and miserable sinner. Say *me* then with all thy might, and print this pronoun *me* indelibly in thine heart. Not doubting, no—not for one moment, but that word is written for thee, to make it thy very own and to make Christ and His death for sin thy very own also.' And in yet another place Luther teaches us that ' all the religion of the Psalms lies in the right use of the personal pronouns, *I*, and *Me*, and *Thou*, and *Thee*.'

' I never can separate the two names of Paul and Luther,' says Coleridge in his *English Divines*. And again, ' How dearly Luther loved Paul, and how dearly would Paul have loved Luther !' exclaims Coleridge. But not more, I will add, than John Bunyan loved him. For much as has been said and written by Coleridge and by many others in praise of Luther, there is nothing that excels the classical text of this evening's discourse :

'Methinks I must let this fall before all men, I do prefer this book of Martin Luther upon the Galatians (excepting the Holy Bible), before all the books I have ever seen, as most fit for a wounded conscience.'

XX

'Oh! many a pull hath my heart had with Satan for that blessed sixth of John.'

HE name of 'Satan' was not a profane jest to John Bunyan. Satan was as real and as terrible and as diabolical to John Bunyan as he was to Adam and Eve, and to Job, and to Joshua the high priest, and to Luther in the Wartburg, and to our Lord in the Wilderness. John Bunyan was little child enough to take literally and truly all that he read in his Bible. He downright believed every syllable that he read in his Bible. And then with his great eyes of genius and of grace he actually saw and felt and acted upon every syllable that he read in his Bible. 'If ever Satan and I did strive for any word of God in all my life, it was for this good word of Christ; Satan at one end of it, and I at the other end. Oh, what work we did make! It was for this in John, I say, that we did tug and strive. He pulled and I pulled. But, God be praised, I got the better of him.' The old serpent, you see, was as real and he was as diabolical to John Bunyan in Bedford as he was to Adam and Eve in Eden, and to the second Adam in the Wilderness.

But to come to some particulars: 'We two, Satan

and I, had the most terrible pull for the natural force of every syllable in that blessed sixth of John': so our autobiographer tells us in another paragraph. Now, since all that was so, and since all that has been written by Bunyan for our learning, let us go back to Bedford to-night, so as to be present at that trial of strength between the prince of darkness and John Bunyan, that poor and oppressed servant of Jesus Christ. And as we look on we shall lay up some lessons as to how we also must play the man when we are in the same arena, and are in the same death agony with the same enemy.

Take, then, 'the natural force,' as Bunyan calls it, of this syllable 'him' in that blessed sixth of John —'him that cometh to Me I will in no wise cast out.' Now there are times when I cannot enter on my text till I have seen what Mr. Spurgeon has to say upon it. And I felt just in that way about this supreme text of to-night. And accordingly I sent up two or three postage stamps to Messrs. Passmore and Alabaster in London and they sent me down by return three sermons by Mr. Spurgeon on this blessed sixth of John. And I read those three sermons with salvation and with thankfulness in my heart, as I always read Spurgeon's sermons, and as multitudes of men and women have read them all the world over. None of us preachers nowadays can hold the candle to Spurgeon. I suppose after John Wesley, and perhaps William Booth, Charles Spurgeon will have the most names of saved sinners read out to his everlasting honour on that day when every minister's work shall be revealed. Well I will give you an example of the way in which that

great preacher brings out 'the natural force' of this
syllable 'him' in this blessed text now open before
us. 'Him,' says Spurgeon, 'means the rich man,
the poor man, the great and famous man, and the
small and obscure man, the moral man, the
debauchee, the man who has sunk into the worst
of sins, the man who has climbed to the highest of
virtues, him who is next of kin to the devil, and him
who is next of kin to the archangel. The sixth of
John,' continues Spurgeon, 'is one of the most
gracious and generous texts in the whole Word of
God. I cannot tell what kind of men may be in
this house to-night,' he said ; 'but if burglars are
here, and if dynamite men are here, him that
cometh to Christ this night, He will in no wise be
cast out.' [As I copy these divine lines out of
Spurgeon's Gospel, I read in the papers that even
Orchard professes to have been awakened and converted. That is to say, he also, who is the horror
of the whole world, has had a pull with Satan for
this blessed sixth of John, and has not been cast
out.] But let Spurgeon proceed with ourselves.
'If amidst this great congregation there should be
some men here whose characters I had better not
begin to describe ; yet if they come to Christ He
will not say one word of upbraiding to them, but
will welcome them with open arms. Be your past
what it may : wrapped up as it may be in such a
mystery of iniquity that nobody would believe it
about you ; nevertheless you come, and all your
sins will be cast into the depths of the sea. Any
'him' in all the world, let that man come, and it
will never be asked where he comes from. Come
he from a slum, or from a shebeen, or from a gamb-

ling hell, or from a brothel, or from the hulks, and if he is cast out he will be the first.' Powerful as that is, it is only one of a thousand illustrations of the way in which Spurgeon in his day pulled so many sinners out of Satan's clutches.

But, then, with all that, *your* sins may have been such that nothing that Bunyan or Spurgeon ever preached comes at all near your awful case, as you now see it to be. Satan who tempted you to those awful sins now turns round on you and accuses you of those very sins, as his diabolical habit is to do; and you cannot deny or extenuate his accursed accusations. Your sins are such, he tells you to your face, that they were not anticipated, and consequently were not provided for, in the one great atonement for sin. The blood of Christ, Satan says he feels sure, was never shed for such horrible sins as yours. I defy you in all your vaunted New Testament, he says, to point out a single sinner to match you among all the saved. I can understand David being saved, says Satan, and Peter, and Paul, aye, and even Judas Iscariot himself, had he come back to Christ; but none of them all, no nor all of them taken together, ever sinned against God such scarlet sins as yours. Now, like John Bunyan, you must silence Satan and your own accusing conscience with this same blessed sixth of John. And you must silence him in this way. Admit at once, and quite frankly, that all he says about you is quite true. For the worst he has said is less than the simple truth. Tell him that your past sins are no news to you; no, nor to your Saviour. Tell him that if you are to die the second death, as you so richly deserve to do, you will die on Christ's

doorstep. And if Christ shuts His door of mercy
against you for ever, so be it: that is only as it
should be. Only, God helping you, if you are to
be cast out for ever, it will not be for want of a
broken heart for ever for your unpardonable past.
'Holy peevish Satan!' cried Luther to the great
accuser on a similar occasion; 'He, to whom I
look in my sin, is able to save to the uttermost:
which uttermost Martin Luther is.' Borrow you
that from Luther, and apply it to yourself. And
always mix that with this blessed sixth of John.

Then again, Satan almost sophisticated Bunyan
out of his soul by the way he worked upon the
Saviour's words—' him that *cometh* to Me.' ' " Had
you been born in Galilee or in Judea you could
easily have come to Christ," Satan admitted. " But
the Son of God is not going about Bedford, as He
was wont to go about Jerusalem. The times are
wholly changed since He invited those contem-
poraneous men to come to Him. He is now
exalted far above all heavens. He is now sur-
rounded and encircled by His glorified saints and
by His elect angels. And how can a contempt-
ible creature like you venture near such exalted
majesty as His ? The thing is preposterous ! You
have a Bible : open it and read about Job. Oh,
cried that eminent saint, that I knew where I
might find Him ! That I might come to His seat !
Behold, I go forward, but He is not there. And
backward, but I cannot perceive Him. On the
left hand, where He doth work, but I cannot
behold Him : He hideth Himself on the right
hand that I cannot see Him. Read that chapter
every night before bedtime," said Satan, " and con-

tent yourself with your lot. Go to church twice a Sabbath if you choose. You can even join Mr. Gifford's young communicants' class if he will admit you; but put going up to heaven to pray to Christ, put that out of your foolish head.'' Thus was I tossed between the devil and my own ignorance, till I could not tell what to do or what to say. Then again, when I would do my best to go to Christ in spite of Satan and his false reasonings, he would set on me with this: "Was I elected, or no? And what if my day of grace was over and gone?" One night, as I sat by the fire and mused on election and predestination, Satan took up my New Testament and opened it at this passage in the ninth of the Romans and bade me read it. And I read this: "It is neither in him that willeth, nor in him that runneth, but in God that sheweth mercy." With this Scripture I could not tell what to do. I evidently saw that unless the great God of His infinite grace and bounty, had voluntarily chosen me to be a vessel of mercy, though I should desire and long and labour until my heart did break, no good could come of it. Therefore this would still stick with me—how can you tell that you are elected? And what if you are not? How then? But when I had been long vexed with this fear, these words one day broke in on my mind: "Compel them to come in, that My house may be filled; for yet there is room." These words, *yet there is room*, were sweet words to me. For, truly, I thought that by them I saw that there was place enough for me also in heaven. This I then verily believed. And one other day this great word came in upon me: "I will cleanse their blood that I have

not cleansed, for the Lord dwelleth in Zion."
These words I thought were sent to encourage me
still to wait upon God, and they signified to me
that if I were not already, yet the time might
come when I might in truth be converted to
Christ.'

Now, who can tell, but among so many, there
may be some man here to-night who is being
sophisticated by Satan in this same way concerning
his coming to Christ. Well let that man remember
this : John Bunyan did not need to be born in
Jerusalem in order to go to Christ and be welcomed
by Him, and no more do you. At the same time
you will find great guidance, and great encouragement, by reading continually about Jerusalem and
Samaria, because Christ is the same ; aye, and
much better to-day. The Father draws sinners
much better to-day to Christ than He did then.
Indeed, *that* is the Father drawing your heart to
Christ His Son at this evening hour. And, always
remember this : Coming to Christ, whatever Satan
may say, does not necessitate any change of time
or of place on your part. Just where you now sit ;
just where you now dwell at home ; Christ says to
you individually and urgently, Come thou to Me
from condemnation to justification. Come thou to
Me from all thy guilt to all My Father's forgiveness
and Mine. Come thou to Me from thy fearful
looking for of judgment, to that peace with God
which passes all understanding. Leave all your
election, and all your predestination, and all your
final perseverance to their proper time and place, and
come you even now to Christ, and come just as you
are. These are the true and proper Scriptures for

you: 'Come now, and let us reason together, saith the Lord; though your sins be as scarlet, they shall be as white as snow; though they be red like crimson, they shall be as wool.' And this: 'Come unto Me, all ye that labour and are heavy laden, and I will give you rest.' And this blessed sixth of John: 'Him that cometh to Me I will in no wise cast out.' And then such psalms and hymns and spiritual songs as these:

> Come unto Me, ye weary,
> And I will give you rest.
>
> Come, ye souls by sin afflicted.
>
> Come, ye sinners, poor and wretched,
> Weak and wounded, sick and sore.
>
> Come, take by faith the body of your Lord,
> And drink the blood of Christ for you outpoured.

Read these Scriptures, and chant these psalms and hymns and spiritual songs without ceasing, and Satan will flee from you to try his sophistications on less well-taught and less believing sinners.

And, then, '" Him that cometh to Me I will *in no wise* cast out." O the comfort that I had from that word " in no wise "! For it is as much as to say, by no means, for no thing, and at no time, will I cast you out. But Satan would greatly labour to pull this promise from me by telling me that Christ did not mean *me*, but sinners of a lower rank, and who had not done as I had done. But I should answer him again: O but Satan, there is no exception here: it is him, any him: it is him that cometh to Me I will in no wise cast out. And this I well remember, that Satan never did so much as put this question to me—Do you come aright? And I think the reason was, because he thought that I knew full well what coming aright was. For I saw that to come aright was to come just as I was, a vile and an ungodly sinner, and to cast myself at Christ's feet, condemning myself for all my sin.'

And now to all that I will only add this to you: Beginning to come to-night keep always coming, never missing one single night, no not one single hour, all your days. In his *Supersensual Life,'* Jacob Behmen says to his disciple who has asked him, 'How shall I be able to live aright amid all the temptation and tribulation of my circumstances?' 'If thou dost once every hour throw thyself by faith beyond all creatures and into the abysmal mercy of God, into the sufferings of Christ, and into the fellowship of His intercession, then thou shalt receive power from above to rule over the devil, and death, and hell itself.' And again: 'O thou of little faith, if thy heart could but break itself off every half-hour from all creatures, and plunge itself into that where no creature is or can be, presently you would be penetrated with the splendour of the divine glory, and would taste a sweetness that no tongue can express.'

And I shall wind up with this out of our own Scottish Analecta: 'Mr. James Durham, of Powrie Castle, when he was on his deathbed, was under a great darkness as to his interest in Christ, and he said to Mr. Carstairs, "Brother, for all that I have preached and written, there is but one promise to which I can now dare to grip; tell me if I am safe to lay the whole weight of my salvation upon that promise. The only Scripture promise I can remember, or can get a good hold of, is this : Him that cometh to Me I will in no wise cast out." "Sir," said Mr. Carstairs to him, "you may depend upon that promise, though you had a thousand salvations to hazard." '

XXI

'My whole soul was then in every word.'

OHN BUNYAN'S whole soul was then
in every word of his prayers, he
means to say. For there were no
other words in all the world but
the words of prayer that could
receive and could contain John Bunyan's whole
soul. John Bunyan's was a big soul, and by that
time his whole big soul was swelling and heaving
within him with his original sin, and with all
manner of misery because of both his original and
his actual sin. So much so that his heart would
have burst and he would have died before his time
had he not got some real outlet for his heaving
and bursting heart in agonising prayer. But with
all the outlet and all the relief his burdened heart
could get even in his most outpoured prayer, there
still remained in his mind and in his heart a whole
world of what he describes as 'irrepressible groan-
ings.' 'Oh,' he exclaims, 'how would my heart at
such times put itself forth! I should cry with
pangs after God that He would be merciful to me.'

Take some examples of how Bunyan would pour
out his whole soul in every word of his concerning
his sin and concerning his misery on account of his
sin. 'By these things my whole soul was now so

turned that it lay like a horse-leech at the vein, still crying out, Give! give! it was so fixed on eternity.' And again: 'In those days I was never out of my Bible, still calling on God for the right way to heaven and eternal life.' And again: 'Now also I should pray wherever I was: whether at home or abroad: in the house or in the field: and should often, with lifting up of my soul, sing to God and to myself the fifty-first psalm.' And again: 'I went up and down, bemoaning my sad condition, and counting myself far worse than a thousand fools for spending so many years in sin as I had done, and I was still crying out, Oh that I had turned to God seven years ago!—Gold! could my salvation have been gotten for gold, what gold would I not have given for it! Had I possessed a whole world made of gold, it had all gone a thousand times over for this that my soul had been in a truly converted state.' And again: 'If now I had been burned at the stake, I could not believe that Christ could have any love for me. For, alas! I could neither see Him, nor feel Him, nor savour any of His good things. I was driven as with a tempest; my heart would be unclean.' And again: 'I was more loathsome in my own eyes than a toad. Sin and corruption would as naturally bubble out of my heart as water bubbles out of its fountain. I thought every one had a better heart than I had, and I could have exchanged hearts with any one. I thought none but the devil himself could equalise me for inward wickedness and pollution of mind.' Now that is not so much rhetoric. That is not mere declamation. There is not one syllable of exaggeration in that. For that is the universal way that every truly awakened sinner feels and speaks about himself, if he is a man of sufficient mind and sufficient heart, and if both his mind and his heart are sufficiently broken.

Listen in the second place, to the way in which John Bunyan put his whole soul into every word of his concerning his Saviour. And mark here also the genuine reality and the intense sincerity of the man. 'One day about ten or eleven o'clock, as I was walking under a hedge, full of sorrow and guilt God knows, suddenly this bolted in upon me —the blood of Christ remits all guilt. At this I made a stand in my spirit, and with that this word took hold of me—the blood of Jesus Christ, His Son, cleanseth us from all sin. Wherefore I felt my soul greatly to love and to pity Jesus Christ, and my bowels did yearn toward Him. For I saw that He was still my Friend, and one who did reward me good for evil. Till I felt so to Him that if I had had a thousand gallons of blood in my veins I could then freely have spilt it all at the feet of my Lord and Saviour. There was nothing now but Christ before my eyes. O, methought, Christ! Christ! Christ in His blood, Christ in His burial, and Christ in His resurrection. Christ in all His virtues, relations, offices, and operations. Now Christ was my all. All my wisdom, all my right-eousness, all my sanctification, and all my redemption.' Again, there is no idle word there and no rhetorical word and no overstated word.

See also how he puts his whole soul into some single and separate words of Holy Scripture. As for instance into the single word 'able,' in that Scripture—able to save to the uttermost. 'At last,

when I was quite worn out, this word did sound
suddenly in my ear—He is able! Methought that
word able was spoken so loud to me; it seemed to
be writ in such large letters to me; and it gave
such a justle to my fear and doubt as I had never
before experienced from any one word, no nor
since. And it was the same with the single word
"sufficient," in Christ's own words—My grace is
sufficient for thee. One morning, when I was
again at prayer, that piece of a sentence darted in
upon me—My grace is sufficient. About a fort-
night before, I was looking at this very passage,
but got no comfort out of it, and that made me
throw down my book in a pet. But now, this one
word "sufficient" had its arms of grace so wide
that it could not only enclose me, but many more
besides me. And, one day as I was in a meeting
of God's people, these words also did with great
power suddenly break in upon me: "For thee, for
thee, My grace is sufficient for thee!" three times
together. And O, methought, every word was a
mighty word to me. These words were then, and
they sometimes are still, far bigger than any other
words to me.

'And yet again: "I will in no wise cast out."
That word, "in no wise," did most sweetly visit
my soul. O the comfort that I had from that one
word, "in no wise"! For it was as if He had said
to me—By no means will I cast thee out. For no
thing thou hast ever said or done will I cast thee
out. O! what sweetness I got out of that!'

And then it is to that same noble and fruitful
habit of mind and heart that we owe the *Holy War*
and the *Pilgrim's Progress.* Take the *Pilgrim's*

Progress. No man had ever poured his whole soul into that one Bible word a *pilgrim*, till God gifted and moved John Bunyan to do that. From the days of Abraham and Isaac and Jacob, God's people had all confessed that they were strangers and pilgrims on the earth; but none of them all, neither patriarch, nor prophet, nor psalmist, nor apostle, had ever put their whole mind and heart and experience and imagination and full assurance of faith into that word and that thing till John Bunyan arose. And thus it came about that the same high habit of mind and heart that made John Bunyan such an eminent saint, made him also such an eminent author; made him, indeed, one of the most eminent in some things of all our authors.

Now in all that there is a whole world of lessons; intellectual lessons for intellectual people, and spiritual lessons for spiritual people. And let us take first what God Himself says on this same matter: for God Himself both felt and spoke on this same matter long before He made Bunyan feel with Him and speak with Him. 'For, thus saith the Lord, I know the thoughts that I think towards you, saith the Lord, and these are thoughts of peace and not of evil, to give you an expected end. And ye shall seek Me and find Me, when ye seek for Me with all your heart.' That is to say, in John Bunyan's words, we shall always find God when we put our whole soul into every word of our prayers to God. And the thing stands to reason, and to our everyday experience, as well as to divine promise. For when we put our whole soul into our prayers, even to our fellow-men, they cannot long resist us. We carry men's hearts

captive to us as soon as we put our whole soul
into our appealing words to them. When we are
wholly moved and wholly melted ourselves we
always move and melt other men. 'Weep yourselves,' said Horace to the young poets of his day,
'and you will make me weep with you.' And just
look back at some of the Old Testament men
and women who moved and melted God Himself.
Abraham in his prayer for Sodom. Jacob in his
prayer for himself at the Jabbok. Moses in his
prayer for Israel on the mount. Hannah in her
prayer for Samuel. And David continually in
every prayer and in every psalm of his. David
was the father indeed of all of us who put our
whole soul into our every word toward God. John
Bunyan especially came of the direct race and
pure lineage of David. And they both showed
their intellectual and their spiritual genius in nothing more than in the way they put their whole
soul into every word they wrote. Let us all be
like them in that. Let us all serve ourselves to be
sons and heirs to their genius, and to their grace,
and to their rich salvation.

I have often told you about Luther and his use
of the personal pronouns. I have told you how he
both reformed the church, and saved his own soul,
by the way he made such believing use of the
personal pronouns. He reformed the church, and
he revolutionised the nation, far more by his
powerful use of the personal pronouns than by his
burning of the Pope's bulls. 'I, Martin Luther,'
he said continually in his confessions of sin, and in
his prayers for pardon: 'I, Martin Luther, the
chief of sinners. Out of the depths, if ever there

were depths, do I cry to Thee, O Lord'; putting
his whole soul into every personal pronoun of his.
I myself have a pastoral memory about that way
of prayer which I will now take boldness to tell
you for your good. I once tried Luther's so personal way of prayer with a young man who was
fast dying. His heart-broken father had come to
me and had told me that his only son was on his
unprepared death-bed. The fast-dying youth had
been a prodigal son and his heart was now as hard
as a stone. Day after day I did my very best with
that sin-hardened youth, but with no result. Till
one day I betook me to Luther's personal way with
him. I said to him, would he follow me in asking
of God for himself, and by his own name, what I
would now ask of God for myself, and by my own
name. He was a courteous and a gentlemanly lad,
and as soon as he fully understood what I said he
answered me with his weak voice that he would.
Forgetting him and every one else for the moment,
I knelt down and prayed for myself by name just
as Luther would have done. And as soon as I had
risen from my knees the fast-dying lad raised himself up in his bed, and said : ' I, James Wedderburn,
pray also and say pardon, O God, the sins of my
youth. Enter not into judgment with me. But
wash Thou me, for Thou canst make me whiter
than the snow.' And then he lay down never
again to rise. But if ever I stood by and saw a
sinful soul born again it was in that room that day.
And it was a sight to see his father's radiant face
that day and to this day as often as he speaks to
me about his departed son. Try Luther's personal
way with yourselves and with others, on occasion.

For there is a wonderful power and reality in it, as you will soon find to your happy surprise, and to your lasting blessedness.

You all know what a fossil is. You have all seen and handled and mused over the pathetic sight of a fossil. For a fossil is a hard and dead stone that was once a soft and a living thing. It is stone-dead now, but at one time it was a living creature; at one time it was as full of life and fruitfulness as any of its kind now living on the earth. But long ago the life died out of that living creature till in the lapse of time it was turned into absolute stone. Now just so has it been with many Scripture words, and Scripture doctrines, and Scripture experiences, and Scripture prayers, and Scripture praises, that were at one time all palpitating with life; all blossoming and blooming with holy beauty and with spiritual productiveness. All these things were at one time full of the most heavenly life in the minds and in the hearts and in the lives of the prophets and the psalmists and the apostles and the reformers; but they are now all but turned to stone in our degenerate hands. Now, I never heard of a fossil bone or a fossil branch being brought back to life by any art or science or quickening touch of any man. But believing and praying and praising men are working a far greater miracle than that every day. Take any petrified psalm of David, or any petrified epistle of Paul, or any petrified creed of the Fathers, or any petrified catechism of the Reformers, and put it into a living man's mind and heart and life, and straightway it will soften and swell and bourgeon and bring forth fruit, as it did in the great days of old. Let but a

Luther or a Bunyan arise, or any man of their faith and their life and their power, and this whole desert all around them will rejoice and will blossom as the rose. Now my brethren, the whole point to-night is this—Will you take your part henceforth in this great resurrection and reanimation of dead prayers and dead psalms and dead doctrines and dead creeds and dead catechisms and all the other dead ordinances in the public and private worship of God? If you do so, you will live to say with the prophet Ezekiel: So I prophesied as I was commanded, and the breath came upon them, and they lived, and stood upon their feet, an exceeding great army.

I will wind up with a few words taken out of Father John of the Greek Church. 'When you are at your prayers,' he says to us, 'do not hurry on from one word to another. Stay with every word till you feel in yourself its full truth and power. Lay every single word well to heart, and strive hard to feel every word that you speak. Always when you kneel down keep this of Paul well before your mind, that it is better to say five words from the depth of your heart than ten thousand words with the tongue only. And when at any time you feel that your heart is not a heart at all, but a hard and a cold stone, then stop attempting to pray for a few minutes, and warm and melt your heart by thinking of your sinfulness and your misery and what you deserve at the hands of God and man. Set the four last things before your eyes; death, and judgment, and heaven, and hell, and then return as fast as you can to the throne of grace.' So far Father John. Now, is it not beautiful; is it not full of instruction and of hope, to see how the Greek High Churchman and the Evangelical English Puritan so agree in pouring their whole soul into every word of their prayers? That is the true union of churches. That is the true communion of saints. Will you join with John Bunyan and Father John as they pour their whole soul into every word of their prayers? Be sure you do! And you also will live to write in your autobiography say: 'My whole soul was then in every word.'

XXII

' I thought now that every one had a better heart than I had, and I could have changed hearts with anybody.'

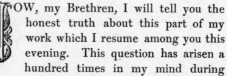OW, my Brethren, I will tell you the honest truth about this part of my work which I resume among you this evening. This question has arisen a hundred times in my mind during these past weeks,—Shall I go on with John Bunyan's terrible book about the chief of sinners, or shall I stop these distressing discourses? And no later than last Saturday afternoon, when I was taking my farewell walk among the hills above Plockton and Strome Ferry, that same question challenged me, and indeed assaulted me, and that in more ways than one. Till suddenly, just as I was almost determining never to mention indwelling sin to you any more, what seemed to me to be a Divine Voice spoke with all-commanding power in my conscience, and said to me as clear as clear could be: 'No! Go on, and flinch not! Go back and boldly finish the work that has been given you to do. Speak out and fear not. Make them, at any cost, to see themselves in God's holy law as in a glass. Do you that, for no one else will do it. No one else will so risk his life and his reputation as to do it. And you have not much of

either left to risk. Go home and spend what is left of your life in your appointed task of showing My people their sin and their need of My salvation.' I shall never forget the exact spot where that clear command came to me and where I got fresh authority and fresh encouragement to finish this part of my work. I know quite well that some of you think me little short of a monomaniac about sin. But I am not the first that has been so thought of and so spoken about. I am in good company and I am content to be in it. Yes, you are quite right in that. For I most profoundly feel that I have been separated first to the personal experience of sin, and then to the experimental preaching of sin, above and beyond all my contemporaries in the pulpit of our day. And I think I know why that is so. But that it is indeed so I cannot for one moment doubt. Well then, with His support who so spoke in my heart last Saturday, and with your continued patience who have been so long patient with me, I shall go on for a few more Sabbath evenings with John Bunyan under the character of the chief of sinners. As thus :

' Now, my inward and original pollution, that, that was my plague and my affliction ; that, I say, at a dreadful rate, was always putting itself forth within me. That I had the guilt of, to absolute amazement. By reason of that I was more loathsome in my own eyes than was a toad, and I thought I was so in God's eyes also. Sin and corruption would as naturally bubble out of my heart as water would bubble out of a fountain. I thought now that every one had a better heart than I had, and I could have changed hearts with anybody. I thought none but the devil himself could equalise me for inward wickedness and pollution of mind. And thus I continued a long while, even for some years together.' Now I quite admit that chapter was not written for Sabbath-school children, any more than was this kindred chapter that we have from the same master hand. ' The Interpreter then has them into the very best room in his house, and a very brave room it was, so he bid them look round about and see if they could find anything profitable there. Then they looked round and round, for there was nothing there to be seen but a very great spider on the wall, and that they overlooked. Then said Mercy, " Sir, I see nothing," but Christiana held her peace. Then said the Interpreter, " Look again." She therefore looked again, and said, " Here is not anything but an ugly spider, who hangs by her hands upon the wall." Then said the Interpreter, " Is there but one spider in all this spacious room ? " Then the water stood in Christiana's eyes, for she was a woman quick of apprehension, and she said, " Yes, lord, there are here more than one. Yea, and spiders whose venom is far more destructive than that which is in her." The Interpreter then looked pleasantly upon her, and said, " Thou hast said the truth." This made Mercy blush, and the boys to cover their faces, for they all began now to understand the riddle.' Now, what do you say to all that ? How do you feel about all that ? Is John Bunyan out of all reasonable bounds in all that ? If you were to speak out what you think, is he simply beside himself in such passages as those about the spider, and about the toad, and about the devil? Or on the other hand, do you subscribe, and that with tears and blood, to all he says and to more than even he dares to say? Do you have all those awful passages of his by heart? Do you turn to them and dwell on them till you feel that you are not wholly alone or wholly hopeless in your valley of the shadow of death? When you count up and go over all your best blessings, do you ever put God's servant John Bunyan, and his *Grace Abounding to the Chief of Sinners* high up among them? I hope so. I most fervently hope so. And I shall continue to labour and to pray that it may more and more be so.

'But my original and inward pollution, that, that was my plague and my affliction.' These are very dreadful words, my brethren; but no words of God or of man are half so dreadful as is the simple truth. To begin with, this awful pollution of ours is 'original.' That is St. Augustine's word about it, and his word about it has been accepted by the whole Church of Christ ever since he first uttered it. Yes, our pollution is original—that is to say, it is native and natural to us. We were all born with it, and it grows and grows with all our growth. And even when we fain would outgrow it and cast it out and leave it behind us, we cannot. With all we can do, we cannot. And all the time it is *the* pollution of all pollutions. It is the parent pollution. Without it there would be no pollution anywhere. Take away our original pollution and there would be nothing to be called pollution in all the world. And then this original pollution is so inward that we cannot get down to it, all we can do, so as to cast it out. There is no bottom to the original pollution of our sinful hearts. It is an abyss. Our sin-polluted hearts are the true bottomless pit and there is no other. It is this same original and inward pollution that makes the man after God's own heart to cry continually, 'Wash me thoroughly, O my God. Purge me with hyssop, O my God. And create in me a clean heart.' And it is this same thing that makes Job answer the Lord and say, 'Behold, I am vile: wherefore I abhor myself, and repent in dust and ashes.' And Isaiah, 'Woe is me, for I am undone.' And Daniel, 'All my comeliness is turned to corruption.' And the holiest of men, 'O wretched man that I am! Who shall deliver me from the body of this death?' 'I had that original and inward pollution to amazement,' says John Bunyan. How true and how fit is that word amazement! You must all have felt the truth and the power and the fitness of that word. You must often be simply amazed and overwhelmed with the original and inward pollution of your own hearts. Where does that sudden and awful pollution come from? you must often stand amazed at yourself and say. It is the mystery of all mysteries to you. 'Who can understand his errors?' the psalmist exclaims; that is to say, his own sin-polluted heart. I greatly like that word amazement. Amid all the unspeakable bitterness of the thing, to have it so aptly described by a master of spiritual language gives me a genuine delight. There is such child-like simplicity in this word amazement. There is such manhood reality in it. There is such a sure note of personal experience in it. And, withal,

there is such true literary genius in it. Yes,
'amazement' is the very word. Amazement at
my original and inward pollution, at such a dreadful rate always putting itself forth within me.
What a delight there is in John Bunyan's English, even in his most dreadful passages, such as
this!

'I thought now that every one had a better heart
than I had, and I could have changed hearts with
anybody.' What do you say to that offer, my
brethren? Suppose you had been in Bedford in
Bunyan's day, and with your present heart, would
you have struck an exchange of hearts on the spot
with Bunyan? *I* would, and I would have given
him good boot to the bargain. With all that he so
honestly says in crying down his own goods, I
would at once have negotiated the exchange, and
been glad to do it. And I feel certain that the foolish
and precipitate man would have repented all his
days the bad bargain he had made with me. The
sin-polluted heart so knows its own bitterness that
it simply cannot believe that there is its match on
earth or even in hell.

And now to return to this gospel in Ezekiel
before I let you go: 'A new heart will I give you,
and a new spirit will I put within you.' Only there
is no good in going back to that, unless you have
first gone through John Bunyan's eighty-fourth
paragraph and have made it your very own. For
you will not understand one syllable of what a new
and a clean and a holy heart means unless you are
amazed and are in despair at your own polluted
heart. But to those of you who are so amazed and

are in such despair, to you are all Ezekiel's promises
sent. And all his promises about a new heart and
a right spirit are to you yea and amen in Jesus
Christ; that is to say, you must always go directly
and immediately to Jesus Christ for your new
heart and for your right spirit. And you must
plead with Him and press Him day and night as
long as you live for a copy of the heart that His
Father so graciously gave to Him. Reason and
expostulate with Him first about His own heart,
and then about yours. Be bold with Him; be
very bold with Him. A lost soul, half down
into hell, cannot be expected to choose soft and
sleeping words. Remind Him then, remind Him
that with all His horror and all His amazement in
the Garden and on the Tree, He never had any
such horror at Himself, or any such amazement at
Himself, as you always have at yourself. With all
the hell into which He descended He never came
near the mouth of a hell like your heart. Tell
Him that. Go to your closet and shut your door
and fasten it firm and fall down on your face and
open your whole fearful heart to Him, and plead
with Him to take your heart at once in hand.
Implore Him not to spit upon you, or to loathe you,
or to hate you, or to cast you out of His presence.
Ask if in all His experience He has ever had a
heart on His hands quite like yours. Tell Him
that if He wishes ever to see the full travail of His
soul that it must be seen in you and in your
holiness-healed heart. Tell Him that He has an
opportunity in you, the like of which He will never
have again to all time. Tell Him that you are
quite the uttermost sinner on this side hell, and

that your new heart and your right spirit will be by far His highest trophy in His Father's house. And to encourage you, I must, and I will, tell you this. When He gave me my new commission in this matter last Saturday afternoon near Duncraig, He added this, as I shall always remember: 'Comfort My people,' He said. 'Speak comfortably to My people, and say to them that I know all their sorrow. Cast them down with all your might,' He said. 'Cast them down continually to death and hell: they have not far to go. But always hasten, after that, to lift them up. Tell them,' He said, 'about all the chief sinners that I have had written out and put in a book for their encouragement. All the Old Testament and all the New Testament sinners whose names they know so well. And add to them,' He said, 'all those great sinners whose books are on your table at Balmacara.' You know yourselves how homely and how home-comingly He sometimes speaks to yourselves. 'Tell them,' He said—at any rate, I took it for His voice, for no one has a voice just like His voice—'tell the congregation and the classes this season about St. Augustine and his sin,' He said, 'and about Dante and his sin, and about Luther and his sin, and about Behmen and his sin, and about Teresa and her sin, and about Hooker and his sin, and about Shepard and his sin, and about Bunyan and his sin, and about Brea and his sin, and about Halyburton and his sin, and about Andrewes and his sin, and about Goodwin and his sin, and about Marshall and his sin, and about Pascal and his sin, and about Law and his sin, and about the Catechism and its teaching about sin and salvation, and about the Hymn-book and its songs of sin and salvation.' And when His voice ceased, I answered and said, Spare me this year also, and by Thy grace I will do what Thou hast so clearly commanded me to do in the pulpit and in the class.

XXIII

'Counterfeit holy.'

'COUNTERFEIT holy' is another of John Bunyan's so arresting and so illuminating expressions. But in order to get at his exact meaning, what exactly is a counterfeit? Well, a counterfeit is a spurious imitation. It is a fabrication and a fraud. It is a sham and a make-believe. It is base metal. In the words of His Majesty's mint, it is Brummagem coin. And it is in all these base senses that John Bunyan employs this contemptuous and contumelious word when he tells us that in those early days of his spiritual life the Tempter was 'so counterfeit holy' with him that he would not let him so much as eat his meals in peace. The old Counterfeit would come to the young tinker when he had just sat down to his well-earned dinner, and would insist with him that he must leave his half-eaten meal that moment, and must go hence to pray. 'Now that I am sat down to my meat,' Bunyan would remonstrate, 'let me make an end.' 'No,' insisted the old impostor, 'you must go pray *now*, else you will displease God, and will despise Christ.' 'So counterfeit holy would the devil be,' says Bunyan, as he looks back to those neophyte days of his. Now that so

characteristic passage arrests us : it makes us stop
and think. And when we stop reading, and begin
to think about counterfeit holiness, a thousand
things arise in our minds.

' It is a very difficult thing to counterfeit genuine
gold and silver,' says Professor Jevons in his Political Economy Primer. Perhaps so. But it has been
done nevertheless. For do we not read to our
amazement that counterfeit Christs arose and had
their disciples even in the days of the true Christ
Himself? Lo, here is Christ! and lo, there! it
was preached, till the very elect were all but
deceived and led astray. We need not wonder
then that certain counterfeit Christs—evolutionary
Christs, and historical Christs, and socialist Christs,
and exemplary Christs, and such like, are preached
far and wide in our so easily satisfied and so easily
deceived day. And not in our day only. As to an
exemplary Christ, it was only last night that I read
an old book which used to have a great vogue in
Scotland till it must have all but deceived the sons
and daughters of the Covenanters themselves.
The example of Christ is set forth with such power
and with such beauty in that old classic that the
reader is almost carried away to think that the
exemplary Christ is the true and the only and the
all-sufficient Christ. Our Lord's unresting dili-
gence in doing His Father's will is so dwelt on :
His unceasing devotion to prayer is so dwelt on :
His charity, His meekness, and His humility are
all so dwelt on, that, for the moment, the fair
picture fills the mind. But as I finished the
beautiful old book, this question began to arise in
my mind and would not be silenced in my mind,

this question : Did that 'sometime Professor in Aberdeen' ever really try to make Christ his own example for a single day? I do not know. He does not say. But as for myself I had been doing that all yesterday, with the result of many a sad breakdown during the day, and with a crushing load of remorse on my conscience at the end of the day. So much so that I could not attempt or expect to sleep last night till I had turned again to the one true Christ for me, as I always find Him, for one place, in the contents and in the text of Paul's first chapter to the Colossians. Calvin was the first commentator, so far as I know, who called Paul's Christ in that passage 'the true Christ.' 'He describeth the true Christ,' says the fine analysis also at the head of that fine chapter. And remembering that I read that great passage again, and then the great commentator's exposition of that great passage, till my greatly defeated and greatly dejected soul found rest and peace again in the one true Christ for me. Let Paul and Calvin describe their true Christ to you also in every defeat and dejection of yours. For this is He : 'In whom we have redemption through His blood, even the forgiveness of sins. For it pleased the Father that in Him should all fullness dwell. And having made peace by the blood of His cross, by Him to reconcile all things to Himself. And you that were sometime alienated and enemies in your mind by wicked works, yet now hath He reconciled in the body of His flesh through death, to present you holy, and unblameable, and un-reproveable in His sight. If ye continue in the faith, grounded and settled, and be not moved

away from the hope of the Gospel which ye have
heard, and whereof I, Paul, am made a minister.'
As always, the true apostle puts the true Christ
first and foremost; and then, when the saints and
faithful brethren have received the sin-atoning
and peace-speaking Christ into their minds and
hearts, Paul then passes on, with all his apostolic
power and impressiveness, to set the Christ of
God before them in His proper order, that is to
say, in the second place, as their one and true and
supreme example. For myself, as often as I glance
at the sometimes beautiful but always superficial
sermons of our day on Christ as our example, I
turn again to Paul's divine order of preaching and
presenting the true Christ. That is to say, the
divine order and the rational order of preaching
Christ as first and last and always our Redeemer
and our Righteousness. And then, after that, as
our example and our pattern. That was Paul's
apostolic order in every sermon and in every epistle
of his. That was Luther's order, who most took of
Paul of all our great preachers. That was Calvin's
order, and that was Bunyan's order. And in this
matter I often remember how the anger of the
Lord was kindled against Uzzah for that he sought
not God after God's due and appointed order.
For myself, as I hear this man and that calling on
me, and saying, lo here! and lo there! lest I be
fatally deceived in this all-momentous matter, and
have God's anger kindled against me, I anxiously
ask, Hath He marks to lead me to Him if He be
my Guide? And I am always and immediately
and infallibly answered, In His feet and hands are
wound-prints, and His side. 'Take Christ in His

personal excellencies,' says Goodwin, 'and He is
the Object of love rather than of faith. But the
faith that justifies the ungodly looks upon Christ
not so much in His personal excellencies, but
rather as He is made sin for us, in order that we
may be made the righteousness of God in Him.'

The narrow way comes to its very narrowest in
that valley where it lies crushed in between a
counterfeit Christ on the one hand, and a counterfeit doctrine of the true Christ on the other hand.
Never can any better counsel be given to any
escaping sinner than to tell him to look to Christ
for his salvation : and to look to Christ always and
in everything. But that Scriptural and soul-saving
counsel is turned into its soul-destroying counterfeit when the corrupt-hearted sinner is told to
avoid all 'morbid introspection,' and all over-
anxious self-examination, as his counterfeit counsellors are wont to have it. In offering his great
Temple prayer Solomon said that as soon and as
often as any man in Israel should come to know
the plague of his own heart, that divinely enlightened man would immediately, and would
always thereafter make his way up to the temple,
and to the atonement that was made in the temple.
But the devil and his counterfeit clergy are wiser
than Solomon. There is really no such plague as
all that in your heart, they say to the too easily
deceived sinner. Or if there is ever anything in
the state of your heart that is not altogether right,
look away from it. Do not brood and break and
mourn over it. As your Bible has it, look only to
Christ. While, if those counterfeit teachers and
their deluded disciples only had grace enough to

know it, nothing is more certain than this, that no
man has ever really and truly looked to Christ with
a saving faith, who has not really and truly and
always looked with shame and pain and horror and
hatred at himself and at his own sin-plagued and
sin-possessed heart. Look unto Me and be ye
saved, is the very truth of God, and the whole
truth of God, as God says it. But the devil has
often put his own diabolical sense upon God's
truth, and has often got his counterfeit preachers to
preach it. It was this same counterfeit Gospel
that put Luther beside himself in those antinomian
days when he cried out in every sermon of his,
Beware of the devil when he comes with the words
of the Gospel in his false mouth! Beware of that
master of mountebanks! Beware of that prince of
impostors! Beware of that arch evangelical counterfeit! But better than even Luther, John Bunyan
puts the whole spiritual situation in his own
inimitable and never-to-be-forgotten way. 'I saw
also in my dream that so far as this valley reached
there was on the right hand a very deep ditch;
that ditch is it into which the blind have led the
blind in all ages, and have both miserably perished.
Again, behold, on the left hand, there was a very
dangerous quag, into which if a good man falls, he
can find no bottom for his feet to stand on. The
pathway here also was exceeding narrow, and therefore good Christian was all the more put to it.
For, when he sought in the dark to shun the ditch
on his right hand he was ready to tip over into the
mire on his left hand. Also, when he sought to
escape the mire, without great carefulness he would
be ready to fall into the ditch. Thus he went on,

and I heard him sigh bitterly.' I sometimes
wonder that Bunyan did not bring in the old
Counterfeit himself at this point to rebuke Christian
for his so bitter sighs. I sometimes wonder he did
not introduce Satan himself to command the downcast pilgrim to march on with a 'light heart,' as
you will remember he got the French army to
march out of Paris on their way to Berlin: a march
that ended not at Berlin but at Sedan.

Then, again, there is a counterfeit conscience,
more or less, in every one of us, though we may
not all know it and admit it. That is to say, there
is a counterfeit strictness, in some things, in all of
us; and then that counterfeit strictness is always
accompanied with a corresponding slackness in
some other things. There is a spurious conscience
in all of us that winks at the most serious evils in
our own hearts and in our own lives, and then
it compensates itself by raging loudly against some
things in other people that are not real sins in
them at all. Our counterfeit conscience will sometimes deal with the utmost scrupulosity and
stringency with the most microscopic matters of
Church doctrine and practice; it will resist to the
death the least departure from a traditional ritual,
while, at the same time, it will allow and well abet
the most flagrant insults and injuries to our neighbours. James Fraser of Brea, who was one of the
profoundest masters of the things of the soul that
ever lived, has set down this as the devil's thirteenth device directed against his soul: 'When I
could not be wholly deluded from laying to heart
matters of religion, Satan, for the most part of my
time, busied me with the externals and the for-

malities of religion, and made me all but forget
the fundamental matters. Nice points were much
studied, and were much talked about by me,
whereas the great matters of my own soul, and of
other men's souls, I forgot to think or speak much
about.' To my mind it is not a good sign of our
Church and our day that such a masterpiece of
spiritual analysis as Fraser's autobiography commands so little sale. To my mind it is one of the
greatest books of that great century in Scotland.
In its own special field I have never met its equal.

But I find I must sum up before I am well
begun: so endless is this subject of counterfeit
holiness, so absolutely endless. For every spiritual
and saving grace in our hearts and in our lives has
its own special and inseparable counterfeit standing
and working beside it. There are a multitude of
counterfeit graces against which we must watch
and pray, with a far from counterfeit watchfulness
and prayer. Take a counterfeit humility as a good
example of that; and take that counterfeit
humility in its most subtle and its most spiritual
shape. Santa Teresa warned her spiritual daughters
that Satan never so nearly had her soul in his
clutches for ever as when he tried to sophisticate
her into a counterfeit contrition of conscience and
into a counterfeit humility of heart. 'Fie, woman!'
he would say to her, 'if it is only for decency's
sake, wait a little! Would you rush into God's
pure and holy presence with your over-hasty repentance, and with your soul still reeking with your
sin? Wait, woman, till your fall is sometime past.
Wait till you have had opportunity to do some adequate penance to show to God and to yourself that

you are not wholly insincere in your repentance and in your prayer.' And the same subtle spirit tried the same sophistical indignation and the same spurious solicitude with that great Scottish saint of whom I have already spoken. 'After my slips and my stumbles,' says Brea in his masterly book, 'Satan tried hard to shock me into despair. He tried to amaze me and to confound me with what I had again done. He tried hard to hold me down. He did his best to keep me from ever getting on my feet again. Whereas, my best way was immediately to seek a fresh pardon, and then to go back to my work.' And yet another outstanding spiritual genius gives us—and word for word —the deceptive debate that the devil dictated to him when he was in the same sad plight in England as Teresa was in Spain and as Brea was in Scotland. 'Oh,' reasoned Walter Marshall with himself, in the great bitterness of his soul, 'Oh, let me first have some true hatred of my sin before I prepare to return from it to God! Let the raging of my lusts be somewhat abated! Let the stinking kennel of my corrupt heart be somewhat cleansed and sweetened! Let me first be more humbled for my sin, and more ashamed of it; let me have a far more godly sorrow on account of it. At any rate, I would first be able to pour out my soul to God, and not be the lifeless lump of sin that I now am.' But Bunyan beats them all at that also. 'Oh, 'twas hard for me to have to pray to this Christ, against whom I had sinned with such vileness! 'Twas hard work again to look Him in the face, against whom I had sinned so frequently and so abominably! Oh, the shame that did now attend me! I was ashamed, yea even confounded, because of my villany committed against Jesus Christ! But I soon came to see that there was only one way left to me. I must go humble myself before Him, and must beg of Him that, in His amazing grace, He would again have mercy on this wretchedly sinful soul of mine.'

My brethren, before we part for the night, I do beseech you to lay all these things well to heart, and that before you sleep. For when any one heareth the word of the kingdom, and understandeth it not in its application to himself, then cometh the wicked one, and catcheth away that which was sown in his heart. 'Nevertheless, the foundation of God standeth sure, having this seal—the Lord knoweth them that are His. But in a great house there are not only vessels of gold and of silver, but also of wood and of earth; and some to honour, and some to dishonour. If a man therefore purge himself from these, he shall be a vessel unto honour, sanctified, and fit for the Master's use, and prepared unto every good work.'

XXIV

'Those who had writ in our days, I thought (but I desire them now to pardon me) had writ without themselves going down into the deep.'

F John Bunyan had lived in our day he would, I fear, have been in the same difficulty that he describes so feelingly and so powerfully in his hundred and twenty-ninth paragraph. The difficulty, that is, to get a book writ in our day that would prove itself most fit for a conscience wounded as his conscience was wounded. I will tell you some of the ways in which John Bunyan's conscience was wounded, and then I will put it to yourselves to say if you know any book writ in our day that you could recommend Bunyan to buy and to read and to find his condition so largely and so profoundly handled, as if the book had been written out of his own broken heart. Take, then, some specimens of poor Bunyan's wounded conscience and broken heart. And I will not water down my great author one iota. I will boldly and honestly read to you what he so powerfully writes about himself in his own unmitigated words.

'Now, thought I, now I grow worse and worse. For I felt such discouragement in my heart as laid me as low as hell. I was driven as with a tempest. My heart would be unclean. The Canaanites would dwell in the land. My original and inward pollution, that, that was my plague and my affliction; that I had the guilt of to amazement. By reason of that I was more loathsome in my own eyes than was a toad. Sin and corruption would as naturally bubble out of my heart as water would bubble out of a fountain. I thought now that every one had a better heart than I had; and I could have changed hearts with anybody. I thought none but the devil himself could equalise me for inward wickedness and pollution of mind. Man, indeed, is the most noble, by creation, of all creatures in the visible world; but by his sin he has made himself the most ignoble. The birds, the beasts, the fishes, I blessed their condition, for they had not a sinful nature; they were not obnoxious to the wrath of God as I was. I could therefore have rejoiced had my condition been as theirs is. And now was I a burden and a terror to myself. Oh how gladly would I have been anybody but myself! Now was the Gospel the greatest torment to me. Every time I thought of the Lord Jesus, of His grace, love, goodness, kindness, gentleness, meekness, death, blood, promises, blessed exhortations, comforts and consolations, it went to my soul like a sword. Aye, I said to myself, this is the Jesus, the loving Saviour, the Son of God, whom I have parted with, whom I have slighted, despised, and abused. Oh! thought I, what I have lost! Oh! what I have for ever parted with! Then there would come flocking into my mind an innumerable company of my sins and transgressions, namely, my deadness, dullness, and coldness in holy duties; my wanderings of heart, my wearisomeness in all good things, my want of love to God, to His ways, and to His people, with this at the end of all—are these the fruits of Christianity? Are these the tokens of a blessed man? But one day, as I was walking up and down in the house, as a man in a most woful state, that word of God took hold of my heart—thou art justified freely by His grace, through the redemption that is in Christ Jesus. Then, O what a turn that made upon me! But with all that I find to this day these seven abominations in my heart. First, inclinings to unbelief; second, to forget the love and the mercy of Christ; third, a leaning to the works of the law; fourth, wanderings and coldness in prayer; fifth, to forget to watch for that for which I have prayed; sixth, apt to murmur because I have no more, and at the same time making a bad use of what I have; seventh, my corruptions of heart will thrust themselves into everything I do. When I would do good, evil is present with me.'

Now if you have been attending to all that, and if you have been understanding all that, and feeling all that in yourselves, then, tell me, do you know any book, writ in our day, that goes down into depths like these? Tell me, I say. For I confess to you I do not know any such book myself, though I have searched for it as for hid treasure. Yes; I have most anxiously searched for such a book, and in this way. I already possess Luther on the Galatians, and concerning Christian Liberty, and Goodwin on the Ephesians, and Davenant on the Colossians, and Shepard on the Ten Virgins, and Marshall on Sanctification and many such like.

But I am man enough of my own day to wish to read something writ in my own day, and writ in the style and in the physiognomy and in the atmosphere of my own day. And, with that view, I have most anxiously searched all the publishers' lists for this autumn and this winter and this coming Christmas. With something of John Bunyan's own hunger I have repeatedly gone over all the advertisements in the *Quarterly*, and in the *Edinburgh*, and in the *Dublin*, and in *Blackwood*, and in the *Athenæum*, and in the *Academy*, and in the *Spectator*, and in the *Nation*, and in the *British Weekly*, and in the *Scottish Review*, and so on. But, would you believe it, among those hundreds upon hundreds of books written in our day, I have only found two or three that I could order and open with any hope. And even the two or three that I did order I found that my money was as good as thrown away upon them; so far that is as my present pursuit is concerned. I enjoyed to read the great promises of great books soon coming out in theology, and in philosophy, and in morality, and in sociology; in history, in biography, in poetry, in fiction, and in pure letters. But I found nothing at all that John Bunyan would have preferred, next to the Bible, for a wounded conscience and a broken heart. Till in my deep distress of soul I turned again to some of my old books that are ready to fall piece from piece if I do but turn them over. Books, that is, about sin, and about the sinfulness of sin, and about indwelling sin; books also about the sending and the substitution and the sacrifice of the Son of God; about faith in His blood; about justification, adoption, and sanctification, and eternal life, and such like. Yes, I said to myself, the old are indeed better; out of all sight better!

'I grow worse and worse,' says Bunyan about himself. 'My heart lays me as low as hell. I am driven as with a tempest. My inward and original pollution of heart, that, that I have to amazement. I am more loathsome to myself than a toad.' Do you know any book, writ in our day, that even so much as professes to deal with a state of things like that? Do not blame your booksellers because they do not display the deep books of the soul on their crowded Christmas counters. They are business men and they display what they know you will buy. But one or two of you will turn upon me in self-defence and will say to me that all you can do you cannot find the books that I am continually instructing you to read for the real and the sure and the everlasting salvation of your souls. O no! that does not deceive me nor silence me for one moment! The great books of the soul are quite easy to be got by those who truly love them and who truly desire to possess them. You know quite well where to find old furniture, and old plate, and old pictures, and old lace, and old wine. And the sellers of those old things know you and send you from time to time their lists of rare and ancient things. And when you become spiritual experts, and collectors of the masterpieces of the soul, you will discover those out-of-the-way shops where such books are still to be bought. It is not the authors of the day who are to be blamed, nor is it the publishers, nor is it the booksellers—it is yourselves. When you are once bent with all your mind and heart on *the one thing needful* in books, you will then importune your bookseller, and he will importune his publisher, and they will both importune our religious authors, and the right sort of book will be produced, and will be sold, and will be bought, and will be read even by you.   Speaking about publishers—just as I am writing this page I come on this paragraph among the literary notes in last Monday's *Westminster*: 'It argues no small amount of courage,' says the writer of the notes, 'for a present-day publisher to issue a new edition of Baxter's *Saint's Rest* in a handsome format. Yet the thing has been done by Grant Richards. This book, famous in its day, and commended for its style by no less a person than Archbishop Trench, is in these days not so frequently read. But, perhaps, in this artistic form it may yet attract a select band of readers.'

Then again : 'My deadness and my coldness in holy duties. My want of love to God, and to His ways, and to His people.' Now suppose you were to come to your minister with that complaint about yourselves. He would not know a book, writ in your day, to recommend to you. There are masterly and immortal books that deal with all such complaints, but they were not writ to-day nor yesterday. You like to hear about classics and to talk about classics. Well, then, you order *The Religious Affections of Jonathan Edwards,* edited by Dr. Smellie. That true classic deals with all those complaints, and deals with them in a way worthy of a writer who has been competently called 'one of the greatest of the sons of men.' The book will only cost you half-a-crown, and if you have mind enough and heart enough to read it once, you will go on to read it till you have read it as often as Benjamin Jowett had read James Boswell.

Then again: 'As I was walking up and down the house, that word of God took hold of my heart—being justified freely by His grace, through the redemption that is in Christ Jesus, whom God hath set forth to be a propitiation through faith in His blood.' Have you ever read that old book called The Romans? Well, that central passage in the Romans was William Cowper's conversion; and it was when one was reading in his hearing Luther on the same subject that John Wesley passed from his darkness of heart into the full light of God's countenance. My own special father in God, Thomas Goodwin, has a whole massive volume on this same subject of justification. Since my student days I have carried about that golden volume with me in trains and in steamers, at home and abroad, till I know it as well, I think, as the Master of Balliol knew his Boswell. But if any salad student here is shy of Goodwin, he can surely hold up his head for Hooker. Everybody honours Hooker and Hooker's readers. And Hooker was a Paul and a puritan at heart in the foundation matter of justification; though, on the surface, and to sciolists, he has a far more popular name.

The very vocabulary of scriptural and evangelical religion has been scorned and set aside by the novice authors of our superficial day. As I have read those ephemeral writers I have honestly tried to fit their new-fangled words and phrases into my mind and into my heart and into my conscience and into my imagination, but, I am bound to say, they do not fit into me at all. The new vocabulary of the new books has all been fashioned by men who are wholly different from me in their whole mental upmake and operation. So different are they from me that they seem to me to belong to another race of men altogether. To me the religious phraseology of the present day wholly lacks the apostolicity, and the authority, and the height, and the depth, and the substance, and the strength, and the intellectual, and the spiritual satisfactoriness and finality of the old phraseology. I entirely agree with what Dr. John Duncan says about John Foster, great man and great preacher as John Foster was. 'You find it in a very noble man,' says Dr. Duncan, 'John Foster. That essay of his entitled, "The Aversion of Men of Taste to Evangelical Religion," I dislike exceedingly. You do no good by changing the vocabulary of your religion. If you change the words you change the things. The more I study language the more I am convinced of this, that particular shades of thought are wedded to particular words. If you cut the one, you wound the other; they are dermis and epidermis. I find that my best words are scriptural words, and my next best words are ecclesiastical words.' So far that true genius and profound scholar, Dr. John Duncan. And a writer of a very different school, Dean Stanley, says: 'Use them to the utmost, use them threadbare if you will; long experience, the course of their history, their age and dignity, have made them far more elastic, far more available, than any we can invent for ourselves.' And Dr. Forsyth has a fine passage to the same effect in his new book on preaching. Yes, the old, both in doctrine and in the vocabulary of doctrine, is the best. Like Marcus Aurelius, even where the new is *true*, the old is *truest*; even where the new is *verus*, the old is *verissimus*.

Now, you will be sure to ask me why it is that our day is so barren of the best books of the soul? Well, I often ask myself that same question. And I confess I cannot answer that question so as to satisfy myself about it. But this may be said. There have been great flowings and great ebbings of spiritual truth and spiritual life all along the history of the Church of Christ. There was a great and an incomprehensible ebbing of spiritual truth, if not of spiritual life, at the very beginning of the Church of Christ. To this day it is an amazement and a mystery to students why the Apostle Paul and the Epistle to the Romans should have so fallen out of sight for hundreds of years in the early Church. And, indeed, what an astonishment it is to see that the greatest of the apostles and his special gospel never once got their true place in the pulpit of Christendom all down the ages till Luther was raised up of God to give them their true place. And then again even since Luther's great gospel day there have been whole generations, even in evangelical Christendom, in which both Paul and Luther and justification and sanctification by faith have been all but completely misunderstood and misrepresented. And this present generation, if we do not take good care, may yet be written down to our shame in Church history as one of those wholly misunderstanding and wholly misrepresenting generations. Then again, some of the ablest and best men of our day have been drawn away from the deepest and the most central

doctrines of the Christian faith, and have wholly
given themselves up to the study of sacred history,
sacred scholarship, and sacred criticism. Noble and
fruitful studies, in their own place. But even such
legitimate and necessary studies may wholly take
the place in our minds that belongs by right to
Christian doctrine and to Christian experience.
Dr. Duncan, already quoted, was wont to say that
his Semitic studies were the wine and the whore-
dom of his heart. Then, again, account for it as
we may, there have been whole generations when
the spiritual sense of sin; the spiritual sense of the
depth and the deceitfulness and the malignity of
sin has been all but completely lost, and that even
among God's best taught and most deeply exercised
people. And so far as I can read the heart of my
day that is one of its most deadly and most
deplorable declensions. For myself I scarcely ever
hear a sermon or read a page or kneel under a
prayer in which the unspeakable evil of my own
sinfulness is at all felt or is at all attempted to be
expressed. All these things combine with some
other things to make both our preachers and our
publishers somewhat ashamed and somewhat shy of
the Gospel of Christ. And yet I feel sure that
the apostolic doctrines of grace and truth must be
far more preached in our pulpits than the silence
of the press would lead us to think. There must
be many able, deeply doctrinal, and genuinely
evangelical preachers who feel that they do not
possess enough of the gift and grace of English
style to justify them in challenging a place among
the literary men of our day. Paul himself must
have felt something of the same shrinking. He

must have felt tempted to water down certain of
his pulpit doctrines in Greece and in Rome, else he
would never have written, and with such emphasis,
that he was not going to be ashamed of the Gospel
of Christ; and, especially, that he was not going to
be ashamed of the scandal of the cross, but was
determined at all costs to preach everywhere that
so scandalising doctrine.   'I was with you in weakness,' he says to the Corinthians, 'and in fear, and in
much trembling.'   But Paul was a strong man; and
he conquered and cast out his fear and his weakness
far better than some of his successors have done.

But the true and proper point of all that for you
is this: You are independent both of your new
preachers and of your new publishers.   That is to
say, if your new preachers are at all like those
preachers of William Law's day who preached in
the morning on the wind called Euroclydon, and
in the evening on the times when the Gospels
were writ.   You are happily independent of such
preachers.   For you have the Psalms, and the
Gospels, and the Epistles at home.   And you have
the Confession—one of our elders died with the
chapter on Justification open on his pillow beside
his Bible—and the Catechism, and the Hymn-book
at home.   And you have Bunyan, and Baxter, and
Rutherford; and perhaps Shepard and Brea and
Halyburton.   And you have Boston's Life, and
Chalmers's Life, and McCheyne's Life, and Spurgeon's Sermons.   'How are you getting on?'   I
said to an old saint who was so full of years and
rheumatism that she never got across her doorstep,
and never saw her so-called pastor.   'O,' she said,
'I get on fine, for I have Spurgeon's Sermons.'

XXV

'Upon a time I was somewhat inclining to a consumption.'

CONSUMPTION is sometimes said
to be the most deceitful and the
most dangerous of all our diseases.
And that is so because in a consumption, as in no other deadly
disease, the patient hopes on and hopes on till at
last he is suddenly summoned away. Well, if that
is a danger and a disadvantage, on the other hand,
the consumptive man has this immense benefit and
advantage over all other dying men in that he
usually has a long warning afforded him beforehand, and has thus a long time given him in which
to prepare himself for his coming translation. As
Dante has it, 'The arrow seen beforehand slacks its
flight.' That is to say, if a man foresees his death
long before it actually comes to him, that gives
him time and opportunity to step aside and to
evade the fatal arrow. In most cases of consumption the arrow is shot so slowly, and has such a
long way to travel, that the dying man has a long
time given him to prepare himself for its last
attack. According to our own proverb, when the
dying man is forewarned he is thereby forearmed.

'Upon a time I was somewhat inclining to a

consumption, wherewith, about the spring, I was suddenly and violently seized with much weakness in my outward man, inasmuch that I thought I could not live.   Now began I to give myself up to a serious examination into my state and condition for the future, and of my evidences for that blessed world to come.   For it hath, I bless God, been my usual course, as always, so especially in the day of affliction, to endeavour to keep my interest in the world to come clear before my eyes.'   Then there follow five paragraphs of spiritual experience the like of which, in some respects, I do not know where to find in any other spiritual writer.   In his own incomparable way Bunyan goes on to tell us what a time of terror he had at the prospect of his un-prepared deathbed.   How all his past sins came flocking round his bed like so many harpies of hell hungering for his soul.   And now his inward man was seized with a far worse consumption than was that which had seized upon his outward man. And that went on till one day as he was walking up and down the house in a most woful state this word of God took hold of his heart: "Being justi-fied freely by His grace through the redemption that is in Christ Jesus, through faith in His blood." But O!   What a turn that Scripture made upon me!'   And what a similar turn that same Scripture has made upon many.   For that was Luther's favourite Scripture.   And it was when William Cowper was almost making away with himself that he was led to open this same Scripture which in a moment brought light and peace and hope and joy to his sad heart.   And then this other Scripture came home to Bunyan in his double consumption

of body and soul : 'Not by works of righteousness
which we have done, but according to His mercy
He saves us.' My brethren, it is worth a hundred
consumptions to have those two Scriptures brought
home to our hearts as they were brought home to
John Bunyan's heart. Now, this is the question.
Have they ever been brought home to your hearts?
You will know by this : 'Then was I got up on
high. Now death was lovely and beautiful in my
eyes. For I saw now that we shall never truly
live till we be gone to the other world. This
additional word also fell with great weight upon
my mind : O death ! where is thy sting ? O
grave ! where is thy victory ? At this I became
well again, both in body and in mind : and all
at once. My sickness did suddenly vanish. And
I walked comfortably, again, in my work for
God.'

Now, are any of you, or are any of yours, somewhat inclining to a consumption? And are you,
like John Bunyan, warningly threatened with that
consumption from time to time? Well, it proved
but a threat in John Bunyan's case. He was one
of those threatened men who proverbially live long.
For he lived to write the *Grace Abounding*, and the
Pilgrim's Progress, and much more of that same
kind. Bunyan's threatened consumption was like
Isaiah's. God's righteousness overflowed in both
their cases. And you are to be spared to read the
Grace Abounding and the *Pilgrim's Progress* again
and again, till you have those heavenly books by
heart; and, who knows, perhaps you are to be
spared to write an account of your own case which
shall be not unworthy to be set beside those two

immortal books of Bunyan's.   In any case, you must
more and more read those immortal books before
you go to meet their author.   You would be
ashamed to meet Bunyan, and Faithful, and Hopeful, and Mr. Honest, and Mr. Fearing, if you had
never been at the trouble to read their recorded
lives.   When you are invited to a dinner in order
to meet some great author, if you are not
well read in his writings, you hasten to look into
Who's Who, and then you take a glance into
such of his books as you can lay your hands on
before the day of the dinner.   Now just fancy your
being set down at dinner between Bunyan and
Greatheart and not being able to speak a word to
them about any of their experiences or any of
their exploits!   You would motion to the minister-
ing angels to change your seat to some other table.
You would far rather eat and drink alone than have
to sit stupid and silent beside Bunyan, and Evangelist, and Christiana, and Mercy, and the boys.   I have
seen as much as that you are threatened with a
consumption in order to give you time to have your
depraved taste for books completely changed before
you are ushered in among the great authors and
the great readers who shall sit on thrones in the
celestial city.   The last case of a fatal consumption I have had to do with was that of a Lochalsh
student last summer.   The last thing he had read
to him in this world was the rapturous narration of
how John Bunyan's pilgrims all crossed the Jordan.
Those splendid pages were read to him in the
forenoon by an Edinburgh schoolboy, and then
he crossed the same river himself in the afternoon.
I had promised to see him again in a day or two.

But that was another lesson to me not to say
' to-morrow' to a death-bed.

Then again are you one of those greatly-to-be-
pitied consumptives who through fear of death are
all their life-time subject to bondage? Well then,
would it not be a glorious thing if you used all
your allotted time so as to fight down all your
fears of death, and so as to lay a firm hold on
eternal life, before you leave this world? What a
splendid victory that would be! How you would
bless God to all eternity for the threatened consumption that was made the means of everlasting
life to your soul! What a successful life, be it
long or short, your life would be if you were able
to leave it with the Apostle's shout on your lips—
O death! where is thy sting? And with George
Herbert's song in your mouth:

> Death! thou wast once a hideous thing:
> But, since my Saviour's death
>   Has put some blood into thy face,
> Thou hast grown, sure, a thing to be desired,
>   And full of grace.

On the great advantages of a consumption
Richard Hooker is rich and elaborate after his own
great manner. The prince of English style takes
high ground in this matter of a consumption, as
thus: ' The soul has time,' he says, ' to call itself to
a just account of all things past by means of which
its repentance is made perfect. The joys of the
kingdom of heaven have leisure to present themselves. The pleasures of sin, and all this world's
vanities, are censured with an uncorrupted judgment. Charity is free to make advised choice of
the soil wherein her last seed may most fruitfully
be sown. The mind is at liberty to have due

regard of that disposition of worldly things which it can never afterwards alter. And the nearer we draw to God, we are sometimes so enlightened with the shining beams of His glorious countenance, as shall cause those present at our death-bed to say,—Let me die the death of the righteous, and let my last end be like his! All which benefits and opportunities are by a sudden death prevented.' So far Hooker. But that great writer does not mention what I look on as one of the most outstanding advantages and opportunities of a consumption. I mean the precious time that a slow consumption gives the dying man to drink into his very soul the best books concerning that strange and wonderful world he is soon to enter. That immense advantage bulks very much in my own mind. For myself, if I am to have some spare time to prepare myself finally before I die I know the great masterpieces of salvation that I shall have set on the shelf nearest my bed. Shall I tell you some of them? My New Testament; my *Paradise*; my Bunyan; and, especially, the Jordan scenes at the end. My *Saint's Rest*, and it in my old classfellow William Young's beautiful and fit edition. My life-long Goodwin; my Rutherford; my Catechism on the benefits of being a believer; my Gerontius; and my Olney, and Wesley, and kindred hymns. But since I am not myself constitutionally inclining to a consumption, and will not have the great advantage of that; since I may any day die in a moment let me have my hand on that heavenly shelf for a few minutes every day; and, especially, every night, lest the cock crow in my case suddenly.

And, then, there is this other advantage in a
slow consumption that Hooker should have dwelt
on as he only could. A man whose life has been
full of faults, and offences, and errors, and injuries,
if he is dying of a slow consumption he has time to
write a book of retractations and self-corrections
such as St. Augustine and Richard Baxter wrote before they died. A consumption gives a man time
to write his late, but all the more sincere, apologies
to those men to whom he has been an offence, and
a temptation, and a burden, and a snare. It gives
him authority also to summon the presence of some
of the worst cases to his bedside and there and
then to make a clean breast to them. As, also, he
has time to send to his friends plain-spoken and
outspoken messages of love and prayer and counsel
that he has not had the courage to speak or to
write as long as he was well. I would be bold
enough to add these two immense advantages to
Hooker's rich and richly expressed list of the consumptive man's privileges and advantages.

And, then, there is this last lesson: 'Now
began I afresh to give myself up to a serious
examination after my state and condition for the
future. For, I bless God, it hath been my usual
course, as always, so, especially, in the day of
affliction, to endeavour to keep my interest in the
life to come clear before my eye.' Now, you
would not stay long enough to-night to let me
speak to you about your interest in Christ and in
the life to come. But if you have any care to
possess an interest in Christ and in the life to come
William Guthrie has a little book on that supreme
subject, a little book of which John Owen said,

drawing a little gilded copy of it out of his pocket, 'That author I take to have been one of the greatest divines that ever wrote; his book is my *vade-mecum*, and I carry it always about with me.' 'I think Guthrie is the best book I ever read,' said Dr. Chalmers also. Now, you might set down William Guthrie's *Saving Interest* for a Christmas present to some one who is visibly inclining to a consumption, and whose interest in Christ and in the world to come you would like to see secured before his consumption gallops away with him for ever.

'This did sweetly revive my spirit, and did help me to hope in God. And, at this, I became well again, and all at once, both in body and in mind. My sickness did suddenly vanish, and I walked comfortably in my work for God again.' The curability of consumption is still a great question among our doctors. John Bunyan does not take time to tell us just how Dr. Skill treated his case. I fear the open-air cure would have been scoffed at in Dr. Skill's day. But I suppose there is no doubt whatever that the open-air cure has worked many miracles in our day; and I hope it has many more miracles to work among our consumptive friends. And then their work for God will be all the more comfortable that their consumption, like Isaiah's and Bunyan's, has been overflowed and carried away by God's grace and righteousness. The best programme of the work that our cured consumptives have still before them is so excellently put by my old favourite Thomas Shepard that I will copy the pilgrim father's words for you, and will so close. 'It may be there is much work to be done by thee at home,' says

Shepard, 'at home, and inside thine own doors.
Many odd distempers to be cashiered, and many
spiritual decays to be recovered. Also, it may be,
there is much for thee yet to do out of doors. It
may be there are friends of thine who are still unconverted; and that may be so because thou hast
been an offence to them, and hast stood in the way
of their salvation. And, converted or unconverted,
few will say that they have been much blessed in
their souls, or much helped in any real way by
thee; and that work for God and for thy friends
stands yet to be done by thee. Also, it may be,
God has some deep secrets of His providence, and
some deep secrets of His grace, to reveal to thee
before thou leavest grace for glory. Then, again,
thy talents have not been laid out to the best
usury in the past; thy time, thy means, thy station,
thy opportunities; and thy consumptions have been
suspended in order that thou mayest have a good
account to render on that day. Thou wilt walk
comfortably with God all the time that is left thee
on earth if thou settest about these tasks with
all thy recovered strength. And, then, when thy
appointed work is finished, thou will say: I was
not ready, at that time when I first took ill, O
Lord; but now let Thy servant depart in peace!'

XXVI

'I mused, I mused, I mused.'

THE religiously minded Greeks acknowledged and worshipped the best they knew. And among many other objects of their worship they paid a special honour and showed a special love to the Nine Muses. Those nine deities dwelt on Parnassus, and from that sacred mountain they presided over, purified, sweetened, and greatly ennobled the best life of ancient Greece. The wisest of the Greeks believed that God Himself was the Father of the sacred Nine, and that the human mind when it was at its best was their mother. And thus both heaven and earth combined in the begetting and in the birth of the Nine Muses of the Greek religion and the Greek civilisation. Nor does the greatest of our Christian poets disdain to invoke the assistance of the classic Nine when he is entering on his high enterprise:

> O Muses! O high genius! now vouchsafe
> Your aid! O mind! that all I saw hast kept
> Safe in a written record, here thy worth,
> And eminent endowments, come to proof!

John Bunyan had never gone to school to Clio nor to Melpomene; and yet such was his native genius and such was his Christian experience that

he has left behind him a history and a tragedy—
Dante would have called it a comedy because it all
ends so well—a history and a tragedy that far
excel all Greek and Roman fame. No Greek
philosopher, no Greek poet, has ever spoken to our
hearts as John Bunyan has spoken in his *Grace
Abounding*, and in his *Pilgrim's Progress*. And in
telling us in his own inimitable way all that God
had done for his soul, Bunyan at the same time
shows us how much his lifelong habit of musing
had to do with his religious experience and with
his intellectual and spiritual equipment for his
splendid work.

The first time we find John Bunyan engaged
in his lifelong habit of musing is on the village
green on that memorable Sabbath afternoon. 'A
voice did suddenly dart, as from heaven, into my
soul, which said to me—Wilt thou leave thy sins
and go to heaven, or wilt thou have thy sins and
go to hell? And, all that afternoon, I fell to musing on all my sanctuary sins, and on all my other
Sabbath-day disobediences. Thus I stood in the
midst of my play, before all that were present, but
yet I told them nothing.' You will follow out for
yourselves what line John Bunyan's musings took
that Sabbath afternoon; and when and how those
Sabbath musings of his ended. For myself, I also
have often had a good deal of musing about the
right sanctification of the Sabbath day. And so, I
feel sure, have some of you. I will tell you some
of my own musings on this sacred matter, and some
of them are yours also, no doubt. Musing on this
matter I sometimes say to myself that even if the
Fourth Commandment had never come into my

hands at all, I would still have observed the Sabbath day. As long as the Four Gospels and the Epistle to the Romans have come into my hands, and as often as I believe in my heart that the Son of God was delivered on the Friday morning for my offences, and was raised again on the Sabbath morning for my justification; as long as I truly believe that I would be a stock and a stone if I did not devoutly observe every returning Sabbath morning. As long as I continually stake my soul on my Lord's death and resurrection—nature herself, common-sense herself, not to say the Spirit of Christ speaking in my heart — all that would combine to make me a devoted observer of the Lord's Day. Sufficient, I sometimes say to myself, sufficient surely are six days out of the seven for this fast-passing life. For if there is indeed another life immediately before me, and if it is to be at all such a life as Holy Scripture forecasts it to be, then surely one day out of every seven is not too much to give up to the preparation of my mind and my heart and my habits and my character for that future life. I spend a large part of my life among books, and I often muse over my books on a Saturday night and on a Sabbath morning and say to myself—Six days and six nights are surely quite enough, in all conscience, to give to the books that bear upon this fast-dissolving earth, and one day and one night is surely not too much to give to the books that bear upon the new heavens and the new earth and upon my preparation to enter them. Six days and six nights to the history, and to the biography, and to the philosophy, and to the poetry, and to the fiction of time, and one day with one night to the

whole literature of eternity. So I sometimes muse
to myself. And as I so muse, the fire burns; till I
again determine that as for me and my house, so
far as I can secure it, we shall more and more
observe, and more and more sanctify, and more and
more enjoy, the Lord's own Day. There is a
two-hundred-year-old and a very musical voice
which exactly expresses not a few of my own musings on this whole matter, and it is this:

> Bright shadows of true rest; some shoots of bliss;
>   Heaven once a week;
> The next world's gladness prepossessed in this;
>   A Day to seek
> Eternity in time; time's bower;
>   The narrow way;
> Transplanted paradise; God's walking hour;
>   The cool o' the day;
> The creation's jubilee; God's parle with dust;
> Heaven here; man on those hills of myrrh, of flowers;
> Angels descending; the return of trust;
> A gleam of glory after six days' showers.

Passing on into our author's ' life of conviction,'
as he calls it, I come on this paragraph which I
shall neither curtail nor water down one single
drop. 'Thus was I always sinking, sinking, sinking, whatever I did think or do. So one day, I
was walking on the street of a neighbouring town,
and I sat down upon a settle in that street. And
as I so sat, I fell into a very deep pause about the
fearful state into which my sin had brought me.
And, after long musing, I lifted up my head: but,
methought, I saw as if the sun that shineth in the
heavens did grudge to give me his light, and as if
the very stones in the streets, and the tiles on the
houses, did bind themselves against me. Methought
that they all combined to banish me out of the

world. I was abhorred of them, and was unfit to
dwell among them, or to be a partaker of their
benefits, because I had so sinned against their
Maker who was also my Saviour. O how happy
was every creature over I was! For they all stood
fast and kept their station, but I was lost and gone.'
These were some of that poor tinker's musings on
the depth of his fall and on the unspeakable awful-
ness of his sin and misery. Now listen to a great
bishop's similar musings some time before that in his
episcopal palace. 'Two things, O Lord, I see in
myself; nature which Thou hast made, and sin which
I have added to my nature. Oh! take away from
me this depravity that I have brought upon myself!
Truth, Lord, I deserve damnation; but no offence
of mine can surely be so great as is Thy compassion.
Infirm, therefore, I come to the Almighty.
Wounded, I hasten to the Physician. Unclean, I
flee to the Fountain.' From a settle on a Bedfordshire street, and from one of the most luxurious
palaces in England, the same sad self-musings rise to
heaven.

'At another time, I sat by the fire in my house,
and was musing on my great wretchedness, and on
death as the wages of my sin, when the Lord came
and made this word a most precious word to me:
"Forasmuch, then, as the children are partakers of
flesh and blood, He also Himself took part of the
same; that, through death, He might destroy him
that had the power of death, and deliver them
who through fear of death were all their lifetime
subject to bondage." I thought that the glory
of these words was then so weighty on me that I
was, both once and twice, ready to swoon as I sat.

Yet not with guilt and trouble, but with solid joy and peace.' We have the very same wretchedness, and the very same issue out of it, in that half chapter of Paul's which stands away out at the head of all the literature of wretchedness, ancient and modern, sacred and profane. Melpomene had her own tragical experiences in wretchedness, and she had her own triumphs in the literary expression of her wretchedness. But all her experiences of wretchedness were shallow and superficial, and all her expression of it was feeble and ineffectual, compared with the concentrated wretchedness, and the transcending expression of it, in the Fifty-first Psalm, and in the seventh of the Romans, and in certain chapters of *Grace Abounding*. 'Rightly to feel SIN,' says Luther, 'is THE torture of all tortures.'

'Especially that word *Faith* put me to it. So that, sometimes, I must question as to whether I had any faith, or no. On this I mused, and could not tell what to do.' Till at last Martin Luther came to John Bunyan and told him with all clearness what to do. 'Do this,' said Luther. 'Saving faith is nothing else but this. It is nothing else but a sure and steadfast looking to Christ. It is nothing else but a fixed and an unwavering taking hold of Him, and of Him alone, as the alone Giver of righteousness, and salvation, and eternal life. This,' said Luther to Bunyan, 'this is the reason that Paul sets Jesus Christ forward so often in his Epistles ; yea, almost in every verse. And, like Paul,' said Luther to Bunyan, 'you, John Bunyan, must do nothing else but look to Christ. For *this alone* is true faith.' And at another time Luther

spoke with great point and great power and said to
Bunyan: 'These words—who loved *me*, and gave
Himself for *me*—these words are full of the right
sort of faith. And he who will utter this one word
me, and will apply this one word to himself, as Paul
the chief of sinners did, he will be a successful disputer with the broken and the angry and the soul-
accusing law. Say always, therefore, *even for me*, a
most miserable and a most wretched sinner! Read
and repeat with a great vehemency these words *me*,
and *for me*, not doubting but that thou art of the
number to whom these words belong.' And
Bunyan obeyed Luther and did all that till he
became the Bunyan that we all know and love;
that is to say, one of the most blessed of all our
great believers, and one of the sweetest and most
consoling of all our great authors. And all that
came of his much musing on that one word Faith.

The next time we find Bunyan musing it is on a
subject which is twin-sister to saving faith; that is
to say, God's imputation of Christ's representative
and suretyship righteousness to all true believers.
This was the true open-air-cure of Bunyan's
threatened consumption as you will see if you
study the passage. 'At this I was greatly
lightened in my mind, and bettered in my body,
and was made to understand that God could justify
and establish a sinner at any time. It was but
His looking upon Christ and imputing of His benefits upon us, and the work was forthwith done.'
And my brethren, when we read it aright we discover that the whole of our Bible is one long muse
upon this same imputation. As far back as the
fifteenth of Genesis we find the God of Abraham

Himself laying the foundation of Gospel imputation in His gracious treatment of the father of the faithful. And when we come to Moses and Aaron we find that they are the divinely appointed ministers of imputation, far more than of anything else. And the God of Israel gave His two servants their first lesson in imputation when He said that as often as He saw the blood of the pascal lamb on any door He would make His destroying angel to pass by that house on which the atoning blood was sprinkled. And David, who so much needed God's imputation, sings a fine psalm celebrating his own experience of it :

O blessed is the man to whom
Is freely pardoned
All the transgression he hath done,
Whose sin is covered.
Bless'd is the man to whom the Lord
Imputeth not his sin.

And Isaiah in his great Gospel sermon : 'Surely He hath borne our griefs and carried our sorrows. He was wounded for our transgressions, He was bruised for our iniquities. The chastisement of our peace was upon Him, and with His stripes we are healed. All we like sheep have gone astray; we have turned every one to his own way; and the Lord hath laid on Him the iniquity of us all.' And the Apostle Paul, that mighty muser, he muses on little else but on Gospel imputation. His great masterpiece the Epistle to the Romans is the very Magna Charta of Gospel imputation. And it was when Luther, Paul's great scholar, mused on this same subject in his cell, that the chains fell off his sin-enslaved conscience when he burst out of his prison-house and became the creator of an emancipated Christendom. The Westminster divines also mused on imputation till they asked and answered their three great Gospel questions, to which all our children know the answers : 'How doth Christ execute the office of a Priest ?' And, 'What is justification ?' And, 'What is faith in Jesus Christ ?' All the hymns of the Reformation also, and of every true revival of religion ; all the Olney Hymns, all the Wesley Hymns, all the Bonar Hymns, and indeed all the hymns that are worthy to be called hymns, they are all so many musings on Gospel imputation. Let every Sabbath day of ours begin then, and go on, and wind up, with a constant musing on Gospel imputation ; for, without Gospel imputation there is nothing left for you and me but a fearful looking for of judgment.

And then as the end of all and the best of all, 'As I was musing and in my studies how to love the Lord, and how to express my love to Him, I felt my soul greatly to go out in love and pity to Him, and my bowels to yearn towards Him. For I saw that He was still my Friend and did reward me good for evil. Yea the love and affection that did then burn within me to my Lord and Saviour Jesus Christ, did work at this time such a strong and such a hot desire of avengement upon myself for the abuse I had done unto Him, that had I had a thousand gallons of blood within my veins, I could freely then have spilt it all at His feet.' To such a heat did the fire burn, as Bunyan mused, and mused, and mused upon sin and salvation, upon himself and upon his Saviour.

Now, my brethren, that is John Bunyan ; or rather that is a small selection and a poor specimen

of that great spiritual writer on his lifelong habit
of musing. But what do you say yourselves to all
that? Marcus Aurelius 'to himself' says this in one
place, this : 'If we were of a sudden seized upon
and turned inside out how would we appear? If
our secret musings were all openly discovered and
read from the house-tops, how would we stand?'
My brethren, if you are wise, and if you would be
found among the wise, besides these offered lessons
out of John Bunyan to-night, you will take home
with you this added lesson out of the Stoic Emperor.
'Suddenly surprised,' and searched to the bottom
of your heart, what would your most secret self-
musings be found to be? Would they ever be
found to be, like John Bunyan's, about the Lord's
Day, about its past history, about its weekly message from Christ's empty grave to you, and about
the rest that remains for you in heaven? Again,
would your musings ever be like those of Bishop
Andrewes and John Bunyan, as to how your sinfulness has degraded you and defiled you and enslaved
you? Again, would your musings ever be suddenly
found to be about that great word faith, and what
faith does, and on Whom faith rests? And on imputation? With all your knowledge, do you know
the great imputation chapters in your Bible? And
the great passages on that supreme subject in
Luther, and in Hooker, and in Bunyan, and in all
the other greatest authors in the Church of Christ?
If we could but overhear you musing and singing
to yourself what would it be? Would it ever be,
' O blessed is the man '? Would it be, 'Just as I
am '? Would it be, 'Nothing in my hands I bring '?
Would it be, ' Jesus ! Thy blood and righteousness '?

Would it be, 'Standing on His merit I know no safer stand'?   Would it be, what we sometimes go home from the class on Sabbath nights singing :

> Jesus! how precious is Thy grace!
> When in Thy Name we trust,
> Our faith receives a righteousness
> That makes the sinner just?

XXVII

'When comforting time was come.'

JOHN BUNYAN was immensely in-
debted to the Puritan preaching of
his day. It was the Puritan preaching of his day that first opened John
Bunyan's eyes to see himself. It was
the Puritan preaching of his day that first opened
his eyes to see his Saviour. It was the Puritan
preaching of his day that so settled and grounded
his heart on Jesus Christ as made of God to him
his wisdom, and his righteousness, and his sanctification, and his redemption. And it was when his
comforting time was come that he heard one
preach a Puritan sermon on a sweet passage in the
Song of Solomon. And then it was his own
Puritan preaching all his days that was so much
blessed, first to himself and then to all his spiritual
children, as he so often and so eloquently testifies.
Do you know, my brethren, and from your own
experience, what a truly Puritan sermon is? Do
you know what it is that differentiates and exalts
a genuine Puritan sermon above all other sermons?
And can you trace in yourselves, and can you trace
up to Puritan preaching, such a succession of
spiritual blessings as John Bunyan traces here, and
indeed traces all through his *Grace Abounding*?

For the very title of this spiritual masterpiece of
his may very well be taken as the title of every
genuine Puritan sermon; that is to say: first, sin
abounding, and then grace much more abounding.
Besides, that is the supreme theme of the true
Puritan pulpit, and of no other pulpit that I have
ever sat under. The sermon that John Bunyan
heard from the lips of a Puritan preacher when his
comforting time was come was, as we say at college,
an eminently Christological sermon. That is to
say, it was a mystical, an evangelical, and an
intensely experimental sermon on that passage in
the Song. It was the kind of sermon that was
wont to be so much relished by our fathers and our
mothers when, like John Bunyan, they were in
deep spiritual distress and when their comforting
time was again come to them.

Walter Marshall's Ninth Direction is to this
effect: 'We must first receive the comforts of the
Gospel in order that we may be able to perform
sincerely the duties of the law.' Now, the atten-
tive student of John Bunyan's great autobiography
is able to trace quite clearly that same spiritual
sequence, and that same evangelical and experimental order, in John Bunyan's life, first of Gospel
comfort, and then of consequent obedience. I
shall not attempt to incorporate into this short
discourse one hundredth part of the passages in
Grace Abounding that bear upon Walter Marshall's
Ninth Direction. But he who is wisely interested in
the one thing supremely interesting, he will find that
rich chain of John Bunyan's spiritual experiences
for himself, which is a far better way than any
one else finding them for him. As to the special

sermon of this comforting time after many years
Bunyan remembers the preacher's text, and his five
heads, and his application of his fourth particular.
And no wonder. For it was that application which
sent Bunyan home from church that Sabbath in
such an ecstasy of unearthly joy. 'So as I was
going home that application came again into my
thoughts; and, as I well remember, I said then in
my heart: What shall I get by thinking on what
I have now heard? And, still as what I had just
heard ran thus in my mind, the words of the text
waxed stronger and warmer, and began to make
me look up. Now was my heart filled with comfort
and hope, and now could I believe that my sins
should be forgiven me. Yea, now, I was so taken
with the love and the mercy of God that I could
not contain myself till I got home. I thought I
could have spoken of God's love and mercy to me,
even to the very crows that sat upon the ploughed
lands before me, had they been capable to have
understood me. Wherefore, I said in my soul, and
with much gladness: Well, I would I had a pen
and ink here, and I would write this down before
I go any further. For surely I will not forget this
forty years hence.'

Now like that comforting Sabbath morning to
John Bunyan, so every returning Sabbath morning
of our own is appointed of God to be a comforting
time to us also. Every returning Sabbath morning
the command comes forth from the God of Salvation to all His true preachers: 'Comfort my people,
saith your God. Speak ye comfortably to Jerusalem,
and cry unto her that her iniquity is pardoned.
Say to her that He who was delivered for her

offences was raised again this morning for her justification.' Now all other preachers among us but the Puritan preachers are either afraid, or they are ashamed, or they are in some way not willing, or are in some way not able, to preach the one thing worth preaching : a free and a full justification by faith in Jesus Christ that is ; and, then, out of that, a life of evangelical obedience. You never hear the one divine message of a free and a full and an immediate forgiveness from any other pulpit but the Puritan pulpit. Or if you ever hear it, all other preachers mix it up and adulterate it with the wood and the hay and the stubble of our own impossible performances. For my part, the older I grow and the wiser I grow, I both preach and pray and sing more and more every Sabbath morning Paul's gospel, that is to say, the Puritan gospel. Summer and winter, fair and foul, dark and clear, I open my Divine Day with Charles Wesley's Sabbath morning words :

> Dark and cheerless is the morn
> Unaccompanied by Thee :
> Joyless is the Day's return
> Till Thy mercy's beams I see.

And almost more with this of Charles Wesley's also :

> His blood can make the foulest clean,
> His blood avails for me.

And Jonathan Edwards, that mighty Puritan, says to us that we are on this day specially to meditate upon and to celebrate the work of our redemption. We are with especial joy to remember the resurrection of our Lord, because His resurrection was the full finish of our redemption. This was the

Day of the great gladness of His heart. For this was the Day of His deliverance from the chains of death, as it was the day of our deliverance from the chains of hell.' And as John Bunyan has it in his own inimitable and incomparable way: On every Sabbath morning he always asserted that he saw Jesus Christ leaping and dancing and singing around his deserted grave, because He had that morning finished for ever John Bunyan's justification. Hooker himself was a true Puritan as often as he preached on justification on a Lord's Day morning. Would that that wonderful man had given more of his time and more of his strength and more of his style to the pure Gospel, and less to the ecclesiastical polity of only one section of the Church of Christ; great as his services have been to all our Churches in some parts of his great debate. Keep up your hearts, all you Puritan preachers. For yours is the only truly heart-comforting and soul-satisfying preaching in all the world. That preaching of yours made Paul, and it made Luther, and it made Hooker, and it made all the English and Scottish reformers, and it made the pilgrim fathers, and it made the Wesleys, and it made Chalmers, and it made Spurgeon and Parker. It made them all, because there is nothing else to be called true preaching; there is nothing else to make true preachers in all the world. There is no other preaching with such Scripturalness, and such depth, and such strength, and such insight, and such adequate and expert treatment of the case, and such adequate and expert treatment of the Cross, and out of all that such Pauline treatment of a sinner's Sabbath morning justification. The true comforting time comes again to every truly Puritan and truly evangelical preacher, and to every truly Puritan and truly evangelical people, with every returning Lord's Day morning.

And then above all other comforting Sabbath mornings the communion Sabbath morning comes to us here next Lord's Day with its special and its supreme comfort to all true communicants. For the God of Salvation is at His best on a communion morning, and His Puritan preachers are at their best, and His prepared people are at their best also. Not that Jesus Christ can be any more or any better to you on a communion day than He is every Sabbath day, when you again receive and rest upon Him alone for salvation as He is offered to you in the Gospel. Only, the Lord's Supper has a Gospel impressiveness about it all its own. For as the Apostle says to the Galatians: 'Christ crucified is more evidently set forth before your eyes in the Lord's Supper.' You hear Christ preached every Sabbath, and as often as you hear you again believe to the saving of your souls. But on the communion Sabbath you both hear, and see, and touch, and taste your salvation, till all your bodily senses are, so to speak, sanctified to the salvation of your souls. As Robert Bruce has it in his magnificent sacramental sermons: 'Speers thou what new thing we get in the sacrament? I say, we get Christ better than we did before. We get a better grip of Christ in the sacrament. The same thing which thou possessed by the hearing of the Word, thou possesses now more largely. For by the sacrament my faith is nourished and the bounds of my soul are enlarged; and so where I had but a small grip

of Christ before, as it were betwixt my finger and
my thumb ; now, I get Him in my haill hand. For,
ay the more my faith grows the better a grip I get
of Christ Jesus.' So far that great Puritan preacher
in Reformation Edinburgh.

And then when you prepare yourselves for the
communion day and for the Lord's Table by some
previous days and nights of recollection of your
past life, and by retired reading of the Word of
God, and by much secret prayer to Him, then the
Supper comes home to you with an immense power
and an immense impressiveness. So much so, that
at the very moment when the elder puts the bread
and the wine into your hand, that very moment
Almighty God again puts His Son and His salvation into your heart. And then Christ Himself
comes and speaks in your heart and says to you :

> My broken body thus I give
> For you, for all : take, eat, and live.

> My blood I thus pour forth, He cries,
> To cleanse the soul in sin that lies.

And that very moment the sin-cleansing efficacy of
His atoning blood is anew experienced and anew
possessed by every believing and appropriating
heart. Yes: Jesus Christ is at His very best on
the communion day, and your Gospel preachers are
at their very best. And you are at your very best
yourselves. And then your great comforting time
has again come round to you once more in this sad
and sinful world.

But it is not your Puritan weekly Sabbath, nor is
it your Puritan communion Sabbath, nor is it your
best Puritan preaching that is your truest and your
best and your consummating comforting time ; it is

—will you let me say it?—your death-bed; yes, it is your death-bed if you are prepared for it. It will be sure to startle some and it will almost anger others to hear a good word said for death; for death, which is the last of all our enemies, as Paul himself in one place calls it. But a great Pauline preacher, Thomas Shepard, who is by far the deepest and the most spiritual of all the pilgrim fathers, he says again and again and again of death that to a true Christian man his death is his most comforting time; it is by far and away his best means of grace; it is by far and away his best Gospel ordinance. Far away better than the weekly Sabbath, far away better than the Communion Sabbath, and far away better than the best preaching. For, says Shepard, the Sabbath and even the Supper itself and even when they are both at their very best, they only bring Christ down to us for another short season. But our death, if we are thoroughly prepared for it, and if we accomplish it aright, will immediately take us home to be with Christ for ever; never again to be parted from Him, and never again to be found unlike Him. But for Thomas Shepard or any one else to speak of death in that bright and eager and entrancing way will seem I fear to some of you to be simply monstrous and insufferable and impossible. You would rather have the so-called Puritan gloom than an unnatural and an impossible hilarity like that about death. But all the same, it was David's hilarity, and it was our Lord's hilarity, and it was Paul's, and Luther's, and Shepard's, and Rutherford's hilarity and that of many more. Read the Revelation of John the Divine, and the *Paradise* of

Dante, and the death-beds of John Bunyan's pilgrims, and Newman's *Gerontius,* and your own Rutherford's *Letters.* Read in all those so masterly and so heavenly-minded books, and you will see that death, as we are wont to call it, is not death at all to them, but is the true beginning of everlasting life. It is the true comforting time to all those who have been for so long saying to themselves secretly like David that they shall be satisfied only when they awake with His likeness. And again like David: I wait for God, my soul doth wait, my hope is in His word. And like Paul: To me to live is Christ, and to die is gain. And like Rutherford:

> There to an ocean fullness,
>   His mercy doth expand,
> And glory, glory dwelleth
>   In Immanuel's Land.

And again:

> Amid the shades of evening,
>   While sinks life's lingering sand,
> I hail the glory dawning
>   In Immanuel's Land.

And like George Herbert:

> *Death!* thou wast once an uncouth, hideous thing!
> But since our *Saviour's* death
> Has put some blood into thy face,
> Thou hast grown, sure, a thing to be desired,
> And full of grace.

And like James Montgomery:

> So, when my latest breath
>   Shall rend the veil in twain,
> By death I shall escape from death,
>   And life eternal gain.

And like Alfred Tennyson :

> Sunset and evening star,
>   And one clear call for me !
> And may there be no moaning at the bar
>   When I put out to sea.
>
> For, though from out our bourne of time and place
>   The flood may bear me far,
> I hope to see my Pilot face to face,
>   When I have crossed the bar.

And almost best of all—for your tombstone and mine
—this : 'The souls of believers are at their death
made perfect in holiness, and do immediately pass
into glory.' Yes ; our death, says Thomas Shepard,
is our best means of grace ; it is our best Gospel
ordinance ; and it is by far and away our best
comforting time. Comfort ye, therefore, comfort
ye, my dying people, saith your God.

XXVIII

'O methought, Christ! Christ! Christ!'

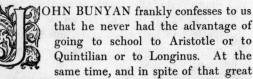OHN BUNYAN frankly confesses to us
that he never had the advantage of
going to school to Aristotle or to
Quintilian or to Longinus. At the
same time, and in spite of that great
disadvantage, he is able to employ their rhetorical
figure of apostrophe to absolute perfection. Genial
and generous Nature, very Genius herself, was the
tinker's sole and sufficient teacher in his oratorical
style. And then the grace of God came to him
and gave him his unparalleled impulse and opportunity. Till he is as good at this literary figure of
those ancient masters as if he had taken first-class
honours in one of their famous schools. And till we
carry this great apostrophe of his in our memories
and in our hearts beside the great apostrophies
of the prophets and the psalmists and the apostles.
And till we borrow this great apostrophe of his and
make use of it on our own account and on our own
occasions almost as much as if it were Holy Scripture itself. 'O methought, Christ! Christ! There
was nothing but Christ that was now before my
eyes! O Christ! O Christ! O Christ! My Lord
and my Saviour! O Christ! O Christ!'

Let us take in his own order some of John

Bunyan's experiences of the grace of Christ that led him to apostrophise Christ in this so impassioned and so impressive way. You all have the first of those great passages of his by heart, and therefore you will enjoy it all the more when I again repeat it in your hearing. Out of Paul himself I know nothing to equal this passage: 'But one day as I was passing in the field, and that too with some dashes in my conscience, fearing lest yet all was not right, suddenly this sentence fell upon my soul, Thy Righteousness is in Heaven! And, methought, withal, I saw with the eyes of my soul, Jesus Christ at God's Right Hand. There, I say, was my Righteousness. So that wherever I was or whatever I was doing, God could not say of me that He wanted my righteousness, for, there it was, just before Him. I also saw, moreover, that it was not my good frame of heart that made my Righteousness better, nor my bad frame that made my Righteousness worse. For my Righteousness was Jesus Christ Himself, the same yesterday to-day and for ever.' And again: ''Twas glorious to me to see His exaltation, and the worth and the prevalency of all His benefits. And that because I could now look from myself to Him, and should reckon that all those graces of God that were now green on me, were yet but like those crack-groats and four-pence-halfpennies that rich men carry in their purses, when their gold is in their trunks at home! O, I saw that my gold was all in my trunk at home! Even in Christ, my Lord and my Saviour! Now Christ was my all! He was made of God to me all my Wisdom, all my Righteousness, all my Sanctification, and all my Redemption!'

Now, righteousness, you will remark, is the one foundation of all those glorious passages. And righteousness is the one foundation of a thousand passages elsewhere, far more glorious than any passage even in *Grace Abounding*. For righteousness is the one foundation word and the one foundation thing of all the great foundation passages in the prophets, and in the psalmists, and in the greatest of all the apostles. If you will take the trouble to consult your Cruden on this great subject you will see that for yourselves. And as you think over all that, this reflection cannot but occur to you that of all the preachers of the Gospel, old or new, John Bunyan and his Puritan contemporaries come, by a long way, the nearest to David, and to Isaiah, and to Paul in this fundamental matter of righteousness: what it is, in whom we have it, how it is to be obtained, and how it is to be held fast and for ever made our own. Now as regards righteousness, true and pure and complete righteousness of heart and of life, you yourselves know as well as Paul and Luther and Bunyan, how the holy law of God condemns you to your face every day and every hour you live: condemns you, and all but executes you on the spot. God's holy law arrested and condemned and executed David, and Isaiah, and Paul, and Luther, and Bunyan every day, and on the spot, as you will read in their great autobiographies. And what those great sinners did when they were so executed and slain we read in all their apostrophes, and in all their prayers, and in all their praises.

Now with all that the main point for us is this, not what Paul and Luther and Bunyan did, but

what you and I do when we are in the same awful
condemnation. To us the priceless importance of
the Psalms and the Romans and the Galatians and
the *Grace Abounding* stands in this, that they all
show us what all those sinful men did in their
dreadful extremity. And it was what they were
enabled to do, or rather it was what Christ came
and did for them, that makes them all so to apostrophise Him in every psalm and epistle and paragraph of theirs. And as many of you as are taken
by the throat continually by God's broken law, it is
for you above all men that the Psalms and the
Romans and the Galatians and the *Grace Abounding*
were all written. Nobody but you, and the like of
you, will understand a single line of those divine
books: no, not one single syllable. And then if
you will take your lesson in all this matter of
righteousness and life from John Bunyan, he will
do you a service in this respect that neither Aristotle, nor Quintilian, nor Longinus, nor Dionysius
of Halicarnassus can do you. That is to say, he
will take you to his own school of Christian doctrine and Christian experience and Christian eloquence, and he will there teach you how to adore
and how to magnify and how to apostrophise and
how to cry continually, O Christ! O Christ! O
Christ! And that with more and more passion
and more and more rapture every new day: O
methought, Christ! Christ! There was nothing
but Christ that was now before my eyes! I was
not now only for looking upon this or that benefit
of Christ apart, as of His Blood, His Burial, or His
Resurrection. But I considered Him now as a
whole Christ. As He in whom all these and all

other His Virtues, Relations, Offices, and Operations met together: and that too, as He sat on
the Right Hand of God in Heaven.

Sometimes, so Bunyan tells us about himself, he
would be like David in the Hundred and Third
Psalm and like our own Shorter Catechism. That
is to say, he would sometimes look at some one
benefit of Christ alone and by itself. As David
looked in that fine psalm of his now at the forgiveness of all his iniquities, and now at the healing of all his diseases, and now at the redemption
of his life from destruction, and now at the satis-
fying of his mouth with good things, and now at
this, that God had not dealt with him after his
sins, nor had rewarded him according to his iniquities. Or again as our Catechism looks in one
place at our assurance of God's love, and then at
our peace of conscience, and then at our joy in the
Holy Ghost, and then at our increase of grace, and
then at our perseverance therein to the end. And
again our Catechism looks at the benefits believers
receive from Christ at their death, and then again,
at the benefits they receive at their resurrection.
And Bunyan sometimes looked at his salvation
benefits one by one and apart in that way. But
as he became better and better skilled in this
matter, so far as he himself was concerned, and
not finding fault with the Psalm, nor with the Catechism, he was now not only for looking upon this
or the other benefit of Christ apart and by itself.
But he got more and more into the great evangelical way of gathering up all Christ's benefits into
Christ Himself. In his own so expressive words,
he more and more accustomed himself to consider

Christ as a whole Christ and as a complete Christ. He more and more trained himself and practised himself to see Christ and to treat with Him as the true Christ of God in whom it has pleased the Father that all God's fullness should dwell. And out of whose fullness, day after day and hour after hour, he was to receive the assurance, and the experience, and the personal possession of all his salvation benefits, as often as he felt his need of them, and again went back to Christ for them. And it was as he continually returned to Christ for all his salvation benefits that he more and more broke out into this adoring and rapturous apostrophe: O Christ! O Christ! O Christ! My Lord and my Saviour! O Christ, the alone source and spring of all my saving benefits! O Christ! O Christ! O Christ!

Now after all that, was it any wonder that the very Name of Christ, as often as he read it in the Word of God, was made to spangle in John Bunyan's eyes. 'Spangle' is his own expressive word in this matter. And no wonder. For whose eyes would not spangle at that glorious Name? Whose eyes that were once opened truly to see Him to whom that glorious Name belongs? I have often seen your own eyes spangling in this house and in your own house at home as I read that Name to you in the Gospels and in the Epistles. I saw some of your eyes spangling like the sun itself this forenoon and this afternoon as often as the Name of Christ fell again upon your open and hungry ears as you sat at His Table. How could it be otherwise? As John Bunyan says, you would be so many Philistines if your eyes did not spangle at that Name which is above every name. Far better be born and die without having eyes at all than have to give an account of two eyes that had never once spangled at the Name of Christ. You will need nothing more to secure you a great welcome and an abundant entrance on that Day than just the light and the love that will spangle in your eyes at your first sight of Christ. I always think of our own Samuel Rutherford as having two of the most Christ-spangling eyes in all the world. You will all remember how he was wont to protest that from the day when he first saw Christ in the beauty of His holiness, he had so fallen in love with Christ, that he could give up his whole heart to no one else. He was wont to write to his more spangling-eyed correspondents that if he loved wife or child or Anwoth, and he loved them all with all his big and warm heart; yet, all the time, it was in Christ, and for Christ's sake, that he so loved them. And in the spangling of his heart he was wont to declare that he loved his very banishment in Aberdeen because it was for Christ's sake that he was living in silence there. And he was wont to declare also that he would welcome the stake and the gallows for the same Name, and that his eyes would spangle and that he would apostrophise Christ as he fell bound among the flames. Happy people! who besides your Bible have the spangling books of John Bunyan and Samuel Rutherford. Happy people who possess spangling eyes wherewith to read the Name of Christ in those spangling books! Now it was to teach and to constrain and to compel a multitude that no man can number to exclaim, O Christ! O Christ! O Christ! and that with spangling eyes: that was the final cause, as Aristotle would have said had he known it, and the chief end of all created things and all redeemed things and all restored things. Yes, the very creation itself, and then the fall, and then the cross, and then the Lord's Supper; all law and all righteousness, all grace and all glory; all, all was intended and was overruled to lead all God's saints up to this apostrophe: O Christ! O Christ! O Christ!

Aye and all your own personal experience of sin, with all your unspeakable misery and shame and degradation all your days on account of your sin, with all your inward agony from that never-ceasing war in your own soul between sin and grace, a war and a bondage past all imagination of mortal man; it has all been appointed you and ordained you in order that you might be brought at last to exclaim, with spangling eyes: O Christ! O Christ! O Christ! And if any of you have been so exclaiming all this communion day, then your households should keep their eyes on you and watch well both your going out and your coming in lest you be not left much longer with them. For the days of the years of your pilgrimage among them must be fast nearing their accomplishment when that communion day comes on which your heart is so carried captive all the day that you are heard to utter nothing so articulately as this: O Christ! O Christ! O Christ! Then the heavenly elder will soon be at your door with your communion card for the Table above. And when it is all over here I will tell you what will happen to you on your arrival there. Make way! it will be proclaimed as with the sound of a trumpet: Make way for this great lover of our

Lord! Make way for this communicant with the rich voice and the spangling eyes! And then you will begin fully to see and fully to understand and fully to accept why it was that you had to pass through such a hell upon earth while you were here, through such a lifetime of such sinfulness and such spiritual suffering on account of your sinfulness. And why also you were so emptied from vessel to vessel till now you are to be for ever sanctified and for ever satisfied with the love of Christ and with your everlasting likeness to Christ. Only, your heart will be so full when you first see Christ that you will not be able for a time even to say to Him so much as His Name. But He will say your name to you. And to hear your name even once from His lips, with His eyes spangling when He sees you — let the bride describe your feelings: 'He brought me,' you will say, 'to the banqueting house, and His banner over me was love. Stay me with flagons, comfort me with apples; for I am sick of love. His left hand is under my head, and his right hand doth embrace me.' 'Beloved,' says one of the friends of the Bridegroom to you and to all such as you are, 'Beloved, now are we the sons of God, and it doth not yet appear what we shall be; but we know that when He shall appear we shall be like Him, for we shall see Him as He is.' 'O methought, Christ! Christ!' says another friend of the Bridegroom. 'There was nothing now but Christ before my eyes. O Christ! O Christ! O Christ!'

XXIX

'I will in this place thrust in a word or two concerning my preaching.'

THE beginning of John Bunyan's preaching was something like this. It was something like what we ourselves have sometimes seen in Scotland and in our own day. At a time of religious revival, or some other season of refreshing, the Spirit of God lays hold of a young man: a ploughman, or a tradesman, or a student. 'Some of the most able for judgment and godliness of life' immediately have their eyes on that young man. 'Some of the most able among the saints' with us also will prevail with that young convert to accompany them to some of their meetings in such and such a kitchen, or carpenter's shop, or barn, or hayloft. I have seen it myself a hundred times in Padanaram, and in Airlie, and in Kirriemuir, and in Logiealmond, and in Huntly, and in Aberdeen, and in Hopeman. I have seen Duncan Matheson and John More taken in hand by the 'most able for judgment and godliness of life,' and gradually led on till their names became a great fragrance to all the country round about. And this same went on in Bedford till the 'priests and doctors' set the civil arm in motion. And till one evening just as the tinker was entering a little prayer-meeting the village constable laid his hand on the unordained preacher's shoulder. 'At the sessions after, I was indicted for an upholder and maintainer of unlawful assemblies and conventicles, and for not conforming to the National Worship of the Church of England. So being by the justices delivered up to the gaoler's hands, I was had home to prison again, and there have lain now complete twelve years, waiting to see what God would suffer those men to do with me.' It cannot, I should think, but interest us all to learn what sort of a preacher the Bedford tinker was before he was shut up into Bedford jail, there to learn to be a still better preacher before he came out.

Well then to begin with, it was the old story. 'Unworthy wretch that I am! Such a fool as I am! Of all unworthy men, the most unworthy!' And then as to his literature. To the end they never made John Bunyan a doctor of divinity nor anything else of that honourable sort. But three degrees had already been granted to Bunyan that neither Cambridge nor Oxford could either give or withhold. 'To wit, union with Christ; the anointing of the Spirit; and much experience of temptation. All of which go to fit a man for that mighty work of preaching the Gospel of Christ, much more than all the University learning that can be had.' So says John Burton of Bedford in his excellently written preface to John Bunyan's *Gospel Truths Opened*. 'In my preaching of the Word,' says Bunyan, 'I took special notice of this, that the Lord did lead me to begin where His Word begins. Yea, it was for this reason I lay so long at Sinai so

as to see the fire, and the cloud, and the darkness,
that I might fear the Lord all the days of my life
on earth, and tell of His wondrous works to my
children.' God's Word, and Bunyan's own conscience and heart, were about all the books he ever
had; and in his preaching he always took the Bible
view, and the view that his own conscience and
heart took, of what true preaching is; with what
all true preaching begins, and with what it all ends.
Bunyan always began where Paul always began,
and where Luther always began, and where all the
Puritan preachers always began.

And then, beginning as he always began, Bunyan
shall tell you in his own words how he went on.
'Now, this part of my work I fulfilled with great
sense; for the terrors of the law, and guilt for my
transgressions, lay heavy on my conscience. I
preached what I felt; what I smartingly did feel;
even that under which my poor soul did groan and
travail to astonishment. Indeed, I have been to my
hearers as one sent to them from the dead. I went
myself in chains to preach to them in chains. And
I carried that fire in my conscience that I persuaded
them to beware of. I can truly say, and that without dissembling, that when I have been to preach,
I have gone full of guilt and terror to the pulpit-
door, and there it hath been taken off. I have
been at liberty till I had done my work, and then,
immediately, even before I could get down the
pulpit-stairs, I have been as bad as I was before.
And yet, God carried me on, but surely with a
strong hand, for neither guilt nor hell could take
me off my work.' 'Now, this part of my work
I fulfilled with great sense.' Canon Venables's

editorial note upon 'great sense' is this: 'With
great sense: that is to say, with great feeling and
with great sympathy. As in Shakespeare, Othello
says:

> O brave Iago, honest and just,
> Thou hast such noble sense of thy friend's wrong.

And our own Highland Brea, speaking like Bunyan
about the beginning of his own ministry, says: 'The
preacher must have the sense of his charge; the
danger of immortal souls deeply imprinted on his
heart. He that hath but slight impressions of his
charge will never faithfully perform it.' And Newman, though he does not use the word 'sense,' has
the very same thing under the word 'earnestness.'
I like to give you Newman's fine English when I
possibly can. 'He'—says that great writer—'he
who has before his mental eye the Four Last
Things will have the true earnestness, the horror
of one who witnesses a great conflagration, or the
rapture of one who discerns some rich and sublime
prospect of natural scenery. His countenance, his
manner, his voice, all speak for him; and that in
proportion as his view has been vivid and minute.
The great English poet has described this sort of
eloquence when a calamity had befallen:

> Yea, this man's brow, like to a title leaf
> Foretells the nature of a tragic volume.
> Thou tremblest, and the whiteness in thy cheek
> Is apter than thy tongue to tell thine errand.

It is this earnestness, in the supernatural order,'
continues Newman, 'which is the eloquence of
saints; and not of saints only, but of all Christian
preachers, according to the measure of their faith
and their love.' Now John Bunyan should have

satisfied the Cardinal so far at any rate as his mental eye was concerned. For not St. Francis himself, not Dante himself, has ever held the Four Last Things before their eyes better, and to more earnestness and impressiveness, than John Bunyan has done. 'God gave me some utterance wherewith to express in some measure what I saw. For still I preached as I saw and felt.' And it was because Jacob Behmen had the same eyes as St. Francis and Dante and Bunyan had that there would continually arise within him what he calls a 'fiery instigation' to tell to others what he had seen and heard when he was caught up by the hair of the head, and was carried away into the Vision of God, as the captive prophet was carried away at the river of Chebar.

'Wherefore I did labour so to preach the Word, as that thereby, if it were possible, the sin, and the person guilty of the sin, might be particularised by my preaching.' 'The Lord,' says Halyburton, 'did point out to me particulars wherewith to try me. But when I saw that it behoved me to quit these particular sins, then I begged a little delay: Augustine-like, I was willing to be pure, but not yet.' And out of that experience like Bunyan, Halyburton, in his pulpit particularisations, was very home-coming and very heart-searching. And he was wont to complain that most preachers were much too general and much too remote in their application of truth. And Fraser says this on this same subject: 'I felt called to preach plainly, particularly, and authoritatively: yet courteously, wisely, meekly, and gently; not to speak in a cloud of words, but to say, Thou art the man!'

'Again, I never cared to meddle with things that were controverted and in dispute, especially things of the lowest nature.' Old Thomas Shepard shall comment on this of John Bunyan. 'Divisions,' says that great Pilgrim Father, 'pull down kingdoms without foreign enemies. It is the delight of hell to see churches at variance among themselves. This is Satan's continual attempt in the best churches and he is too often successful. It is most distressful to see what a small thing the devil will make to do his work : a word, a gesture, a garment will do it. One must have liberty to speak one thing, and another another thing. I am of this mind, saith one. But I am not of that mind, saith another. Even a breath of suspicion will not seldom do it. O, tremble to entertain a thought of contention ! Love one another sincerely, and you will live together quietly.' So far dear old Shepard. 'Besides,' says Bunyan, 'I did let alone the things that engendered strife, because my proper work did run in another channel, even to carry an awakening word : to that therefore did I stick and adhere.'

'Again, when, at sometimes, I have been about to preach upon some smart and searching portion of the Word, I have found the temper suggest and say—What! will you preach this ? This, of which you are yourself guilty ? Do not preach upon that subject to-day. Or if you do, mince it down so as to escape the condemnation yourself. But I thank the Lord I have never consented to these satanic suggestions. Let me die, said I, rather than water down the Word of God.' Plutarch-like, I like to give you parallel lives in all these matters. To me parallel lives are very instructive and very impressive. You see how John Bunyan's mouth was almost shut sometimes by reason of his own sinfulness. And listen to Jacob Behmen on the same experience. 'Leave all these matters alone, it would be said to me. And so have I often said to myself; but the truth of God did burn in my bones till I again took pen and ink. All this time, do not mistake me for a saint or an angel. For my heart is full of all evil. In malice, in hatred, and in lack of brotherly love, after all I have experienced, I am like all other men. I am surely the fullest of all men of all manner of malignity and infirmity.' And, wholly unlike Bunyan and Behmen in everything else, I myself am only too like them in my temptation to mince matters and to be mealy-mouthed in my preaching. Like them I would flee the pulpit if I only could, and for the same reason. Often when the church officer is bringing in the Bible I think of escaping by the back door. You will not believe me, but it's true. And when you are settling yourselves down in your luxurious seats I am holding on by the banister behind, and am pleading with God that He would not cast me away from His presence, but would uphold me with His free Spirit! And when the organist is welcoming you in with sweet music I am staggering in with this prayer: O! sprinkle the pulpit, and the preacher, and the sermon, with the peace-speaking and the power-giving blood! And I never once come along Melville Street on a Sabbath morning or on a Sabbath evening that I do not have to reason with myself in this way: Be quiet, O my conscience! Be sensible, and look on

things as they are! Remember that you are but a
postman, as it were, to the people. You are not
proposed as a pattern to them. Go boldly, then,
and declare your message to them. It is not
because you have attained, or are already perfect.
If you follow after that is enough for you. And
that, well considered, and laid close to my conscience and to my heart and to my imagination
carries me through; when, otherwise, I would flee
from before your faces. 'It is far better,' said
Bunyan and Behmen to themselves, 'that we
condemn ourselves in what we preach, rather than,
to escape condemning ourselves, we imprison the
truth in unrighteousness.

Every self-observing preacher will read with a
humbled heart what Bunyan says about his temptations now to vainglory and now to a too great
depression of spirit in and after his pulpit work.
Again and again he returns to that, and not once
too often. But there is one of his passages on
that subject which I must give you. 'I have also,
while found in this blessed work, been often
tempted to pride and to liftings up of heart. Yet
the Lord, of His precious mercy, hath so carried it
toward me, that I have had but small joy to give
way to such a thing. For, it hath been my every
day's portion to be let into the evil of my own
heart, and still made to see such a multitude of
corruptions and infirmities therein, that it hath
caused hanging down of my head under all my
gifts and attainments.' I have often wondered—
and I say it with all reverence—how it was with
our Lord Himself in this matter. He could not
but have felt satisfied, and happy, and hopeful after
such a sermon as the Sermon on the Mount: nor

could it have been sinful in Him so to feel, could it? And Paul could not but have known that he had spoken eloquently and impressively on Mars Hill. Now, was it vainglory in the Apostle so to feel? And when he felt buoyant and generous-hearted and affable all day after such a sermon was he in that sinfully puffed up? What do you think? Or did the Apostle protect himself and justify his happiness by saying, 'It is no more I that preach good sermons, or offer good prayers, but it is the Spirit of Christ that preacheth and prayeth in me'? Both in their elation and in their depression, our preachers must often be thrown back upon such problems and such patterns as these.

There are many more points of the greatest interest in Bunyan's account of his experiences in preaching. But I have time to mention only one more. 'Now, I altered my preaching. Now, I did labour to hold forth Jesus Christ in all His Offices, Relations, and Benefits, to His Church. And with this God led me also into something of our mystical union with Christ. Therefore that I discovered and shewed to them also.' Now this raises a question that I have often thought about. And that is how much, how far too much, a congregation is dependent on the attainments, and on the experiences, and on the labours, and on the alterations of their minister. For years John Bunyan's congregation heard next to nothing of Jesus Christ as their Prophet Priest and King. And nothing at all of their mystical union to Him. It is true, they had five years of all that from Bunyan before he was caught, as he says, and was cast into prison. But there must be multitudes of our ministers who are caught and cast into their graves before they have

ever preached a single sermon on the Mystical
Union, or so much as know what it is. Now, in
what way is that famine of the Word to be met? I
do not know any other way but by all our ministers
setting themselves to grow deeper and deeper into
the divine life every day themselves; and then
their preaching on the Sabbath day will grow
deeper and deeper also. But here again, and most
happily, our people are not wholly dependent on
us. They need not be starved of evangelical, and
spiritual, and mystical doctrine, even though we
who preach to them know little or nothing of these
great matters ourselves. You will all remember
James Stewart of the cab office down at the Dean
Bridge. Holding up his well-worn Walter Marshall
to me on his death-bed, he said, 'I read little else
now but Marshall's *Third Direction*. It is pure
gold!' he exclaimed. 'It is pure honey out of the
Rock! It is heaven upon earth to me to read it
again and again!' Now James Stewart to most
men's eyes was a plain man and an unlettered man.
He was just the sort of man, you would have said,
who would be wholly and entirely dependent on his
minister for the deepest things of the spiritual life.
Not at all! Not at all! James Stewart, plain man
as he was, was a spiritually-minded student of
spiritual things, and he was a much-experienced
man of God. And it was largely Walter Marshall's
Sanctification, and it was largely his *Third Direction*, that made James Stewart the man he was, and
the man he now for ever is. Blessed be the God of
Walter Marshall and the God of James Stewart!
And may He be your God and my God for ever
also! Amen!

XXX

'I find to this day seven abominations in my heart.'

HE number seven has been a mystical and a sacred number in all ages and in all literatures and in all religions. But it is in Holy Scripture and in Christian literature alone that the number seven has taken to itself that special height and depth and breadth and completeness with which we are so familiar. As for instance, there are the seven gifts of the Holy Ghost: Wisdom, and Understanding, and Counsel, and Fortitude, and Knowledge, and Piety, and the Fear of God. Then there are the seven Penitential Psalms. Then, again, there are the seven deadly sins: Pride, and Lechery, and Envy, and Wrath, and Covetousness, and Gluttony, and Sloth. And over against them there are the seven chief virtues: Humility, and Chastity, and Love, and Patience, and Bounty, and Abstinence, and Vigilance. Then, again, there are the seven spiritual works: to convert sinners, and to instruct the ignorant, and to counsel doubters, and to comfort the sorrowful, and to bear wrongs patiently, and to forgive enemies, and to pray for all men. And, lastly, there are the seven works of charity: to feed the hungry, and to give drink to the thirsty, and to clothe the naked, and

to shelter the homeless, and to visit the sick, and
to come to the imprisoned, and to bury the dead.
And then, after the Bible examples of the number
seven, the seven scars that were cut on Dante's
forehead have made by far the deepest impression
on our minds and our hearts :

> Seven times
> The letter that denotes the inward stain,
> He on my forehead, with the blunted point
> Of his drawn sword, inscrib'd.   And 'Look,' he cried,
> 'When enter'd, that thou wash these scars away.'

But all that only serves as so much preface and intro-
duction to the seven arch-abominations that John
Bunyan still finds in his own unsanctified heart.

Now my brethren, those seven arch-abominations in John Bunyan's heart have given me
more deep thought, and more perplexing thought,
than I can well attempt to tell you.   And
in this way.   When first I took those seven arch-
abominations of John Bunyan's heart, and laid
them alongside the whole Law of God, I did not
know where I was : I did not know what to say or
what to think.   For in the Book of Exodus I read
that the Lord gave unto Moses two tables of stone
written with the finger of God.   And the tables
were written on both their sides, and the tables
were the work of God, and the writing was the
writing of God, graven upon the two tables.   Now,
the first table contained all the commandments
concerning our duty to God ; while the second
table contained all the commandments concerning
our duty to our neighbour.   And just here arose my
great perplexity about Bunyan's seven arch-abominations.   For in all his deep self-discoveries, in all

his sometimes almost too awful contritions and confessions, in all his quite extraordinary brokenness of heart and burdensomeness of conscience, he has not recorded one single instance of any transgression of his against any of the commandments of the second table. In speaking of the holy law of God which the Holy Ghost makes use of to show us our sinfulness, John Calvin says that the first table of the law holds by far the higher spiritual rank, but that the second table is far better suited for the purposes of our self-examination: for our severe scrutiny of ourselves. Now, I will not say that John Bunyan never scrutinised himself by the second table; only we have no report of any such scrutiny. In all the three hundred and thirty-nine paragraphs of *Grace Abounding to the Chief of Sinners* there is not so much as one single line that speaks of any single sin of his against either the fifth, or the sixth, or the seventh, or the eighth, or the ninth, or the tenth commandment of the law. And in his enumeration and confession of his seven arch-abominations at the end of his heart-searching book there is not one syllable that refers to any sin of his against man, or woman, or child: not one syllable. In all his openness of heart and in all his brokenness of heart about himself Bunyan has not one word to say about anger, or about malice, or about pride, or about impurity, or about ill-will, or about an unbridled tongue, or about an envying or a grieving heart at the good of his neighbour. And yet you may depend upon it John Bunyan was quite as guilty in all these respects as you and I are. Emerson the American essayist once boasted that he did not care who saw into his heart. But in that boast Emerson only advertised to all the world that he had never seen so much as one inch under the surface of his own heart himself. And thus it is that we find that literary man saying that the Christian Church has dwelt with 'noxious exaggeration' on the Person of Christ. But John Bunyan was not such a born Philistine as that. And just how to account for the seven arch-abominations in Bunyan's heart, and all of them against the first table of God's holy law, and not one of them against any commandment of the second table, that fairly confounded me: I did not know how to explain that. I did not know what to make of that.

And then when leaving Moses I went on to lay Bunyan alongside of Dante, I was only more and more staggered and perplexed and thrown out. You will all remember the successive names of Dante's seven scars. You will all remember them because they are all your own. All your own foreheads have had cut in upon them all those same seams and scars of sin and shame. But not Bunyan's forehead as it would seem. For Bunyan in all his humiliations, does not confess to so much as one of those seven scars of Dante's and yours and mine. Only, on the other hand—and how this more and more perplexes us!—on every red-hot page of his *Grace Abounding* John Bunyan is constantly confessing to kinds of sins, and to aggravations of sins, and to a guilt and to a despair on account of sins, to all of which Dante seems to have been wholly ignorant and innocent. Now, how is all that, and all that on both sides, to be accounted for and explained? If I were to suggest to you that perhaps Bunyan saw deeper into some divine things than even

Dante saw: that for one thing, he both saw and felt the spirituality of sin far better than Dante did, what would you say to me? If I were so much as to hint at my belief that Bunyan's seven abominations are far away more significant, spiritually considered, than all Dante's sufficiently fearful scars, what would you say in answer? Would you not start up and tell me that John Bunyan was not worthy to stoop down and unloose Dante's shoe-latchet? Would you not exclaim that the tinker of Bedford is not to be named in the same day with the greatest of all Christian poets? And I would at once admit that. That is to say, I would at once admit that as far as Dante's aristocratic birth and aristocratic breeding were concerned. And as far as his classical education and his oceanic reading were concerned. And as far as many more such like immense advantages of his were concerned.

But perhaps there may have been one or two very real and very rich blessings left behind for Bunyan that even Dante did not wholly inherit, much less exhaust in his day. For one thing, Bunyan lived after Luther had written; whereas Dante lived and died long before that great epoch in the Church of Christ. And a great saying of our Lord comes to my mind at this moment: 'Among those born of women there hath not risen a greater than John the Baptist: notwithstanding, he that is least in the kingdom of heaven is greater than he.' Now to my mind, Dante is among the very greatest born of women: notwithstanding, at the same time, John Bunyan is greater in the kingdom of heaven than he. Not that Dante is not high up in the kingdom of heaven also: for

so he is and very high up. But the whole point is
this: the kingdom of heaven had made some immense advances between Dante's day and Bunyan's
day: immense advances in inwardness, and in
depth, and in spirituality, and in evangelical
doctrine and evangelical experience: immense
advances of which the best men of Dante's day
had no knowledge and no experience. If Luther
was all that Evangelical Christendom is now
wholly agreed that he was, then simply to have
been born after Luther, and to have heard him
preach Paul's Gospel, and to have read his Comment on the Galatians; all that places a man like
Bunyan in a position of such privilege as to make
all talent, and all learning, and all labour to fall
into a far inferior place. Yes, yes: that great saying of our Lord about John the Baptist gives us the
true point of view in this whole matter now in
hand. The whole explanation of which we are in
search lies away out in that direction. And they
who are willing to receive that explanation, they
will find it sufficient the more they think about it.
For that explanation sheds a great light on all our
confessed perplexities about the two tables of the
law; and about Dante and his seven scars: and
about Bunyan and his seven abominations. And
when once you get a point of view that harmonises
difficulties and perplexities hitherto insoluble and
irreconcilable: however new to you, and however
unexpected by you that point of view may be, you
will be wise to take it, and to hold it, at any
rate till you have found a better.

The sum, then, under this head, is this. These
same seven scars would all have been cut deep into

Dante's forehead, even though Jesus Christ had
never come, and had never died, and had never
risen again, and had never sent down the Holy
Ghost.   But unless the Son of God had come, and
had been made sin, and had been made an atonement for sin, and had sent the Spirit of holiness to
the Church ; and unless Paul and Luther had had
the Son of God and His righteousness revealed in
their hearts, and had had the Spirit of gospel holiness shed abroad in their hearts, Paul would never
have written his seventh chapter, and Bunyan
would never have written his seven abominations.
Nature herself, the law of God written on the
natural conscience, would have secured Dante's
seven scars.   But evangelical illumination and
evangelical experience alone could have opened
Bunyan's eyes to such spiritual sins as he here
laments, and that with such inconsolable bitterness.
Where Dante is so severely ethical, Bunyan is intensely spiritual.   Where Dante is consumed with
the fire of legal and moral righteousness, the zeal
of evangelical holiness has eaten Bunyan up.
Dante's seven scars are seen and are felt and are
bitterly confessed by every righteously-minded
man, pagan and Christian. But Bunyan's seven
abominations are seen and are felt and are bitterly
confessed by the most evangelically-enlightened
and the most heavenly-minded of God's New
Testament saints alone.

' Unbelief' was the first and it was by far the
deepest of all John Bunyan's abominations.   Unbelief, and unbelief alone, was the one baleful
mother of all the abominations in Bunyan's heart.
And when our own eyes are opened we then see

that our unbelief also is the true and the only
mother of all our abominations also. They have all
been begotten in her bosom, they have all been
suckled at her breasts, and they have all been
brought up on her knees. All our sins and all our
scars and all our abominations of all kinds arise out
of our unbelief. Our Lord met with no enemy and
no opposition in all His ministry but unbelief. He
never upbraided any man or any woman or any
city for anything else but for unbelief. He went
about from city to city, and from synagogue to
synagogue, and from one supper-table to another,
asking for nothing but faith. And as soon as He
found faith He straightway praised it and rewarded
it and blessed it. ' O woman!' He said, 'great is
thy faith! Be it unto thee and unto thine according to thy faith!' And so it is, down to our own
day. For I find this illuminating passage in the
spiritual biography of a great believer and a great
preacher. ' Having been much exercised, and for
many years, with troubled thoughts, he had, by
many self-mortifying methods, sought peace of conscience, but notwithstanding all he could do, his
troubles still increased. Whereupon he consulted
several eminent divines, who told him that he
understood the Scriptures much too legally. Upon
giving one of them an account of the state of his
soul, and particularising his sins, that divine told
him that he had forgotten to mention the greatest
sin of all, the sin of unbelief, in not believing on
the Lord Jesus Christ for the remission of his sins,
and for the sanctification of his nature. Hereupon
he set himself to studying and to preaching Christ,
till he attained to eminent holiness and to great

peace of conscience.' So bitterly did Bunyan feel the evil of unbelief that he set down even 'inclinings' to unbelief as the first and the greatest of all his seven abominations, and as the too fruitful mother of all the rest.

All the same, it still remains no little of a mystery to me how Bunyan in all his so severe scrutiny of himself, spiritually and morally, should make no mention at all of pride, or of anger, or of hatred, or of malice, or of revenge, or of impurity, or of envy, and such like. I would have thought that by this time his eyes would have been so opened to all his sinfulness that he would have seen and would have confessed himself to be guilty of all these abominations of heart every day he lived. But no. For some still unexplained reason, no. Well, then, to make a last guess, was it this? Was it because Bunyan by this time had become so absolutely godly in all his views of things, that all his sins of all kinds, and of all degrees, and of all aggravations, he now saw to be committed not so much against man or woman as against God : indeed, as committed against God alone ? Was that it ? Would that be it ? Yes, that was it ; that must be it. That, I feel certain, is the whole of our difficulty resolved and explained. By this time Bunyan has become so like David that he says after every single sin of his of whatever kind, Against Thee, Thee only, have I sinned, and done this evil in Thy sight. And so like Paul and Luther has Bunyan become that to him now faith, faith working by love, is the fulfilling of the whole law in both its tables, and in all that is required and in all that is forbidden in both its tables. And

to him now the lack of faith in Christ and the lack
of love to God involves all sin of all kinds. Yes;
since God is the God He is, and since Christ is the
Christ He is, faith in God, and faith in Christ, is
everything. Only have faith in God, as God is in
Christ, and all things are yours: law and gospel;
Moses and Christ; whether Paul or Apollos, or
Cephas, or the world, or life, or death, or things
present, or things to come; all are yours; and ye
are Christ's, and Christ is God's. Read this now
in the light of all that: ' I find to this day seven
abominations in my heart. (1) Inclinings to unbelief. (2) Suddenly to forget the love and mercy
that Christ manifesteth. (3) A leaning to the
works of the law. (4) Wanderings and coldness in
prayer. (5) To forget to watch for that I pray for.
(6) Apt to murmur because I have no more, and
yet ready to abuse what I have. (7) I can do none
of those things which God commands me, but my
corruptions will thrust in themselves. When I
would do good, evil is present with me.'

' These things I continually see and feel, and am
afflicted and oppressed with; yet the wisdom of
God doth order them for my good. For (1) they
make me abhor myself. (2) They keep me from
trusting my own heart. (3) They convince me of
the insufficiency of all inherent righteousness. (4)
They show me the necessity of fleeing to Jesus.
(5) They press me to pray unto God. (6) They
show me the need I have to watch and be sober.
(7) And they provoke me to look to God, through
Christ, to help me, and to carry me through this
world. Amen.'

XXXI

'Temptations, when we meet them at first, are as the lion that roared upon Samson. But if we overcome them, the next time we see them, we shall find a nest of honey within them.'

N the preface to *Grace Abounding* John Bunyan dedicates that great book to his spiritual children. 'I have sent you enclosed a drop of that honey which I have taken out of the carcase of a lion. I have eaten thereof myself also, and am much refreshed thereby. Temptations, when we meet them at first, are as the lion that roared upon Samson; but when we overcome them, the next time we see them, we shall find a nest of honey within them. The Philistines understand me not.' And so on, all through that wonderful preface to that wonderful book.

Now when we go on to read that wonderful book itself we soon find that the temptations of its author were temptations of no ordinary kind. They were very far from being temptations of that coarse and common kind into which we would have expected to see young Bunyan falling, when we consider his birth, and his upbringing, and his tinker and his soldier life. So inward indeed, so spiritual and so evangelical even, were John Bunyan's temptations all through his wonderful life that the most of us are much too philistine fully to understand either him or them. For there is nothing in which the most of us are more philistine than just in the true understanding of inward and spiritual and evangelical temptations.

'Temptations, when we meet them at first, are as the lion that roared upon Samson.' Now you all know from your childhood the Bible story of Samson and the lion. You all remember how Samson went down, and his father and his mother to Timnath; and, behold, a young lion roared against him. And how the Spirit of the Lord came upon Samson mightily, till he rent the lion as if it had been a kid, and he had nothing in his hand. And when some time after Samson returned to the place to look at the carcase of the lion, behold! there was a swarm of bees and a nest of honey in the carcase of the lion. And Samson took of the honey in his hands, and went on eating, and he came to his father and mother, and he gave them, and they did eat. But he told them not that he had taken the honey out of the carcase of the lion. That is the substance of the old Bible story. And then the classical preface to *Grace Abounding* contains John Bunyan's spiritual interpretation and personal application of that same old Bible story.

Now to John Bunyan and to all Bunyan-like men among us the roar of Samson's lion is never out of their ears all their days on earth. Like Samson's road to Timnath, some men's roads all through this life lie alongside of the lions' dens and up among the mountains of the leopards. To some men every step of their earthly life is just another new temptation. They are no sooner delivered out of one temptation than they suddenly fall into another and a worse. Till their whole earthly lifetime is one long snare to them, one long warfare, one long watching, one long weariness, one long waiting for the deliverance of death.

During a solitary walk along the hillside above the village of Durinish one day last September, all the way as I walked I was thinking about my own unceasing and ever-increasing temptations. Now as God would have it there had been a whole night of the densest sea-fog from the Atlantic, and the wet spray stood in millions of shining gems all over the spiders' webs that were woven all over the broom, and the bracken, and the bushes of whin, and the bushes of heather. Had I not seen the scene with my own eyes I could not have believed it. The whole hillside was absolutely covered from top to bottom with spiders' webs past all counting up. All the spiders in Scotland seemed to me to have conspired together to weave their webs and to spread their snares all over that Durinish hillside that day. To the casual and innocent-minded passer-by the whole hillside would have seemed smiply splendid with its brilliant network of sparkling silver. But the very brilliancy of the scene only made that hillside all the more horrible and diabolical to me, as I thought of the bloodthirsty devil that lay watching for the silly flies at the hidden heart of every silvery web. It was a Saturday forenoon, and it would have been well worth a week-end ticket to some of you just to have stood beside me for a few moments, and to have seen with your own eyes that satanic hillside that September forenoon. For myself, I shall never forget the sight. I see it at this moment as I

stand here. A thousand times that sight has risen
up before my eyes since I came home. If our
Lord had been passing that hillside that forenoon
He would have stopped His walk, and looking at
the spiders' webs He would have said to His disciples: Such is the kingdom of Satan! Which
when the twelve had seen and had laid to heart
they would have been exceedingly amazed, and
would have said: Who, then, can be saved? When
He would have answered them: With men this is
impossible, but with God all things are possible.

It was the rising of the sun that morning that
revealed to me those thousands on thousands of
glistering snares. But for the sunlight falling on
the hillside, and but for the subject of my morning
meditation, I would have wholly missed seeing that
never-to-be-forgotten spectacle, and I would never
have read to myself or to you that so impressive
parable. If I had not been musing all that morning on matters of eternally vital importance to you
and to me, and if the sun had not by that time
been high in the heavens, I would have stumbled
on like any idle-minded holiday maker, and would
never have seen so much as a single one of those
thousands of death-spreading spiders' snares. And
so it is, I said to myself, with the thousands of
Satan's death-spreading snares in the case of every
human soul. Satan's accursed snares are woven
and woven over and over every inch of every
human soul. But those snares of Satan are wholly
invisible till the sun rises and till the soul awakens
to a life of watching and praying and believing.
But when, by the special grace of God to any of us,
we are so awakened, then this whole city in which

we dwell becomes to us a second Durinish hillside, and you and I become those dismembered flies whose blood-sucked wings and legs I saw dangling in the wind all up and down among those glistering spiders' webs. The streets and the squares of Edinburgh, our own houses, and our own churches even, all are that doleful hillside over again to every man who is not a stark philistine. Nay to every man who is not a stark philistine his own soul is that doleful hillside. For the very body which his soul inhabits is all set over with snares for his soul. The very table also at which he eats and drinks, the very chair on which he sits, and the very bed on which he sleeps.

> The close pursuer's busy hands do plant
> Snares in thy substance: snares attend thy want;
> Snares in thy credit, snares in thy disgrace;
> Snares in thy high estate, snares in thy base;
> Snares tuck thy bed, and snares attend thy board;
> Snares watch thy thoughts, and snares attend thy word;
> Snares in thy quiet, snares in thy commotion;
> Snares in thy diet, snares in thy devotion;
> Snares lurk in thy resolves, snares in thy doubt;
> Snares lurk within thy heart, and snares without;
> Snares are above thy head, and snares beneath;
> Snares in thy sickness, snares are in thy death. . . .
> Skill, bugle, poison, steed, bow, raiment pale,
> Decoys, snares, nets, shafts, dogs—make up the tale.

By far the worst of all John Bunyan's temptations, so he himself tells us, was to question the being of God, and the truth of His Gospel. And some of you have had your own worst temptations in that same so fatal direction. But by persevering in secret prayer, and by constant and exclusive reading of your Bible and other devotional and experimental books, and by continuing to do the will of God all through your darkness, you came at last to 'know the doctrine,' as Christ said you would. Aye and to know the doctrine with a certitude that nothing shall ever any more shake in your case. That is what Bunyan in his own sweet style calls a nest of honey taken out of the carcase of a lion. For an assault of unbelief in God and in His Gospel is the lion of all lions, and her roar is the roar of all roars. But then the sweetness and the strength that dropped into your heart when your faith in God came back to you, that was to you like Samson's honey and his honeycomb.

Then again, to come to another side of your awful life of temptation: in the case of some of you that is. You are sometimes so fixed and fastened down inside such a perfect network and woven web of trials and temptations as to make your daily life all but absolutely unbearable by you. Some man that you hate in your heart, some man that is an incessant and a wearing-out temptation and snare to you, is fastened down at the very heart of your life. He lives in the same house with you. Or his house is next door to you. Or his house or his office or his shop is straight across the street from your house or your office or your shop. And so tortured are you in your heart with that man's simple neighbourhood that you often think of going to live in another part of the town so as to get him out of your sight. Nay you have sometimes thought of spending the rest of your days in another country altogether. You sometimes wish in your misery that either he were in his grave or that you were in yours. Nobody would believe the terrible trial

that man is to you. Nobody will ever know what
a snare that man is to your soul. Nobody—but
your minister. Nobody will ever guess at your
terrible torture but that solitary traveller among
the spiders' webs of Durinish that awful September
forenoon. It was of you that he was thinking
when the sun came out and the whole hillside
became so full of personal and pastoral lessons to
him. Only one man on earth, and one Man in
heaven, for one moment understands and sym-
pathises with your fearful sufferings. But they
both understand your case; yes, down to the
deepest and the darkest bottom of it. I have told
you something about your minister. John Bunyan
shall tell you something about his High Priest and
yours. 'Christ Himself was tempted to blaspheme
His Father,' says Bunyan. 'He was tempted to
fall down and worship the very devil. Nay, he was
tempted, like you, to take His own life.' But long
before those recorded temptations of His, you are
invited to imagine His year in and year out of
temptations, so like your own that you alone can
imagine them or believe them possible. His year
after year of temptations and trials in the carpenter's
shop all day, and then every morning and every
night at His mother's fireside, beside all His un-
believing and unsympathising brothers and sisters.
He was in all points tempted like as you and I are.
A whole forest of lions roared on Jesus Christ day
and night for thirty years. But He forgot it all as
often as He again ate the honey that lay hid for
Him also in every overcome temptation. Pray you
and endure you like Him, and you will eat honey
like Him. 'If you pray for an enemy and an

injurious and an offensive man, and speak good
concerning him, and continue to do him good, it
will end in your actually loving him,' so says
William Law to us, and he had tried that way of it,
and had taken the honey out of it that he shares
with us in his so victorious books.   Try much more
prayer on your so offensive and injurious neighbour;
try much more prayer and much more good neighbourhood as God gives you your opportunity; and
some day soon you will find a great nest of honey
opened up next door to you; aye, opened up in the
very house beside you.   And so on, through all the
lions, and through all the spiders, and through all
the men, and through all the devils that are now
ensnaring your soul, and are roaring upon your soul
every day and every hour of your earthly life.

You are in downright desperation some Sabbath
morning. And you stumble into some open church,
as Hannah stumbled up to Shiloh. And you hear
a prayer offered or a sermon delivered, the like of
which you never heard before. And it goes
straight home to your broken heart. It takes
away your breath. You feel as if your whole secret
case had somehow been all discovered to that com-
manding preacher. Already you are not so desper-
ate and so near drowning yourself as you were all
last night. You are not so awfully alone on your
bed in hell as you were all last night. A strength
and a sweetness straight down from heaven entered
your broken heart that never-to-be-forgotten
Sabbath morning. You have always dated your
deliverance from death and your newness of life
from that miraculous Sabbath morning. For it was
both a birthday and an espousal day and a true

marriage day to your lost soul. A true Samson, if ever there was one, shared his nest of honey with you that Sabbath morning. But, though you found him out, and told him something of what his sermon had done for your soul, I feel sure he has never told you where he got his sermon. He has never told you out of what temptations of his he took his sermon, nor what it cost him before he preached it. 'And Samson took thereof in his hands, and went on eating, and came to his father and mother, and he gave to them, and they did eat.' But Samson never told them that he had taken all that honey out of the carcase of a dead lion that had at one time roared upon him.

I have seen as much as that some prodigal son who is all but ready for the Dean Bridge will stop me in the dark lane behind the church on my way home to-night, and will say to me: 'Sir,' he will say, 'I am that blood-sucked fool that you saw dangling among those spiders' webs by the wayside! Temptations, you said, to some men become a nest of honey. My temptations have become to me, for years past, nothing but dust and ashes in my mouth, and I have drunk nothing but blood and tears.' Some thirty years ago I took home a prodigal son from the same dark lane, who is now in his Father's house, where all tears are wiped from off all eyes. But before he was received home in heaven he lived long enough on earth to find his sweet nest of honey not only in all his overcome temptations, but even more, in those temptations that he did not overcome, but that at one time had overcome him. And on many a communion day in this same house of God I have heard him singing with all his heart

and soul after the table this thanksgiving psalm:
'Bless the Lord, O my soul, and all that is within
me bless his Holy Name, who forgiveth all thine
iniquities, who healeth all thy diseases, who
redeemeth thy life from destruction, and who
crowneth thee with lovingkindness and tender
mercies. Yes, truly, bless the Lord, O my soul!'

XXXII

'The Philistines understand me not.'

HE Philistines were the aboriginal inhabitants of Palestine. Philistia was the original name of Palestine, and the original inhabitants of Philistia were known by the name of Philistines. As far back as we are able to trace the Philistines their chief cities were Gaza, and Ashdod, and Ashkelon, and Gath, and Ekron. And their chief gods were Ashtoreth, and Baal, and Beelzebub; three of the most cruel and most obscene of all the cruel and obscene gods of the Gentiles. The Philistines were of a gigantic size and of herculean strength, while in their moral character they were exactly like the gods they made and worshipped. Brutish size and brutish strength of body; brutish grossness and brutish stupidity of mind and heart, with great cruelty and great obscenity, these were the outstanding characteristics of the Philistines among all the heathen peoples of those days. And these are the broad and deep footprints that the Philistines have left to this day on the pages of the Old Testament.

One of the first things that drew the young tinker of Bedford to open the Bible and to return to it was the story of Samson's victorious encounters

with the Philistines of Timnath. But the Philistine that young Bunyan liked best to read about
was that gigantic Goliath of Gath, whose height
was six cubits and a span ; the weight of his coat was
five thousand shekels of brass ; the staff of his spear
was like a weaver's beam ; his spear's head weighed
six hundred shekels of iron, and one bearing a
shield went before him. And he stood and cried
to the armies of Israel, and said unto them, Am not
I a Philistine ? I defy all the armies of Israel this
day ! And when Saul and all Israel heard those
words of the Philistine, they were dismayed and
were greatly afraid.

By the time that John Bunyan had finished his
classical preface to *Grace Abounding*, the opprobrious
epithet of ' Philistine' had already entered the
vocabulary of English literature never again to
leave it. The contemptuous students of the
German universities were not the first to make
the modern application of that ignominious term.
Neither was Thomas Carlyle nor Matthew Arnold
the first to transfer that ignominious term to our
English tongue. The tinker of Bedford was beforehand with the students of the fatherland when he
already penned these so expressive and so plain-
spoken words: ' The Philistines understand me not.'
It was not their want of a university education that
drew down upon so many of Bunyan's contemporaries
this severe description that he here gives them.
Had the want of a university education been the
sure mark of a Philistine there would have been no
greater Philistine in the whole of England in that
day than just John Bunyan himself. But the
author of the preface to *Grace Abounding* is far

deeper in his insight, and he is far more masterly
in his use of such words, than are those home and
foreign critics who use the word philistine with
such studied contempt of their unlettered neighbours. The students of Germany, and our own
Matthew Arnold after them, apply the nickname
of philistine to those of their fellow-countrymen
who do not possess the openness of mind and the
intellectual refinement that a classical education is
assumed to give. But our author employs this
condemnatory term in a far deeper way and in a
far truer way than that. For he finds the true and
the genuine philistines of his day fully as much
among the 'priests and doctors' of the University
of Cambridge as among the tradesmen and shopkeepers of the town of Bedford. With John
Bunyan it is not the lack of a university education
that makes and keeps a man a philistine; it is the
lack of personal religion. It is the fatal lack of a
personal experience of spiritual and divine things.
To John Bunyan there is no ignorance and no
narrow-mindedness like the ignorance and narrow-
mindedness of the man who does not know his own
heart and consequently does not know his overwhelming need of Jesus Christ and His redemption.
To John Bunyan there is no stupidity like the
stupidity of an unconverted and an ungodly man.
And if that man is a member of a famous university
his spiritual stupidity is only all that the more
notorious and is only all that the more mischievous.
Read the preface to *Grace Abounding*—a piece of
English writing of the first order both intellectually
and spiritually considered—and unless you are a
philistine yourself you will at once feel how deep

that preface cuts into yourself. For if you are a man of an enlightened and a spiritual mind, it will cut to the dividing asunder of soul and spirit, and of the joints and marrow, and will be a discerner of the thoughts and intents of your heart.

Now, are there any philistines left in our day? And if so, who are they and where are they to be found? How shall we know them? And how shall we behave ourselves towards them? Well, a proud heart, and a scornful and a blustering tongue, were the sure marks of the original and indigenous dwellers in Philistia. Now if pride and scorn are the indubitable and universal marks of a philistine, how beset and how possessed is the very Church of Jesus Christ with that spirit and that temper in our own day. Our Church parties, our Church divisions, our hostility to one another, our hatred and contempt and scorn of one another, is all due at bottom to our philistine pride, self-conceit, and insolence. The Greek Church in her ancient ecclesiastical pride and insolence despises and excommunicates the Latin Church, and the Latin Church in her turn despises and excommunicates the English Church. And then the English Church, not yet having learned wisdom by all that example and experience, makes herself very unlovely sometimes by her behaviour to the Churches that she thinks are beneath her. Three-quarters of a century ago there was a great outbreak of ecclesiastical philistinism in the Tracts for the Times and in the so-called Lyra Apostolica. The pride and insolence of those productions are a painful study to any man with a spark of brotherly love and Christian humility in his heart. But two can play at that philistine game. And thus it was that when the Tractarians turned away from their evangelical brethren in England to seek an alliance with the Holy Synod this was the proud reply that they got: 'You English separated from the Latin Church three hundred years ago, just as the Latins had separated from the Greeks. We orthodox Greeks think even the Latin Church heretical, but you are an apostasy from an apostasy. You are a descent from bad to worse.' There speaks a very Goliath of Gath. Now how are we to behave ourselves toward the Churchmen of this spirit who are so plentiful among ourselves in our day? Well, our best way is to track the same spirit down to its universal root in our own half-regenerate and half-sanctified hearts. Let us put its proper name upon that so unchristian mind when we discover it in ourselves. And that will work patience in us and even pity toward our brethren who so much allow themselves in this so unchristian temper and attitude toward those for whom Christ died, quite as much as He died for them. Let us put on strength even to love and to pray for the proudest of such men. And let us more and more be clothed with humility and contrition that such a spirit should obtain at this time of day in that body of Christ, which they and we equally are, and which we and they taken together wholly constitute.

Then again, you may be the most polished and the most urbane of men in the world of letters, and yet you may behave yourself toward the far better world of religion so as to prove yourself to be at heart little better than a philistine yourself. You may be the universally recognised scourge of all

stupidity and all dullness and all narrow-mindedness
in your own world of things, and yet you may go
on to act the part of the uncircumcised in a far
better world of things with which you have too
little sympathy. To be plain, you may be Matthew
Arnold himself in your intellectual insight, and in
your matchless criticism of ancient and modern
literature, and yet you may act the part of a
philistine scoffer toward certain religious men and
toward certain religious and social movements of
your own day. Every lover of English literature,
who is also a lover of evangelical religion, must
have often been sorely vexed at the way Matthew
Arnold gibes and jests at such men as Lord
Shaftesbury, and Mr. Bright, and Mr. Moody, and
Mr. Spurgeon; and at such centres of religious
activity and social redemption as Exeter Hall and
the Salvation Army. Poor gibes and jests at the
best, that every true admirer of Arnold could so
much wish to see blotted out of his beautiful books.
For, not to care how much you pain and even injure
good men in their work for God and man, if only
you can make a point and raise a laugh at their
expense—that, surely, is to act the part of the true
philistine. That surely comes down from Gath and
Ekron even when it comes to us by the way of Oxford
and Cambridge. Another writer of much the same
literary rank as Arnold some time ago published a
Life of John Bunyan. And he so patronised and so
belittled and so philosophised over and so explained
away John Bunyan's religious experiences and his
apostolic doctrines as to make his book, practically
and eventually, a powerful plea for unbelief. I
know what I am saying. For I knew in those days

a divinity student who was so dazzled and sophisticated and bewildered by that brilliant book that he
went aside altogether from the study of divine
truth and has landed by this time I do not know
where.   For all the strength and all the high
interests and all the high motives went out of his
life with that book.   Now if that is not to do the
work of a genuine philistine—literary insight and
English style and all—then I do not know what
the work of a modern philistine is.

But the most practical and the most profitable
point of all this study of the philistines, past and
present, is this: it is to carry the inquiry home to
ourselves: first to myself, and then to you.   For
I would be an arch-philistine myself if after all this
I let myself go free.   Well then, I must understand
and must accept this, and you must all understand
and accept this along with me : that the bitter
dregs of the true philistine are still in us all ; aye,
and more than the dregs in many of us.   There is
pride to begin with, if we know what pride really
is, and how it shows itself.   All self-importance
also, and all self-assertiveness, and all self-opinion-
ativeness.   All talkativeness, and all boastfulness.
All indifference to other men's feelings and sufferings and necessities.   All injustice, all injury, and
all cruelty.   All neglect of the poor, and the
oppressed, and the friendless; and so on all
through our sinful hearts and lives.   All that and
everything of that kind is the dominion, or at best
it is the deep dregs and the inward remains of the
philistine still in us all.   In short, it is the old
story : it is sin.   It is all the deep dregs and all
the inward remains of indwelling and unconquered

and unexpelled sin. But in all this the true and genuine philistine will not understand one syllable of what I am saying. Only, beloved, says the Apostle, I am persuaded better things of you, and things accompanying salvation, though I thus speak.